HG 3891 .C64 2010
Cohan, Peter S., 1957-
Capital rising

DISCARD

Courtright Memorial Library
Otterbein University
Courtright Memorial Library
Westerville, Ohio 43081

Capital Rising

Capital Rising

How Capital Flows Are Changing Business Systems All Over the World

By

Peter S. Cohan

and

U. Srinivasa Rangan

CAPITAL RISING
Copyright © Peter S. Cohan and U. Srinivasa Rangan, 2010.

All rights reserved.

First published in 2010 by
PALGRAVE MACMILLAN®
in the United States—a division of St. Martin's Press LLC,
175 Fifth Avenue, New York, NY 10010.

Where this book is distributed in the UK, Europe and the rest of the world,
this is by Palgrave Macmillan, a division of Macmillan Publishers Limited,
registered in England, company number 785998, of Houndmills,
Basingstoke, Hampshire RG21 6XS.

Palgrave Macmillan is the global academic imprint of the above companies
and has companies and representatives throughout the world.

Palgrave® and Macmillan® are registered trademarks in the United States,
the United Kingdom, Europe and other countries.

ISBN: 978–0–230–61231–0

Library of Congress Cataloging-in-Publication Data is available from the
Library of Congress.

A catalogue record of the book is available from the British Library.

Design by Newgen Imaging Systems (P) Ltd., Chennai, India.

First edition: June 2010

10 9 8 7 6 5 4 3 2 1

Printed in the United States of America.

To my parents, Paul and Sue, who provided the intellectual capital that fueled my lifelong quest to discover why.

Peter Cohan

To my wife, Sudha, but for whose care and support the book could not have been written.

Srinivasa Rangan

Contents

Figures

Part I

Definining the Entrepreneurial Ecosystem

I

Introduction

This book is about capital, globalization, and entrepreneurship. When we first thought about writing it in 2006, an enormous capital bubble was building in the world. And as we put our final touches on the book in early 2010, the global financial system was continuing to respond to that bubble's implosion.

One thing that remained constant during these years of research was the powerful force that capital flows exert on global entrepreneurship. While increased leverage helped to expand the capital bubble during the mid-2000s—leading to a boom in private equity deals and cross-border mergers, the subsequent de-leveraging caused the bubble to pop quite suddenly—slowing down that activity. We expect these cycles to persist. Witness the recent report from the respected Institute of International Finance that suggests that net private capital flows to emerging economies will almost double from $349 billion in 2009 to $672 billion in 2010.[1] And a significant part of those capital inflows—$80 billion—headed toward emerging markets' mutual funds in 2009 thanks to the soaring returns they delivered to investors in those markets. Specifically, the MSCI Emerging Markets Index spiked 74.5% in 2009 while Latin America, the top performer among MSCI's developing-market indexes, yielded a nearly 98% return.[2]

What is important to remember is the upward trend in the flows of capital to markets around the world and their impact on firms, industries, and countries.

So, rather than focus our attention on the macro economic impact of capital's *cyclical* ebbs and flows, we chose to write about how capital's rising importance is moving economic history *forward*. To that end, our book seeks to explain why and how capital seeks places to invest and what policymakers in search of such capital can do to attract it. We believe that these international capital flows are a powerful economic force that influences the rise and fall of industries. To help explain these factors, we've created the concept of the Entrepreneurial Ecosystem (EE)—consisting of four key factors: financial markets, corporate governance, human capital, and Intellectual Property (IP) regime—that a country can shape to encourage or discourage capital flows.[3]

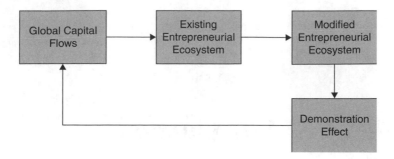

Figure 1.1   Capital Heliotropism Framework

But recently, more and more companies have been trying to reshape their EEs to attract capital. Why? Capital spurs entrepreneurship and entrepreneurship, in turn, creates jobs and tax revenue. What can policymakers do about this? They can lower restrictive barriers to encourage flows from a country with a surplus of capital into one that needs them. And if the demand for capital is sufficiently high, they can upgrade their country's corporate governance standards in order to overcome the reluctance of capital providers to invest in their companies.

Financial markets and corporate governance are among the factors that can determine whether industries rise or fall. If these are attuned to the standards that big capital providers expect, capital will flow toward the countries that do the attuning. And if countries resist such standards, their ability to attract fresh capital will lag behind those that do. The boost to the economic performance of countries that attract the capital creates pressure for all countries to upgrade their EEs.

We formalize the way such opportunities expand ecosystem value for all participants, creating demonstration effects; to be more specific, the Capital Heliotropism[4] Framework (figure 1.1) that describes how recipient countries' desire for international capital causes a gradual evolution toward greater corporate governance and financial market transparency. The Capital Heliotropism Framework links the following three key themes.

- *Capital seeks the highest profit potential.* Specifically, capital flows initially toward countries and companies where investors perceive an opportunity to profit from the existing EE.
- *Investment creates pressure to upgrade the EE.* Investors use their initial access to opportunities as a means to change the EE—so they can profit further by enhancing corporate transparency, streamlining capital markets, and building more globally competitive human capital networks.
- *High investment returns lead to a demonstration effect.* Ultimately, investors hope that the success of companies that benefit from the transformed EE will create a demonstration effect. As such, more companies will alter their EEs to gain access to capital. This can lead to a bottom-up

transformation in the approach toward entrepreneurship within a country.

We believe that if decision makers embrace the concepts in our book, capital heliotropism will yield a world that is safer for global entrepreneurship—spreading jobs and wealth to a broader swath of the world's citizens.

We hope this book is valuable for anyone who makes a living out of creating new opportunities to enrich the lives of workers and the communities in which those workers toil. Those who create such opportunities—including government policymakers, capital providers, and business leaders (both of start-ups and existing companies)—can benefit from reading this book.

This book offers readers a prescriptive and practically focused approach that fundamentally changes the way managers make strategic decisions by highlighting previously hidden risks and opportunities. Specifically, the frameworks presented in the book help managers make decisions such as the following.

Where to perform activities. While traditional economic theory would lead managers to perform business activities in the countries where they can be performed at the lowest cost, our book demonstrates that this is not always the case due to the economic pressures created by global capital. For example, Wal-Mart—which had traditionally expanded into countries such as Germany through acquisition—rethought its India strategy. In response to the risks and opportunities presented by India's evolving retail entrepreneurial ecosystem, Wal-Mart chose a value-chain-splitting strategy in which it joined its back-office skills with its partner's retailing ability. The Indian government, using an industrial policy approach, has forbidden foreign investment in retailing by foreign firms such as Wal-Mart. This has allowed Indian business groups with access to global capital such as Reliance to get into retail.[5] Most observers in India wrote off Wal-Mart's prospects in potentially one of the largest retail markets in the world. Wal-Mart, however, demonstrated its strategic savvy by deciding to exploit its core competence in supply chain and logistics management. It has entered into a joint venture with one of Reliance's local rivals—Bharti Enterprises—to provide supply chain and logistics services to Bharti's retail operations in India. We analyze how Wal-Mart's success in India depends on many factors including its understanding of India's evolving EE, its appreciation of the impact of availability capital to its local competitors, its need to reassess its strategy in the light of other countries' business ecosystems, and its ability to execute an innovative strategy fast in order to preserve its strategic options for the future. The important point here is that Wal-Mart recognized a need to change its strategy given Indian government regulations and the availability of global capital to Indian firms such as Bharti (and its local rivals such as Reliance), if it wanted to take part in an emerging market opportunity. By broadening the way managers think about how to configure their activities globally, our book helps them capture the significant growth opportunities within emerging markets while avoiding costly pitfalls.[6]

Which growing industries to invest in. In most countries, an entrepreneur seeking venture capital would be likely to build a business plan around a patented technology targeting a huge market with a staff of top-notch engineers. Our book shows that due to differences in IP regimes across countries, a Chinese entrepreneur, for example, would be more likely to attract foreign capital by providing a service and hiring people with strong operational skills. How? We've found that due to weak IP protection in China, venture investors are loath to invest in technology-intensive start-ups. Consider the experience of IDG Ventures, that invested in China and had one investment that was worth 100 times what IDG paid for. IDG focused on service-oriented investments with strong management teams and avoided investments involving IP since China does not protect it. Success with such service-oriented growth industries extended to its investments in Vietnam as well—where IDG had a $100 million fund. Examples of such service-oriented investments include Cyworld Vietnam, which has received two rounds totaling $1.7 million from IDG Ventures Vietnam, is a social networking company based on the South Korea's Cyworld brand. YeuAmNhac JSC, whose name means "love music" in Vietnamese, aims to build an online music community. The third company is Vinapay, a mobile payment service offering electronic refill of prepaid cell phone airtime and mobile payment of expenses such as cab fares and airline tickets.[7] Michael Greeley, a former partner in a U.S.-based IDG fund, also thought corruption in China was still a significant concern, which is why he made a series of small investments in companies rather than a few big ones. He implied that in China, the government can take over a company more easily or corruption is more of a threat when a foreign VC invests above a certain amount per transaction.[8] By helping entrepreneurs understand how venture investors view the global opportunities and risks in their markets, our book helps them to choose business models most likely to attract the capital they require to grow.

How to manage mature businesses. Managers typically look to harvest the cash that mature businesses generate—starving them of investment. Our book demonstrates that global capital flows enable managers to revitalize mature businesses—thus making them capital recipients that can reward investors with high returns. For example, we demonstrate how Infosys, Wipro, and TCS of India have become major global players in the software and IT outsourcing industry by using their access to global capital markets. In the process, they have forced major changes in the way IBM, Accenture, and EDS operate globally. For example, Accenture invested in India where it planned to hire so many people that by August 2007 it would employ more people there than in any other country.[9] And in the mature coated paper industry, the role of private capital is opening up entirely new strategic possibilities. Instead of focusing managers on squeezing out costs, private capital is giving managers in mature industries a new competitive weapon—using the power of the U.S. government to raise tariffs against Chinese competitors. How? In March 2007, the U.S. Commerce Department raised tariffs on Chinese coated paper companies—accusing them of lowering these companies' cost of capital through low-cost loans and debt forgiveness. And one U.S.-based coated paper company, NewPage, is owned by

Cerberus Capital Management, a private equity fund whose chairman John W. Snow, served as former president George W. Bush's Treasury Secretary from February 2003 to July 2006.[10] Given private equity firms' access to power, they can spur surprisingly effective government-backed strategies for managers of their portfolio companies. By changing the way managers think about maturing businesses, our book helps them spot investment opportunities that will benefit their employees, clients, and investors.[11]

Whether to exit declining businesses. If an industry is declining, managers traditionally seek to get out of the business or try to shrink it to a profitable core. But we demonstrate that global capital flows enable industries that are declining in developed countries to deliver cheap sources of new capacity that satisfies the needs of the rapidly growing developing countries. As a result, managers might change their perspective—for instance, the decision that it makes more sense to invest in the business so it can fit more effectively with a global acquirer with a proven track record of buying and improving such declining operations. For example, in its 1992 acquisition of a Mexican steel mill, Mittal used its IP—a highly sophisticated pre- and postacquisition process—to transform Mexico's struggling Sicartsa steel plant into a rapidly growing and much more efficient operation which it ultimately bid to acquire for $1.4 billion in December 2006.[12] Having listed its shares on the New York Stock Exchange (NYSE), Mittal enjoys access to massive pools of capital that it uses to finance such deals as part of its global acquisition strategy. Moreover, Sicartsa's investors turned their share of a declining industry into valuable equity thanks to Mittal's application of its IP—funded by the global capital access. By helping managers to identify global partners in declining industries, our book shows how they can brighten substantially the future for their employees, customers, and investors.

Where to seek capital. Traditionally entrepreneurs seek capital from venture investors and/or public equity markets in the countries in which they operate. Our book shows that the emergence of global capital markets creates a wider variety of options for entrepreneurs. For example, Wall Street gave the cold shoulder to the IPO of a Massachusetts-based genetic engineering firm so its CEO flew to London whose Alternative Investment Market (AIM) helped him raise $30 million for Asian expansion.[13] Specifically, Elliot Entis, current director and former CEO of Aqua Bounty Technologies of Waltham, MA is developing genetically modified fish for aquaculture. Entis recounted how potential Wall Street underwriters gave him 15 minutes and showed him the back door while London capital providers held a long meeting with him. In March 2006, Aqua Bounty sold stock in London worth $30 million, which it planned to use to expand in Asia. By providing entrepreneurs an expanded view of where they can raise capital, our book helps them lower their cost of capital and obtain the fuel they need to grow.

How to hire managers and coordinate global operations. When a U.S.-based company seeks to open up operations in a new country, it typically assigns a young executive who has demonstrated his or her potential in the United States. Our book demonstrates that global capital flows make this instinct obsolete. We illustrate the importance of placing managers in new countries that have "cultural bridging skills." For example, the $440 million hedge fund, Monsoon Capital, seeks to invest in Indian companies whose younger generation of management—while part of the founding family—has significant U.S. educational background that enables them to understand the expectations of U.S. investors and manage the business accordingly. Similarly, we explore the example of ChrysCapital, a Mauritius-based venture firm, that demonstrates the importance to investors of finding managers who can apply skills that bridge cultures—say between the United States and India. ChrysCapital financed Spectramind, a call center. Spectramind was started by the GE executives who ran GE's call center in India. The executives sought capital to build their own company to find new clients who would pay for their GE-honed call center management skills. They were so successful that, three years later, Wipro acquired Spectramind for $300 million.[14] By explaining in detail how managers can plan to staff and coordinate global operations, our book seeks to enhance their profits from global expansion.

This book is organized to answer four broad questions:

- How and why are these capital flows occurring?
- What has been the impact of these flows on the global economy and the economies of individual countries?
- How will this phenomenon affect my life as an entrepreneur, manager, or policymaker?
- What are the ways I can benefit from or protect myself from this new wave of globalization?

In general, we seek to describe the phenomenon of capital flows, present new ways to think about what causes them to rise and fall, and describe ways that our readers can profit from this framework. Chapter 2 addresses the first question; chapters 3 through 5 answer the second one; and chapters 6 through 10 tackle the last two—through case studies and methodologies for each of the key EE participants. And here follows the contents of the chapters in a gist.

Chapter 2, "Capital Rising: Globalization, Capital Flows, and the Emerging New Entrepreneurial Ecosystems," introduces the role of capital flows in shaping globalization. It argues that globalization has changed the nature and meaning of entrepreneurship. This chapter suggests that the primal role of capital in shaping entrepreneurship demands a new approach for policymakers—the EE.

Chapter 3, "The Impact of the Entrepreneurial Ecosystem on Countries," explains how the contours of a country's EE can either attract or repel capital. We explore cases to illustrate how countries fall into one of three categories—leaders, loungers, or laggards—depending on their choices about their EE and conclude by highlighting the key lessons of these cases for EE participants.

Chapter 4, "The Impact of the Entrepreneurial Ecosystem on Growing Industries," demonstrates that a country's EE is an essential determinant of the success or failure of growing industries within that country. We explore two cases of successful Indian companies that benefit from certain elements of India's EE and discuss implications of these ideas for EE participants.

Chapter 5, "The Impact of the Entrepreneurial Ecosystem on Maturing and Rejuvenating Industries," argues that changing EEs attract entrepreneurs and capital to industries that formerly did not enjoy much dynamism. We provide case studies of mature industries and rejuvenating ones that enjoyed a boost in economic performance thanks to changing EEs in the countries that host them. We then summarize the implications of these cases for EE participants.

Chapter 6, "Implications for Policymakers," advocates the idea that policymakers must act promptly to shape their country's EE in a way that is consistent with their growth goals. This chapter presents seven mini–case studies that illustrate several benefits and risks of such EE reshaping.

Chapter 7, "Implications for Capital Providers," similarly argues that analyzing a country's EE is essential for capital providers seeking to maximize investment returns. To bolster that argument, the chapter presents 10 case studies of capital providers and their investments, and these case studies highlight both the opportunities of making smart choices about EEs in which to invest and, just as importantly, which ones to avoid. To help capital providers, we present a capital receptivity index (CRI) that we believe ought to be an essential tool in their pre-investment due diligence process. We describe a six-step process for exploring, closing, and exiting successful investments illustrated through interviews with a private equity firm that uses the process.

Chapter 8, "Implications for Managers in Existing Industries," contends that thanks to changing EEs around the world, managing a company in an existing industry is not a life sentence to slow growth. Instead, we suggest that evolving EEs create opportunities for global acquisitions that can spur higher growth. We examine cases of such global acquisitions and provide a methodology based on the lessons of these cases that we believe can help managers grow their companies profitably.

Chapter 9, "Implications for Entrepreneurial Managers in New Firms and Industries," argues that CEOs of start-up companies ought to tread carefully when it comes to global EEs—wonderful opportunities as well as enormous risks await them. We help these CEOs seize the opportunities and shun the risks. We emphasize the importance of using rigor when making key business decisions by exploring 10 case studies of global start-ups. As we explore each of these cases, we examine specific lessons that we believe entrepreneurs can use to help them as they expand their start-ups. And we conclude with a six-step methodology that we believe can help entrepreneurs apply these lessons to their own businesses in a rigorous fashion.

Chapter 10, "Seeking Congruencies and Resolving Conflicts among Ecosystem Participants," recognizes that while the foregoing chapters have explored EE participants in isolation, the complex reality is that these participants interact. When such interaction is harmonious, that harmony boosts the odds that good investments will get funded. Conversely, disharmony among these elements increases the chances for an unhappy outcome. Chapter 10 analyzes the 47 cases we explore in this book and categorizes them based on their success or failure. It draws lessons from these outcomes and recommends a six-step process for business leaders to work with EE participants to find sources of harmony while addressing and resolving sources of conflict.

The globalization of entrepreneurship is a powerful phenomenon with the potential to boost worldwide employment and wealth. To learn more about how to harness that potential, read on.

2

Capital Rising: Globalization, Capital Flows, and the Emerging New Entrepreneurial Ecosystems

Globalization is now on everyone's mind. Journalists like Tom Friedman of the *New York Times* write popular paeans for it. Pundits like Lou Dobbs of *CNN* vehemently criticize it. Academics like Jagdish Bhagwati of Columbia University argue passionately for it. Policymakers like the former U.S. Trade Representative and current World Bank President Robert Zoellick embrace it. Leaders like Hugo Chavez of Venezuela denounce it downright. Researchers everywhere pore over its statistics. Amidst all these, common people, however, remain mesmerized, confused, puzzled, and worried, but not fully informed by it. So, what is globalization and why does it evoke strong views?

Globalization of Trade and Services

The main reason for this state of affairs is that almost all observers—journalists, pundits, academics, policymakers, and elected officials—are focused on largely one facet of globalization, namely, increased cross-border flows of goods and services. Rising imports and growing exports are easily visible. Their impact on local economies through lost jobs and closure of factories and offices are easy to observe. While learned men dissect the reasons for these developments ascribing them all largely to impersonal forces of globalization, the person on the street affected most by these developments remains unenlightened and fearful.

Indeed, global trade flows have been rising since the end of the Second World War almost continuously except for a few hiccups here and there. As a recent *Wall Street Journal* editorial pointed out, global trade has gone up from $2.3 trillion in 1980 to $19.7 trillion in 2008.[1] Recently, global economic recession has slowed down this expansion but most economists expect trade flows to resume their upward trajectory when the global economy revives. What is more, almost all the major countries in the world—developed as well as developing—have participated in the surge of global trade. Witness the increase of China's exports to the rest of the world in the past three decades. Indeed, the growth of Chinese exports has become a major talking point in all the forums where globalization is a topic of discussion. Other countries too ranging from India and Korea to Brazil and Mexico have been able to participate more fully through rising exports and substantially rising imports. True, countries such as the United States and United Kingdom have seen their imports grow faster than their exports but they too have participated in the global growth in trade. Indeed, barring a few, very poor countries in Africa, almost all countries seem to have participated in the growth of international trade in goods and services. So, for the question "Is globalization a fact?" the answer seems to be in the affirmative.

Another interesting question is whether all countries feel they have benefited equally from this surge in global trade in goods and services. Here, opinions vary. Mainstream economists strongly believe that the global growth in exports and imports is a testament to the recognition of how trade growth leads to increased national welfare in all countries. This is strongly in accord with the traditional trade theory that posits that trade leads to optimal exchange between nations on the basis of comparative advantage and optimal usage of resources. In turn, such exchange and usage leads to increased welfare for participants in international trade.[2] Of course, the more nationalistic or mercantile view asserts that international trade imposes unequal burdens on countries. The proponents of such a view suggest that export-driven countries such as China, Germany, and Japan tend to gain in new jobs and register balance of payments surpluses that tend to shift the burden of adjustments on other countries that pursue more market-oriented policies. In this formulation, countries such as the United States end up with balance of payments deficits as well as loss of jobs, especially in labor-intensive sectors.

The response of the classical economists to such carping criticism is to resort to two arguments, one macro and the other micro. The macro argument refers to differences in savings rates in different countries. Since such differences between countries, especially in different phases of economic development, are considered normal, the economists go on to suggest that the resultant differences in balance of payments are also inevitable and the way to deal with them is through macroeconomic policies.[3] The micro argument refers to the notion that international trade allows for better allocation of productive resources between different sectors and that the problems facing countries is merely one of transitory nature. Again, the way to deal with them is through public policies, this time focused on adjustment assistance and retraining for workers displaced by imports.[4] Unfortunately, both the suggestions are somewhat esoteric and rarely do they allay the concerns of people affected by trade policies.

What is more, such a bloodless analytical view of globalization reinforces the popular view that globalization is largely for the benefit of large corporations.

Indeed, many writers on the topic of globalization tend to see the growth of international trade and foreign direct investment as exemplifiers of the phenomenon.[5] Some have suggested that globalization is largely driven by multinational corporations from developed countries that have sought to leverage their presence in and access to markets through internal and external trade in goods and services.[6] Others have stressed the role of spatial agglomeration in industries in various regions of the world as drivers of globalization.[7] What is missing in this formulation is the question of how countries that have been till now in the periphery of global economy are learning to participate in the globalization process and succeeding in it. Herein comes the issue of how entrepreneurial capitalism is spreading in many countries, the issue at the heart of our book.

Globalization and Entrepreneurship

What is the connection between global trade growth and entrepreneurship? Much of the global trade in goods and services is driven through entrepreneurs, and entrepreneurially minded managers in large corporations who see opportunities in the business sector in which they operate. They see new markets in other countries and expand to meet their needs. As more companies see this happening, more of them join in the efforts. This leads to increased competition, which, in turn, leads to a second round of entrepreneurial thinking by new firms and managers. These entrepreneurs and managers decide to focus on new ways of doing business. They may seek newer low cost ways of making the goods and services in demand globally or in other markets. They may introduce new ways of differentiating their offerings of goods and services from other firms' offerings. What is more, in all these happenings, the industry itself may change in dramatic ways with new rivals, with new products and services, with new ways of competing, with new configurations of value chain activities, and so on. All these activities are entrepreneurial in nature. This push toward entrepreneurship—through new firms as well as changes in established firms—is perhaps the most enduring legacy of growth in international trade in goods and services.

Perhaps, the best example of this is the transformation of the global personal computer industry over the past three decades. Far from being a vertically integrated, few-firms-dominated industry as its predecessor main frame industry used to be, the new industry has from the beginning been highly decentralized.[8] The splintering of the vertical chain was facilitated by the standardization of various parts, components, operating systems, and microprocessors. In turn, this led to the springing up of a large number of new manufacturers specializing in key parts of the value chain in many parts of the world and especially in Asia, a classic case of global spur to entrepreneurship we referred to above. This push to new entrepreneurial firms was facilitated by the growth in international trade and its facilitation by micro developments (such as advances in product design and process technology) and macro trends (such as the acceptance of a liberal international trading order) in economic and political realms.[9] Indeed, this splintering and global spread of value chain has also accelerated the spread of innovation in global industries across the globe.[10] A good example is how Apple developed the iPod in collaboration with a number of external partners in several geographic locations across the globe. It worked with United Kingdom's Wolfson for the digital-to-analog sound chip, New York based Linear Technology for a power management chip, California based Broadcom for the video chip, Japan's Toshiba for the hard drive, and Taiwan's Inventec for manufacturing.[11] In other words, global trade has yielded a new global division of labor that in turn drives the growth of new firms and even new industries.

The ramifications of globalization do not stop there. As new opportunities for entrepreneurs open up in many countries around the world, capital providers—banks, venture capitalists, angels, hedge funds, and private equity firms—flock to fund profitable opportunities in those countries. This leads to two additional developments. One, as it becomes known that entrepreneurs have an easier time getting funding, more entrepreneurs and entrepreneurially minded managers decide to make entrepreneurial moves to change the way business is done in their industries. These can range from new innovations to low cost manufacturing. Witness how the availability of capital led to an explosion of entrepreneurship in the latter half of the 1990s when the Internet boom was in full swing. Two, as more such entrepreneurial efforts take hold in an economy, the economy creates more jobs, creates more wealth, and the economy begins to prosper. This leads to even more optimism among would-be entrepreneurs and entrepreneurially minded managers and leads to another burst of innovation and reinvention of industries. This continuous reinforcement of a virtuous cycle of entrepreneurship ➔ capital availability ➔ more entrepreneurship ➔ more capital availability ➔ more entrepreneurship is especially worth recognizing in the global arena as more and more countries partake in the bounty of access to global markets, be it for goods, services, or capital.

If the unleashing of the entrepreneurial potential in various countries is a key aspect of globalization, then why is it that most observers have not recognized it? For that we need to turn to how entrepreneurship has traditionally been thought of and how we need to go beyond that to understand the full import of capital flows for the world economy.

Reconceptualizing Entrepreneurship

Whenever someone talks of entrepreneurship, the first image that comes to most people's mind is that of Bill Gates. That is because we traditionally associate entrepreneurship with the idea of creating a new company. Indeed, much of the current view of entrepreneurship, as articulated in business schools, stresses the notion of start-ups. Indeed, many researchers measure the incidence of entrepreneurship in countries based on measures of start-ups or a variant of them. For example, the widely known GEM Report "studies *individuals'* [emphasis added] activities with respect to starting and managing a business."[12] Such a view is likely to lead to people seeing more entrepreneurship activity in a poor country like Mali than in a rich country like the United States, which is the hot bed of innovative firms such as Microsoft. This is because in poor countries, where opportunities for gainful employment are low, self-employment is the norm than the exception. So, any activity ranging from selling vegetables to delivering newspapers are actively pursued by individuals. Under traditional view of entrepreneurship, the vegetable seller as well as the newspaper delivery person is an entrepreneur. Naturally, based on such a measure of entrepreneurship, Mali would seem a more entrepreneurial nation than the United States!

Indeed, faced with such a dilemma, GEM authors now distinguish between "entrepreneurship of necessity" and "entrepreneurship of opportunity."[13] The idea is that in poor countries ("factor driven" economies in GEM Report's parlance), people are driven to start some self-employment businesses because of economic necessity whereas in more developed countries ("efficiency driven" or "innovation driven" economies in GEM Report's language) such start-ups are driven by identification of some opportunity[14] by an entrepreneur. While this classification system helps in linking the stage of economic development and occurrence of start-up mode entrepreneurship, it still begs the question why entrepreneurship of necessity could not be from the identification of an opportunity and thus be entrepreneurship of opportunity as well. Another problem with such a narrow definition of entrepreneurship is that it suggests that world-class "opportunity-based" entrepreneurial companies are likely to be founded in more developed countries ("efficiency driven" or "innovation driven" economies) rather than in poorer countries ("factor driven" economies). For example, based on such reasoning, India, which is classified as a factor driven economy, is unlikely to produce world class entrepreneurial companies. How do we reconcile this hypothesis with the reality that India in the past three decades has produced several world-class entrepreneurial firms—Infosys, Tata Consulting Services, and Wipro—to take just one industrial sector, namely, computer and software services?

Indeed, this raises a more fundamental question: What is entrepreneurship?

It is quite likely that identifying entrepreneurship with start-ups may not be a very helpful way to think about this question. We would be better off starting with Schumpeter, the economist often associated with a modern view of entrepreneurship. For him, an entrepreneur is one who has a capacity for innovation and who then may combine his innovation with such things as risk taking, forming an organization, and using management skills to create a new firm.[15] Witness, how Schumpeter does not concern himself so much with start-ups as with innovation. Clearly, innovation can occur in large, established firms as well in the mind of an individual. And, innovation itself could be defined broadly as Schumpeter did. It could be a new product or service. It could be a new production method. It could be a new way of combining different processes and products. The combinations are endless. All these innovations, as Schumpeter pointed out, could lead to "creative destruction" of firms, industries, and economies. Thus entrepreneurial minded people do play a role in the economic development of nations. In more recent years, other researchers have sought to delineate entrepreneurship as relating to opportunity assessment, resources mobilization, and team building.[16] This is fully consonant with Schumpeter's view since innovation could be in any of these activities be it opportunity espying, mobilizing resources, or in building a team. Either way, entrepreneurship is best viewed as nothing more than entrepreneurial thinking and action in a range of organizations, large and small, and start-ups as well as established ones.

Reconceptualizing entrepreneurship along these lines has profound implications. One, such entrepreneurial thought and action could manifest itself in a variety of organizations ranging from small start-ups to large corporations. It is indeed such entrepreneurial vitality that keeps a country like the United States in the forefront of economic growth and economic development. Here small, medium, and large firms alike constantly reinvent themselves through innovation and the resultant entrepreneurial behavior. Witness how IBM, the computer hardware giant, had reinvented itself first as a nimble player in the personal computer industry and then as a major computer services firm. Like Schumpeter, we too would say that IBM behaved as a quintessential entrepreneur finding new opportunities, mobilizing resources to exploit those opportunities, and adapting its organizational capabilities to realize those opportunities.

Two, if entrepreneurial thought and action is at the heart of economic development, we need to understand why some countries such as the United States consistently outperform other countries in the act of creative destruction of which Schumpeter spoke. Again, the record of the United States has been stupendous. Here the economic competition is so intense that, over several decades, the lists of top companies such as the Fortune 500 show considerable churn as new companies ascend and old firms disappear altogether. In none of the other developed countries, such a churn is witnessed.

The Entrepreneurial Ecosystem

To understand why some countries excel in "creative destruction" we need to look at how the legal, political, and economic environment of a country influences the behavior of entrepreneurially minded individuals and managers. In other words, the entrepreneurial ecosystem of a country largely determines how would-be entrepreneurs behave and whether they thrive or not. In a broader sense, the entrepreneurial or business environment that businesses confront in a country has a considerable say in how the firms behave in the marketplace and how effective the competitiveness of firms is. This is an area that scholars from various fields have sought to look at from various angles.

There are no magic formulas to build competitiveness. According to recent evaluations, both the United States of America and Singapore are often deemed to have a high degree of international competitiveness.[17] Their histories and backgrounds could not be more different. The United States has a long history as a nation-state, is endowed with enormous natural resources, and is now widely acknowledged as the only militarily dominant superpower in the world. Singapore, on the other hand, is a small island in Southeast Asia, has no natural resources to speak of, and its history as a nation-state goes back no more than 50 years since its independence from British colonial rule. Given such wide disparities among nations in general, competitiveness is a difficult concept to do research on. Interestingly enough, while the United States has been in the forefront of the creation of new entrepreneurial firms, Singapore has not been so successful in that area.

The work of such scholars as Professor Porter has inferred several possible factors that go into helping a country gain competitiveness from the past development path followed by various countries. Unfortunately, though, such work often sounds like retrospective rationalization.[18] Moreover, like Professor Porter, researchers in this field tend to view competitiveness from the perspective of a country in the context of an industry rather than from a country level analysis per se. What is needed is an institutional perspective. Such a perspective will look at those institutional mechanisms that seem to enhance the entrepreneurial behavior of firms within the countries.

In recent years, a sociological and economical school of thought has come to recognize that each nation's national business system formed by the interaction of several key factors, many of them institutional and some policy choices, uniquely determines the competitive opportunities open to firms in that nation.[19] However, these are key factors that permit enhanced international competitiveness over time. Together, they constitute the national business system (NBS). While national business systems differ from country to country, they tend to be internally consistent within each country. Moreover, national business systems tend to be deeply rooted in the culture, history, and political institutions of each country. Taking such a holistic approach to competitiveness through institutional and policy mechanisms makes sense since it is now widely recognized by scholars that institutions play a major role in economic development of countries and thus in the strategy choices firms make within countries.[20] Indeed, one suspects that the same mechanisms that constitute the national business systems of countries are likely to influence the entrepreneurial ecosystem of countries.

Past research suggests that four major institutional arrangements are crucial to understanding the entrepreneurial ecosystems of countries. They are: Corporate Governance, Financial Markets, Intellectual Property Regime, and the Human Capital Development System. All of these evolve over a period of time in response to business needs and to an extent shaped by policymakers. These institutions interact with and influence each other as to create a self-reinforcing and thus supportive or mutually contradictory national level entrepreneurial ecosystem (see figure 2.1).

The entrepreneurial ecosystem framework integrates both the sociological perspectives on national business environments[21] as well as the new institutional perspective that places emphasis on economic rationale of institutional arrangements.[22] Since economic underpinnings of institutions cannot be isolated from social and political contexts, such a synthesis indeed makes intuitive

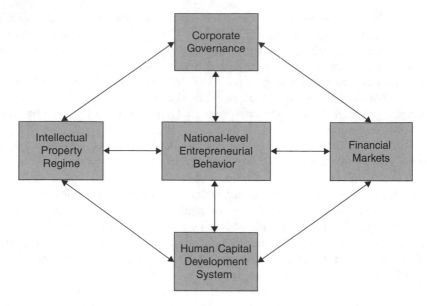

Figure 2.1 Entrepreneurial Ecosystem Framework

sense. In its broadest approach, the entrepreneurial ecosystem approach takes into account the historical, cultural, and social aspects of the country under scrutiny. In this book, though, our stress is only on the four institutional arrangements we have identified above. In our assessment, these four provide enough of a conceptual lens to understand both the phenomenon of entrepreneurial ecosystems and its implications for "creative destruction" of economies through the actions of entrepreneurially minded individuals and firms. Indeed, as we shall suggest in later chapters, more and more countries are taking steps to shape these factors in a way to facilitate the promotion of strong entrepreneurial ecosystems within their borders. Hence our focus on this parsimonious choice of four variables to delineate the national level entrepreneurial ecosystem of countries seems reasonable. In the following paragraphs we briefly outline details on and the logic for the choice of these variables for the entrepreneurial ecosystem paradigm.

It is easy to recognize that the quality of the *human capital* available within a country has a major impact on whether or not entrepreneurial firms are able to take advantage of the opportunities they identify as worth exploiting.[23] In any country, human capital development occurs through formal schooling, vocational programs, and corporate training programs. Therefore, in assessing human capital development in a country, one has to look at the educational infrastructure, training systems, curricula, and values. Moreover, an evaluation of the human capital development system in a country should include more than the system of education and training in that country. It should extend to healthcare systems since even the most educated person will not be productive if he or she is seriously ill.[24] The human capital development system in a country also links educational institutions and labor markets. Thus, labor governance, often seen as separate in discussions of national business systems, is closely influenced by the human capital systems of countries. As many observers have recognized, the often harmonious labor relations in many large firms in Japan is largely due to the collectivist values that are imparted to students in Japan in their formative school years. Human capital development systems also affect how individuals see opportunities in the environment. Societies that tend to foster individualistic values may promote entrepreneurial behavior among individuals and managers. Some researchers have also argued that corporate governance and labor governance practices in countries are also influenced by human capital development systems.[25]

It is easy to recognize how *corporate governance* practices could influence entrepreneurial ecosystems. By corporate governance we refer collectively to the incentives, safeguards, and dispute resolution mechanisms to control and coordinate the actions of various stakeholders and to improve the efficiency of the commercial system. For example, the Anglo-American and Japanese systems are vastly different yet are highly effective for each country. While the Americans stress allocative efficiency through antitrust laws, ownership restrictions, separation of stakeholder interests and market for corporate control, the Japanese stress transactional efficiency through relational contracting, reciprocal trade, cross-shareholding and interlocking directorates.[26] In a country where shareholder interests are not protected well and where lender prioritization is lacking, entrepreneurs will have a difficult time raising capital to implement their ideas. Thus, we need to recognize the importance of corporate governance for the promotion of an effective entrepreneurial ecosystem.

Interestingly enough, at least part of the reason for these differences among corporate governance practices between countries lies in the organization of *financial or capital markets* in these countries. In the United States and United Kingdom external financial markets (stock markets, bond markets, venture capitalists, private equity firms, hedge funds, etc.) tend to dominate whereas in Japan and Germany internal capital markets (group banks, closely related institutions, etc.) tend to be predominant. It is no accident that, in general, the former group of countries (United States and United Kingdom) ranks higher in new firm creation while the latter (Japan and Germany) lags in that dimension. Entrepreneurial efforts, be they from individuals or from existing firms, tend to be risky and as such availability of risk capital is crucial for a positive entrepreneurial ecosystem. An external financial market with a variety of players and instruments[27] is in a position to fund such risk taking by marrying the right type of investors to the right type of entrepreneurial efforts. Internal capital markets that are closely tied to corporations tend to be less inclined to fund risky ventures by new comers. On the other hand, internal capital markets may be more helpful to internal ventures since intricate intercorporate links such as *keiretsus, zaibatsus, chaebols, grupos,* and so on among firms may promote trust among various players.[28]

Finally, as more and more innovation in the market place is tied to technological advances in different industries, countries have come to recognize the importance of *intellectual property regimes* in promoting innovative firms. That property rights are critical for the effective and efficient functioning of a market economy is now widely recognized by economists.[29] Beginning with ancient rights to own property through English philosopher Locke's view that government should be constrained in attenuating property rights to American constitution's recognition that no person shall be deprived of "life, liberty, and property" without due process of law, the line is direct and clear. Property rights are important for a well-functioning economy since these rights encompass more than mere possession of ownership. As legal experts agree, property rights include a combination of rights and relationships that give rise to entitlements in addition to ownership. Property rights entitle a person to use, enjoy, and dispose of property as he or she sees fit. We can recognize the importance of these rights for entrepreneurship when we realize that, only with those rights, an owner, when necessary, will be able to use property as collateral to fund his risky ventures.

Intellectual property laws extend these property rights to intangible property. Under it, owners are granted property rights to a variety of intangible assets, such as musical, literary, and artistic works; ideas, discoveries, and inventions; and words, phrases, symbols, and designs. Copyrights, trademarks, patents, industrial designs, and even trade secrets come under the rubric of intellectual property. The importance of intellectual property rights for innovation and entrepreneurship was recognized early on by America's founding fathers. They included such rights in the constitution itself that provided for limited monopoly rights to holders of copyrights as well as patents.[30] That much of the success of the technology and innovation based firms in United States could be traced to these rights is a testament to the importance of these rights for entrepreneurship.

A Tale of Two Entrepreneurial Companies

The power of the above entrepreneurial ecosystem framework is best seen in the history and evolution of two different firms, in the same technology space, but in two different countries and thus beginning in two different entrepreneurial ecosystems. The short, thumb-nail picture of these companies— Google of United States and Infosys of India—attest to the effect, supporting or debilitating, that entrepreneurial ecosystem has on the fortunes, growth, and strategic trajectory of companies. This is especially striking since both companies could be considered entrepreneurial in the most quintessential sense. Both had visionary founders, both identified unique opportunities, and both had plans to go against the grain and succeed. Still, one company's success was almost effortless while the other company's success was achieved against stupendous odds.

The story of Google is well known.[31] By the mid-1990s, as the World Wide Web expanded and its potential came to be recognized, the need for search services also grew. Alta Vista and Inktomi were already into the market with their search engines that were also adopted by Yahoo!, a major Internet firm. In late 1998, two Stanford graduate students, Sergey Brin and Larry Page, came out with their search algorithm. The effort of two young people, with no prior business experience in a field already dominated by a firm like Yahoo!, to start a search engine company would have been laughed out of office in most countries. But not in the United States. First, the two were able to take advantage of the intellectual property regime in the United States. They were able to patent their algorithm. Next, the sophistication of the financial markets in the United States came to their help. Brin and Page were able to gain first-round venture capital funding from two elite venture capital firms—Sequoia and Kleiner Perkins—in June 1999, a mere eight months after perfecting their search algorithm. This was possible partly because the intellectual property rights allowed the pair to use their patent to support their capital needs. Next, Brin and Page were able to draw on the abundant, high quality human capital available in the United States to staff their fledgling company with talented people, many of them young, who were lured by the chance to strike it rich through stock options proffered by Google. Here, the corporate governance system came to Google's assistance. The system allowed hiring and compensating people on the basis of future earnings (represented by stock options). During the initial phase, the venture capitalists were content to allow such compensation so that the company could grow. Also, since the corporate governance system in the United States secured the rights of key investors like Sequoia and Kleiner Perkins, the latter were content to wait to reap the benefits of their investments without hurrying the two founders— Sergey Brin and Larry Page—to move too quickly to gain short-term profits. This allowed the founders to experiment with different business models and ways to monetize their intellectual property rights. It was in late 2004, five years after their speculative venture investment, that Sequoia and Kleiner Perkins were able to reap their huge returns through a public offering of Google shares. The rest, as they say, is history. Today, just a decade after its founding, Google is one of the largest, most profitable companies in the world. It would not be wrong to argue that Google represents the acme of the success of the supporting entrepreneurial ecosystem of the United States. Perhaps in no other country would such a success have been possible.

Contrast this experience of Google with Infosys of India. Infosys came into being when seven founders—all well educated engineers with several years of experience in the software service industry—decided to form a new company in India in the early 1980s.[32] The key leaders—Narayana Murthy and Nandan Nilekani—did not hail from any of the well-known business families that dominated the Indian business scene at that time. They were middle-class Indians who were truly pioneering entrepreneurs. Unlike Google's founders though, they had to struggle against the unhelpful Indian ecosystem that was largely stacked against entrepreneurial ventures.

First, they faced the challenge of Indian intellectual property rights. Beginning in early 1970s, India had made it difficult to obtain much protection for intellectual property. Ostensibly meant to fight off the multinationals, especially in pharmaceuticals, the system gave out only short duration process patents and not product patents. Software did not qualify for patents either.

Being thus unable to rely on Indian intellectual property rights, the founders of Infosys chose a business model that emphasized low cost, high quality human capital available in India to serve the software development needs of overseas clients. Highly educated engineers and scientists who were willing to work for fairly low wages was the only advantage that the Indian entrepreneurial ecosystem offered to Infosys' founders. And they exploited it to the hilt.

Still, the other aspects of Indian ecosystem worked against them. For one thing, they had no access to risk capital. India, at that time, did not have venture capitalists or angel investors. The only source of capital was a state-owned banking system that was highly risk averse and unwilling to lend to up-start Indians. Indian capital markets, thus, were inimical to truly entrepreneurial ventures.

The Indian corporate governance system was no help either. The Indian business scene was then dominated by family owned conglomerates that did not provide for much protection of minority shareholders. So, used to cavalier treatment by dominant shareholders, no banker worth his salt would invest in new, entrepreneurial ventures.

Indeed, Infosys resorted to bootstrapping. It was funded by Murthy and his associates with an initial capital of approximately $1000 borrowed from their spouses. Indeed, it is reported that, at a later date, when Murthy needed some working capital, he had to hypothecate his wife's gold jewels to borrow the necessary funds. And yet, Infosys turned out to be a success and it owes it not to the Indian entrepreneurial ecosystem.

Infosys succeeded in spite of and not because of the Indian ecosystem. Fortunately, it was able to latch on to the ecosystem of United States, using that country's financial markets to raise capital in New York through the issuance of American Depository Receipts. And to do that it needed to live up to the demands of those markets' corporate governance practices and disclosure requirements.

The narration of these two firms' evolution is an illustration not only of the importance of the entrepreneurial ecosystem for fostering entrepreneurial firms, but also of how global capital flows allow entrepreneurial firms from countries whose own ecosystems are inimical to entrepreneurial firms. Infosys is typical of an Indian company that managed to become a global player because it was able to tap into the global capital markets. In other words, it was able to become a company that changed the competitive landscape in a global industry because access to global capital allowed it to succeed. What is more, the success of firms like Infosys has led Indian policymakers to question their old ways of doing things and to adjust their ecosystem to be friendlier to entrepreneurial initiatives. It is to this idea of how global capital flows are changing the industries and countries that we turn to next.

Global Capital Flows and the Evolving Global Entrepreneurial Ecosystem

Capital has always been a scarce resource. Capital for risky ventures is even more of a scarce resource. Entrepreneurial ventures, be they by individuals or by managers in established firms, by definition, carry risks. A good entrepreneurial ecosystem finds a way to encourage innovative and entrepreneurial efforts by balancing the risks and rewards of investors and entrepreneurs. The American entrepreneurial ecosystem we described earlier is essentially the way such a system works in practice. In other words, while some countries have managed to create a sound entrepreneurial ecosystem, some have not. Until recently, this meant that some countries, because of their helpful entrepreneurial ecosystems, led through entrepreneurial "creative destruction" and the resultant transformation of industries and high economic growth. Others, which did not foster such helpful entrepreneurial ecosystems, remained stagnant; wedded to old ways of doing things, they lost out on global opportunities, ending up as laggards in economic performance leagues.

Global availability of capital has changed all that. It has unleashed the entrepreneurial potential of would-be entrepreneurs and entrepreneurial managers on the world. This has had a profound effect on countries as well as industries. And this is the thrust of this book. Our agenda in this book is to describe how global capital flows are changing the global entrepreneurial ecosystem itself and its implications for managers and policymakers.

First, we show how capital tends to flow in response to the entrepreneurial ecosystem of the countries. Those who already possess even a rudimentarily supportive entrepreneurial ecosystem tend to attract capital from abroad. This sets up a virtuous cycle of improving entrepreneurial ecosystem and flow of more capital into the country. These are the leaders. Others, which do not respond to the need for improving entrepreneurial ecosystem either become loungers or laggards in attracting global capital. The availability of capital helps firms in leading countries to participate more fully in global arena. Witness how companies from India have managed to acquire companies in other advanced countries by tapping into the global capital market.[33] Companies in laggard countries are usually not in a position to do so.

Second, global capital flows have the effect of profoundly changing the competitive landscape of industries. Again, the impact is through the change in the global entrepreneurial ecosystem. Because firms are not constrained by having to depend only on their own country level entrepreneurial ecosystem for their growth and entrepreneurial ambitions, firms have a reach that may exceed their grasp. In turn, this makes the lives of managers and owners of firms in many industries less comfortable. In nascent or growing industries like nanotechnology or biopharmaceuticals, firms from countries like India and China are now competing intensely because they are able to tap into the global entrepreneurial ecosystem through capital access. This has created both threats and opportunities for firms in developed countries. In maturing industries like computer services, firms like TCS, Infosys, and Wipro of India are competing intensely against the likes of IBM, Accenture, and Cap Gemini. What is more, even in industries such as steel, given up by developed country firms as difficult to compete in, new comers with the help of global capital flows are making a difference.

Third, as global capital flows change the competitive landscape of industries and challenge countries to change their entrepreneurial ecosystems, the policymakers too face a challenge. They have to respond to the pressures brought on them for changes in their countries' entrepreneurial ecosystems as global capital flows either offer them the carrot of further opportunities for effective participation in the global arena or the stick of being left behind as other countries steal a march over them in global competition. Policymakers have to rethink ways to improve all facets of their entrepreneurial ecosystem— human capital, corporate governance, financial markets, and intellectual property regimes—if they want their countries to do well in the new world of free capital flows.

Fourth, even as countries and their policymakers are wrestling with the challenges posed by global capital flows, capital providers themselves ranging from venture capitalists and private equity providers through hedge funds to institutional investors are figuring ways to find and invest in places where their capital will generate the best risk-adjusted return. Again, the entrepreneurial ecosystem framework may provide them with ways to assess how well their investments will pan out in different countries.

Fifth, among managers in existing industries, global capital flows are already causing much angst. Managers in industries ranging from steel to plastics and automotive have had to decide whether they want to acquire or be acquired. Again, managers have to rely on our entrepreneurial ecosystem framework to assess their plans to spread their wings abroad. Alternatively, if they are to be acquired by players from countries with different entrepreneurial ecosystems, the managers need to know how the new owners' conditioning by their home country's entrepreneurial ecosystem will affect their strategic choices and how they—the managers in the acquired firm—should deal with those choices.

Finally, the entrepreneurs and entrepreneurial managers themselves face interesting decisions in the new world of global capital flows and converging entrepreneurial ecosystems. They have to learn how to cope with the needs and pressures of investors from another country with a different set of expectations based on their familiarity with their home country entrepreneurial ecosystem. These would-be entrepreneurs and entrepreneurial managers also have to negotiate the shoals of challenges posed by pressure brought on by having to operate in new countries and new markets with different entrepreneurial ecosystems.

Part II

The Entrepreneurial Ecosystem's Impact on Countries and Industries

3

The Impact of the Entrepreneurial Ecosystem on Countries

Why does capital flow into some countries and away from others? Capital seeks growth and it moves to those countries where investors believe that such growth will be the highest. Naturally, there's more to the decision than simple growth. It does not do an investor much good to invest capital that grows until the host country nationalizes the business. Nor will an investor place capital in a country that simply seeks a check for a minority stake that will passively sit by and hope that management of the recipient company makes the right moves.

As we'll explore in this chapter, investors can use the entrepreneurial ecosystem (EE) framework to help them judge which countries should get their capital and which should not. What insights does this framework reveal? Here are four on which this chapter will focus attention.

Capital flows globally from large, but slower-growing countries to large developing ones with the highest growth rates. Capital is attracted to rapid growth because it can earn the highest return the most rapidly in such markets. However, growth is not a sure prescription for high returns. That's because the investment climate in a rapidly growing country may introduce new risks—such as the ultimate confiscation of the investment, complex ownership restrictions, and cultural differences that might limit managerial flexibility. As a result, investors must analyze the EE within the destination country before writing a check.

Emerging markets' hunger for capital creates pressure to change their EEs. The predominance of private capital flows within the walled garden of advanced corporate governance, relatively transparent financial markets, and respect for intellectual property puts pressure on developing nations seeking to attract that capital. Simply put, if a developing country wants foreign capital, it must alter its EE to create a more compelling risk/return calculus for private capital. And those changes must make it more likely that private investors will earn higher returns more rapidly by protecting their interests.

Private capital flows are changing traditional capital gradients among countries. In the past the United States had lent money to South American countries, and the capital flows have reversed in recent years. Relatively depressed regions in North America, such as Canada's nickel mining region, have found themselves receiving capital from more successful South American mining enterprises. As we'll see, this new flow of capital often takes the form of M&A activity in which a highly valued developing country company takes over an undervalued asset in a slower-growing region of a developed country.

New sources of capital are altering the EE of developed countries. Sovereign Wealth Funds (SWFs)—a $5 trillion pool of capital generated from government surpluses in countries such as China and energy producing nations— have different objectives than private equity and venture capital firms. As a result, SWFs challenge the traditional rules established by countries to manage cross-border capital flows. For example, in 2007 and 2008 the United States hosted internal debates regarding the wisdom of allowing SWFs to own significant stakes in U.S. financial institutions (FIs). Opposing such SWF investments were those who feared the risk associated with letting a country that could become a foreign policy opponent own a stake in U.S. FIs. Those who were more afraid of U.S. taxpayer investment in FIs tended to favor the SWF capital.

Entrepreneurial Ecosystem and Intercountry Capital Flows

As we suggested above, when it comes to attracting private capital, not all countries are created equal. Some countries find investors beating down their doors to get a piece of the action while other countries struggle to get potential investors to return their phone calls. To provide some structure to a discussion of how to explain these differences, we define three categories of countries, as follows.

Leaders. The *leaders* are the countries that generate and invest the most capital. These countries set the agenda for other nations seeking to both invest and receive capital. The conditions that they create for accumulating and investing capital are the focus of intense scrutiny by other countries that seek to achieve comparable levels of performance. The leaders we refer to include developed countries such as the United States, the United Kingdom, continental Europe, and Japan; as well as developing countries like India. Despite the global recession that began in 2007, these leaders had accumulated sufficient capital and access to credit to weather the downturn—and their EEs offered hope for their ultimate recovery.

Loungers. The *loungers* are the countries that are most likely to be examining the practices of the leaders and trying to emulate them. These countries do not want to be on the leading edge; however, they are willing to adopt the most effective practices for generating and investing capital and to shun practices that work less effectively for leaders. The loungers include Brazil and Mexico.

Laggards. The laggards lack the ability to generate significant amounts of investment capital and thus they do not concern themselves with investing it. Such countries generally lack comparative advantages that enable them to generate enough wealth to feed and educate their people. They often suffer due to wide disparities in income with their leaders feeding at the trough of global aid while their citizens lack basic necessities. Unless these countries control valuable natural resources, they will have trouble attracting capital to their shores. These laggards include parts of Africa and several Latin American countries.

In chapter 2, we mentioned the EE framework. We'll next explore the various factors within the four components of the framework that investors use when deciding how to allocate capital (figure 3.1). After examining these factors, we explore how the EE framework manifests itself among countries that are leaders, loungers, and laggards.

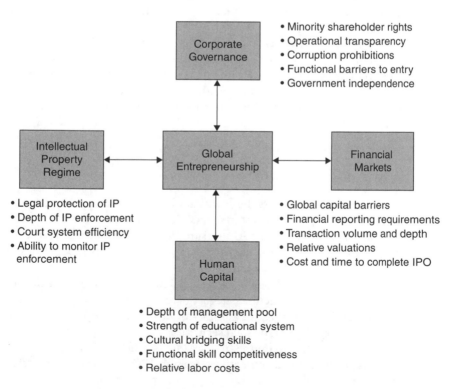

Figure 3.1   Drivers of Entrepreneurial Ecosystem Receptiveness

First let's examine each of the factors. Although it is likely that the relative importance of these determinants will vary for different countries, these determinants can help investors assess which countries in which to invest and how best to structure such investments. These Drivers of Entrepreneurial Ecosystem Receptiveness include the following:

Corporate Governance

- *Minority shareholders rights* assess the extent to which the rights of minority shareholders are respected within a specific country;
- *Operational transparency* measures how well a company within a particular country discloses to minority shareholders the specific opportunities and threats facing the company as well as its financial performance and prospects;
- *Corruption prohibitions* gauge whether a country has laws against corruption and the extent to which those laws are enforced;
- *Functional barriers to entry* include prohibitions against a foreign investor performing specific business activities within a country. One example of this is the Indian government's regulation prohibiting foreign retailers, such as Wal-Mart, from selling goods directly to the Indian public; and
- *Government independence* measures the extent to which a company within a specific country makes decisions independent of government influence. For example, many companies in China and Russia are tightly controlled by the government and thus foreign capital providers must consider the impact that this government control will have on their potential returns.

Financial Markets

- *Global capital barriers* assess the extent to which a capital recipient country permits foreign capital to invest in companies within that country;
- *Financial reporting requirements* measure the comprehensiveness, level of detail, and frequency of financial reporting required to issue securities to the public within a specific country;
- *Transaction volume and depth* gauges the relative volume of securities transactions within a particular category of securities, such as Initial Public Offerings (IPOs) as well as the number of dealers and large institutional investors who regularly trade such securities;
- *Relative valuations* compare the price/earnings ratios and other valuation metrics typically applied to ventures seeking IPOs in various countries' capital markets; and
- *Cost and time to complete IPOs* compares the cost—in terms of fees paid to underwriters, regulators, legal and accounting advisors,

and others—as well as the time required to complete IPOs in various countries' capital markets.

Human Capital

- *Depth of management pool* assesses the extent to which the country in which a capital provider seeks to invest has a deep pool of management talent;
- *Strength of educational system* measures the relative quantity and quality of workers that a country's educational system produces and their relative fitness for performing specific functions—such as general management, computer systems design and development, manufacturing process design, and call center staffing;
- *Cultural bridging skills.* Since weak cultural bridging skills can threaten a global venture, it is important to assess the ability of a country's workers to bridge the culture of their home country and the country supplying capital. For example, many U.S. companies have found that Philippine call centers can serve U.S. customers effectively because Filipinos have a deep cultural knowledge of America and their English-speaking skills are strong;
- *Functional skill competitiveness* gauges how well a particular country's companies can perform specific business functions, such as automobile parts manufacturing, accounts receivable collection, or technical service; and
- *Relative labor costs* measures the price a country's companies would charge to perform these specific business functions. To decide where in the world to perform these functions, managers can combine the measures of specific countries' functional skill competitiveness with their relative cost. Such relative cost analysis should include first order costs, such as shipping goods to their selling destination and second order costs such as coordinating with the people performing the function remotely.

Intellectual Property Regime

- *Legal protection of IP* assesses the extent to which a country receiving capital protects the IP receiving the investment. If a capital recipient country's legal system has more lax protection of IP than the originating country, then capital providers must assess the extent to which this laxity is likely to reduce the expected return;
- *Depth of IP enforcement* helps decision makers to distinguish between countries with tight IP protection in the legal system and lax enforcement from countries with both tight laws and strict enforcement of them. Decision makers can measure the depth of IP enforcement by analyzing the government resources allocated to detecting IP violations and bringing the violators into the court system;

- *Court system efficiency* gauges a country's backlog of IP violation cases and how quickly that country's court system is able to process these cases and bring them to an effective conclusion. Court system efficiency is another measure of how well an investment in IP is likely to be protected by the government in a country that receives global capital; and
- *Ability to monitor IP enforcement* measures the ease of obtaining accurate and timely information on the status of IP protection within a specific country. As we describe below, such transparency is a critical element in creating and reinforcing an IP regime that makes a country a competitive place for capital investment in IP.

So how do these factors in the EE manifest themselves among countries that are leaders, loungers, and laggards? There are no simple answers. Some countries, such as Russia, which excel at *creating* capital by selling their natural resources, lower the barriers to *entry* for *attracting* capital while subsequently building insurmountable barriers that block the capital's *exit*. Other countries, such as China, which are quite hospitable to foreign purchases of their goods produced by relatively inexpensive labor, have very weak intellectual property protection that has the effect of blocking venture capital investment.

In short, the EE manifests itself in complex ways in different countries. To explore how the EE manifests itself in leaders, loungers, and laggards we will describe the EE in each of the countries—exploring that of a leader (the United States), a lounger (China), and a laggard (Russia).

Leader (United States)

The United States, though imperfect (the reasons for saying so are given below), is a leader because the strengths of its EE enable it to generate capital, invest it domestically and globally and attract capital from other countries. The United States has robust corporate governance, open and liquid capital markets, excellent human capital (although with relatively high labor costs), and a relatively strong intellectual property regime.

The United States's EE has distinct flaws—its corporate governance tends to lack sufficient transparency, its labor costs are relatively high and many managers lack cultural bridging skills, and its capital markets do not require sufficient transparency. Nevertheless, relative to other countries, the strengths of the United States's EE outweigh its weaknesses. And as we will see later in this chapter, these strengths enable the United States to generate, invest, and attract more capital than any other country.

Lounger (China)

China is a lounger because the strengths of its EE enable it to generate capital and invest it domestically; however, some weaknesses in its EE make it difficult for China to attract private capital. Its corporate governance enables it to organize efficient manufacturing and its workers are both skilled and willing to accept extremely low wages. Global corporations use of these strengths to purchase goods from China has enabled it to build up enormous capital reserves it invests globally. Some of these investments—such as its 2007 and 2008 infusions of capital into the U.S. banking system—have lost substantial value. However, as a holder of $340 billion of U.S. debt, China is an important provider of outside capital.

Conversely, weaknesses in China's EE have repelled many providers of private capital—particularly those from the United States. Among the biggest weaknesses in China are its lack of intellectual property regime and the lack of transparency in its capital markets. China is known for its willingness to violate copyrights for music and technology. As a result, venture capitalists (VCs) are often uncomfortable placing capital in technology-based ventures. Instead they prefer to invest in services-based ventures where the source of competitive advantage is customer relations and distribution. Moreover, the absence of rigid financial reporting standards for companies listing on the Shanghai exchange, for example, makes it less likely that venture capital firms would seek to list their companies on those exchanges.

Laggard (Russia)

Russia's EE illustrates the dangers to capital flows of weak corporate governance and opaque capital markets. As oil and gas prices rose, thanks in part to high amounts of borrowed money from outside Russia used to prop it up, these foreign capital suppliers convinced themselves that their risk of loss was minimal. However, the centralized control of Russia's companies and its stock market demonstrates the dangers of a flawed EE—particularly when those trends reverse.

And between May and October 2008, the flaws in Russia's EE became more pronounced as its stock market declined and foreign capital flowed out of Russia at a rapid pace. During that time Russia's RTS index fell 71% and Russia's central bank reported that its companies owed $47.5 billion to foreign creditors by the end of 2008 and $160 billion by the end of 2009. Meanwhile the outflow of capital from Russia turned into a flood as falling commodity prices wiped out investment value—specifically, between August and October 2008, $74 billion in foreign investment fled Russia. Not only did foreign capital collapse, but so did that of Russia's so-called oligarchs—their richest 25—who lost a collective estimated $230 billion between May and October 2008.[1]

What makes Russia an EE laggard and how did its EE contribute to this reversal of fortune? As we'll explore with specific case studies later in this chapter, Russia's EE is centrally controlled. Its most powerful companies control natural resources—so wealth stems not from human capital but from the willingness of a select group of financially skilled oligarchs to support the policies of the existing power structure in exchange for control of those natural resources. Russia uses its court system to harass executives who speak in opposition to government policies. And its financial markets lack the transparency and depth to support IPOs.

As commodity prices tumbled, Russia closed its securities markets on several occasions only to watch them tumble further as they reopened. More importantly, through its willingness to oust executives representing Western interests, such as the Hermitage example we'll explore later in this chapter, Russia sent a strong signal to foreign capital providers that it would be happy to take outside capital but would not allow that capital to earn a return on it. Rather, Russia provided a stark example to those foreign capital providers that it would use its court system to drive out the representatives of its Western partners and take full control of the venture once it had the foreign capital it needed to launch it.

Simply put, Russia's EE—particularly its functioning during a downturn—illustrates that foreign capital that takes a chance in Russia is likely to get the worst of all possible outcomes—if it invests in a risky venture that fails, it will have no recourse and if it funds a successful venture, Russia will root out Western executives and expropriate the profit.

Capital Flows among Countries

Can the EE help us understand the flow of capital around the globe? Before examining this question, let's first scrutinize the evidence on capital flows. Specifically, we'll study the flow of capital among the leaders, between the leaders and the loungers, and—to a lesser extent—between the leaders and the laggards. Our analysis of the data suggests the following patterns.

Capital flows in and out of leaders—such as the United States and the United Kingdom—exceed those in other regions. Those countries with the most advanced EEs *supply* and *invest* the most capital. As we will see later in this chapter, while capital seeks growth—which pushes the capital to developing countries with the most advanced EEs—developed nations still generate the majority of capital and reinvest that capital in slower-growing, but less risky countries. One measure of this is the flow of Foreign Direct Investment (FDI) into developed countries. Such FDI inflows increased 33% in 2007 to a record $1,248 billion while FDI outflows grew even faster to $1,692 billion. Due to the financial crisis that began in developing countries in 2007, UNCTAD expected capital flows in 2008 to be much lower—specifically, it estimated that 2008 FDI flows would total $1,600 billion—a 10% decline from 2007. Meanwhile it expected FDI flows to developing countries to remain fairly stable in 2008 compared to 2007. However, in 2007, the United States received more capital than any other country while Canadian inflows nearly doubled as they did in 2006, making it the fourth largest recipient. Meanwhile FDI inflows to other leaders in Europe, such as the United Kingdom, France, the Netherlands, and Spain contributed to a 43% FDI inflow boost to the European Union (EU) to $804 billion. Moreover, much of this growth resulted from entrepreneurial activity in the form of cross-border acquisitions as a result of the restructuring and consolidation of industries.[2]

Merger and acquisition (M&A) activity—spurred by corporate and private equity buyers from developed countries—set a new record in 2007. M&A transaction value of $1,637 billion in 2007 surpassed the previous record set in 2000 by 21%. Global M&As involving private equity funds as the acquirers doubled to $461 billion, a record total which accounted for 25% of cross-border transactions. Global companies from developed countries used their high profits to make 90% of the M&A deals over $1 billion. In August 2007 an abrupt downturn in M&A resulted from a global economy slowdown and financial turmoil. During the first half of 2008, M&A transactions were 29% lower than they were in the second half of 2007.[3]

SWFs represent a new phenomenon, shifting government capital generated in developing countries into troubled FIs in developed ones. A new feature of global FDI is the emergence of SWFs as direct investors, which have accumulated reserves rapidly in recent years and now manage assets estimated at $5 trillion; these are increasingly behind large-scale cross-border M&As and lately have injected large amounts of capital into several troubled FIs in developed countries, particularly in the United States. SWFs made only one cross-border merger in 1980—a figure that peaked at 30 in 2007. SWFs accumulated capital due to export surpluses based on inexpensive labor—as in China—and on oil and natural gas surpluses—as in the Middle East and Russia. In 2007 and early 2008, SWFs saw an opportunity to acquire stakes in the weak U.S. FIs as their stock prices and capital bases plummeted. However, after the rapid build-up of reserves generated by export surpluses, changes in global economic fundamentals created new investment opportunities involving structurally weakened financial firms. Examples include China Investment Corp.'s (CIC) $5 billion Morgan Stanley investment; Abu Dhabi Investment Authority's $7.5 billion stake in Citigroup; KIC (Republic of Korea) and Kuwait Investment Authority's $ 5.4 billion equity stake in Merrill Lynch.[4] However, after losing significant portions of their investment to a continued decline in the value of these FI's stock prices, SWFs lost interest in adding to their positions in these weakened FIs.

China and India have attracted significant private equity and venture capital in recent years. As with other capital sources that peaked in 2007, so did private capital flows to emerging markets, which hit a record $1 trillion in 2007 and were expected to drop to around $800 billion by 2009 according to the World Bank.[5] Nevertheless, private capital invested in China and India grew significantly during 2007 and 2008. For instance, during the first half of 2008, $26.5 billion of fresh capital entered China—33.3% more than in the same period in 2007. Moreover, buyout funds dominated China's capital pool in 2008's first half, accounting for $10.2 billion, or 38.5%. The most rapidly growing type of fund invested in infrastructure—funds boasted the biggest increase, attracting $3.0 billion worth of capital, 13.5 times more than the $222.8 million recorded during the same period of 2007.[6] VC funding to China surged 85% in the first half of 2008, due to large injections of capital into mature Internet ventures. Venture firms invested $2.15 billion in mainland China companies during the first half of 2008, up from $1.16 billion in 2007.[7] India also attracted significant private equity and venture capital. For example, private equity firms invested $2.8 billion in 77 Indian companies during the quarter ended June 2008, higher than the 74 deals for a total of $1.9 billion in the same quarter of 2007. VCs invested $237.6 million in 17 deals in India during the three months ended June 30, 2008—more than twice the $108 million and 12 deals in the same period in 2007.[8]

Nations are changing their laws to encourage the flow of capital globally. Despite rising protectionism in some countries, the majority of regulatory and legal changes have favored increased investment by global companies. In particular, UNCTAD's annual survey of changes in national laws and regulations that may influence the entry and operations of such companies suggests that policymakers seek to encourage FDI by making the investment climates in their countries more attractive to global companies. In 2007, 74% of the 100 FDI-related policy changes were intended to make the host country's investment environment more suitable to foreign capital flows—this despite the growing concerns and political debate over rising protectionism. Some Asian governments, for example, further relaxed ownership restrictions on foreign investors, encouraged private-sector investment in infrastructure industries, and introduced measures to attract FDI. Some countries, for instance, increased the level of investment protection provided under their investment laws or relaxed foreign-exchange controls, improved admission procedures, and offered investment incentives. In 2007, Asian governments also launched new measures to encourage or support outward FDI.[9]

Companies choose to invest in countries with large, rapidly growing markets. Although these legal and regulatory factors influence where companies, SWFs, and private equity firms invest, economic factors play a larger role in the decision. More specifically, according to UNCTAD, market growth, market size, and access to international/regional markets are by far the most important factors influencing companies' choices of investment location (50% of answers combined), followed by quality of business environment, including availability of skilled labor (8%), suppliers (6%), and adequate infrastructure (7%). The relative importance of inexpensive labor is high only for manufacturing activities such as garment production.[10]

Case Studies of Intercountry Capital Flows

How do these broad trends play themselves out in the minds of investors and business executives in different countries? To explore this issue, we will examine case studies that highlight the issues related to how that capital was used and describe the resulting creation and destruction of companies. Through these case studies, we will explore how the capital flows generate both resistance and change—mapping transformations from risk aversion and tax avoidance to prudent risk- and growth-seeking behavior by firms' managers. To do this, we take a couple of countries as examples under each of the three categories—leaders, loungers, and laggards—to demonstrate how the EE framework explains why and how these countries' respond the way they have to global capital flows. What follows are the four examples we'll illustrate in this section.

Boston VCs go global. This example shows how the availability of Venture Capital (VC) expertise in information technology coupled with rapid growth opportunities in developing countries has led these VCs far from their home base to seek opportunities. This proves the importance of the Financial Markets and Intellectual Property components of the EE framework since both of these make it possible for a Boston VC to profit from investing in start-ups in India, China, and Vietnam.

Brazilian mineral company changes Canadian management culture by acquisition. This example illustrates how a rare credit rating upgrade for Brazilian mining company Vale de Rio (Vale) gave it the capital to acquire a Canadian nickel mining company, Inco. After acquiring Inco, Vale applied its more harmonious labor management techniques to the formerly rancorous climate. Ultimately, however, this deal had a less than sanguine ending as declining nickel prices soured the deal. This example also illustrates the importance of the Financial Markets and Human Capital components of the EE framework.

Siemens' acquisition of Michigan plant revives its local economy. This case study is a proof of how the availability of global capital to finance M&A coupled with growing demand in developing countries is enabling a German company to acquire an idled plant in a depressed area of Michigan and use its capital and expertise to manufacture wastewater treatment equipment eagerly gobbled up by countries in Asia and the Middle East. It shows the importance of the Corporate Governance and Human Capital components of the EE framework.

Russian government uses legal system to shut down Hermitage Capital. This example illustrates how a laggard country can lure foreign capital to finance the development of its natural resources and then turn against the capital providers once the investment of money and know-how has been completed. Russia followed this approach when it ousted the founder of Hermitage Capital, a $4 billion investment fund, and used its legal system to scare him into taking his money out of Russia and escaping to London. This example demonstrates how failures in a country's EE, particularly in components such as corporate governance and financial markets, can repel foreign capital.

Boston VCs Go Global

While countries seek to attract capital so they can benefit through the wealth created by those investments, Boston VCs have a very different

challenge. They have a long track record of funding successful companies; however, local investments have accounted for an ever smaller proportion of that
success. In fact, the success of Boston VCs investing in Boston companies may
have peaked in the 1980s with the public offerings of a raft of minicomputer
companies competing with Digital Equipment Corp (DEC). In the 1990s, Boston
VCs had some success with local start-ups, mostly because they sold themselves
to more successful companies in Silicon Valley. At the end of the most recent
decade, very few Boston companies have enriched local VCs and they are looking
around the world for growth.

There are numerous examples of Boston VCs investing outside of the region.
For example, Matrix Partners raised $275 million to invest in Chinese start-
ups. International Data Group announced a $150 million fund for Eastern
European investments. And Battery Ventures has slashed its New England
investments in the past several years—cutting by 50% the amount it invested in
New England between 2002 and 2006 compared to the previous five years. In
the case of Battery, one of its partners, Tom Crotty, said the reason was simple:
higher growth in other regions. As Crotty put it, "That [drop in New England
investments] wasn't because we made any strategic decision to do so. [Rather,
the firm was just] chasing better growth opportunities [in California and outside the United States]."[11]

Other Boston VCs place a similar emphasis on the importance of growth
in the markets in which they invest. For example, another VC fund, Matrix
Partners, expanded a fund dedicated to India from $150 million to $400 million
in late 2007. The rationale was growth. As Tim Barrows, general partner at
Matrix Partners, said, "[The economies of countries like India and China] are
growing faster than ours, and the venture business there is still nascent, which
makes it a good opportunity." Implicit in Barrow's comment is an important
point related to the different EEs of Boston versus India. He seems to believe
that Matrix's accumulated expertise in VC investing—a form of human
capital—will help it to find profitable deals in India. Moreover, Barrow's view
that India's market is rapidly growing and relatively inexperienced with VC
might provide Matrix with a chance to shape India's EE in a way that favors
Matrix. It remains to be seen whether Matrix's skills in investing in U.S. companies will help or hinder its efforts to find profitable investments in India.
However, given the significant differences between the two investing environments, it is likely that Matrix will need to be cautious about how it adapts to
those differences.[12]

Another firm with a longer history of investing outside of the United States
finds several aspects of these countries' EEs compelling. The firm, International
Data Group, set up the first foreign VC firm in China in 1992 and now manages
$2.6 billion there. McGovern started a fund in Vietnam in 2004 and in India in
2006. In 2008, he planned to launch a new fund in a different country, such as
Russia and Brazil, every year or 18 months. McGovern finds both the market
growth and the countries' efforts to upgrade their human capital as increasing the
appeal of investing there. As McGovern said, "We find these developing markets

very attractive. The GNP growth is high, and the government has invested a lot in technical education. They want to see the entrepreneurial sector of their country's economy move up."[13]

Investing in places outside Boston is a recognition by VCs that growth has slowed locally in the industries in which they are accustomed to investing. However, some Boston VCs are willing to admit that global expansion entails risks. For example, Todd Dagres, a former Battery Ventures partner, noted that "To some extent, setting up in India and China and Israel is kind of an admission that the backyard isn't as fertile as it used to be [referring solely to technology investing]. Those are risky places to go."[14]

Going overseas is clearly somewhat of a desperate move by VCs in Boston with a hunger for growth in their area of expertise. This seems to be a requirement for VCs who specialize in information technology investing (e.g., in Silicon Valley, there appear to be more investment opportunities related to information technology). However, other Boston VCs have had success focusing on the life sciences industry. And those investors find ample growth in their own backyards—thus they are reluctant to stray from the local source of growth. One such VC firm is Polaris Venture Partners that reasons that there is no need to take on the additional risk of investing overseas when growth is available at home. Polaris Venture Partners cofounder Terry McGuire put it this way: "This is the most fertile time I've ever seen. Our partners wonder if it's a distraction for us to do offshore deals when there's so much happening here."[15]

What is driving the growth of Boston's life sciences industry? It appears that a combination of government investment and technically trained people in the Boston area contribute to its growth. In fact, its human capital—which leads the world—appears to be attracting government money. This creates a fertile climate in which to place venture funds. According to Michael Lytton, a general partner at Oxford BioSciences Partners, "Boston is still the top recipient of funding from the National Institutes of Health, and there's a steady supply of entrepreneurs who've built companies before. We'd just as soon take the T [Boston mass transit line] to Kendall Square [where much of MIT is located] for a deal than take a plane to Europe."[16]

What is the contour of an EE that attracts venture investment? The Boston VCs suggests that there are three key elements that will open their checkbooks:

- *Rapid growth.* VCs appear to have an appetite for investing in rapidly growing countries. Their logic is that rapid growth increases the odds of earning high returns in a relatively short time frame. The speed to earn a high return lowers the risk of the investment.
- *World-class human capital.* VCs prefer to invest in EEs where the level of human capital is getting stronger thanks to an investment in training and the country's government wants to encourage the influx of foreign capital and its mutually profitable exit. Such EEs appeal to VCs because they lower

the risk that the business will not have the people it needs to operate effectively and the risk that it will not be able to move capital into the business quickly and get it out when market conditions warrant.

- *Opportunity to transfer skills to emerging country.* Finally, VCs believe that the skills they have developed operating in their home country are transferable to a new one. This is particularly true when they are seeking investments in an industry in which they have focused their attention. Since there are differences between the home market and an emerging one, a successful VC skill transfer must be done carefully. And in order to succeed with the skill transfer, a VC might need to hire a partner (who knows its culture, regulatory system, and management practices) in the country where the capital will be invested. Working to adapt to the specific contours of that country's EE increases the odds of successfully transferring the VC skills to the new country.

Brazilian Mining Giant Acquires Canadian Nickel Company

Thanks to its globally dominant position making iron ore and a rare credit upgrade for a Brazilian company, Vale de Rio had the operational ability and the access to capital it needed to make an enormous acquisition of a large Canadian miner of nickel. Through effective management of relationships with the nickel miner's labor union, Vale succeeded in winning over the skeptical Canadian town and settled matters with the union. However, despite its best intentions, a decline in nickel prices turned what had initially been a mutually profitable acquisition into a corporate albatross for Vale.

In 2006, Vale—the world's second-largest mining company, and the biggest miner of iron ore, a key ingredient in steel—spent $17.8 billion to acquire Sudbury, Ontario's biggest employer, nickel company Inco. Following the acquisition, Vale launched a campaign to win over Sudbury's skeptical residents. Vale surprised Sudbury with its rapid acquisition of Inco. According to John Rodriguez, the mayor of Sudbury, Vale "came right out of the blue. We knew nothing about them."[17]

Vale won over many in Sudbury—a town with a history of labor conflict. It donated $375,000 to a local food bank and emphasized the importance of employees. Mark Cutifani, a former Inco executive who now heads miner AngloGold Ashanti Ltd., found Vale to be a model employer. As Cutifani said, "You even had the accountants saying, 'If we are going to be taken over by anyone, it should be those guys.'"[18]

How did Vale get to the point where it could buy such a large company in a developed country such as Canada? Vale has been growing rapidly. In 2007, it hired 9,281 new employees in Brazil, leaving total employment worldwide at 124,013. It generated $39.7 billion in revenue—nearly 10 times what it did in 2001. Moreover, between 2002 and 2006, Vale's average annual return to stockholders—share appreciation plus dividends—was 54.6%, making it the top performing public company with a market capitalization over $50 billion.[19]

Vale has an interesting history. It was formed in 1942 as a state-run company, with loans from the United States as part of a World War II deal in which Brazil agreed to supply minerals to Allied factories. The Brazilian government used its well-known technical skills to undertake projects outside of mining and pulping paper.

In 1997, as part of a Latin America–wide push to privatize, Vale was sold at auction for $3.3 billion. The buyer was a consortium that included Brazil's largest steelmaker, Companhia Siderúrgica Nacional (CSN) as well as banks and pension funds.[20]

Following a 2001 management change, Vale developed a more focused strategy. During 2001 meetings of major shareholders, with consultants from McKinsey & Co. guiding the discussion, Vale decided it wanted to become a global leader in metals such as copper, zinc, and iron ore. Since mining iron ore was considered a declining industry, it did not attract much attention from competitors and annual price increases to steel companies never exceeded 3%. As a result, Vale faced minimal competition as it bought up Brazilian rivals in the iron ore business. By 2005, Vale produced 91% of Brazil's iron ore.[21]

Vale dominated iron ore production at a time when the bargaining power of such steel suppliers increased significantly. For decades, steelmakers had the upper hand in price negotiations with ore producers. But demand from China put the iron ore makers in a much stronger bargaining position. In 2005, the price steelmakers paid for ore rose 68.8%, nearly doubling Vale's profit that year. Ore prices have continued to rise, at a pace Vale executives admit they never imagined.[22]

The growing demand for metals enhances the competitive advantage of the biggest producers, which can make the investments necessary to open new mines, many in remote areas of politically unstable countries. The cost of mining also has been rising. Prices have climbed for many suppliers including explosives and big off-road tires used on mining trucks, which cost $15,000 each. Vale estimates that the cost of opening Southern Range, a new Brazilian iron ore mine that has yet to open, has risen to $10 billion, from $2 billion several years ago.[23]

To diversify beyond iron ore, Vale wanted to grow outside of Brazil, which has almost no coal and not much nickel. But its cost of capital was higher than that of global competitors because ratings agencies regarded it as a riskier credit. So Vale actively courted the metals analyst of Fitch Ratings through frequent visits to New York to provide information about Vale. The investment in building ratings agency relationships paid off when in 2005, Vale received an investment-grade credit rating from ratings agencies—something the Brazilian government still hasn't achieved. The rating enabled Vale to match the lower cost of capital of its rivals in developed countries. As a result, Vale broke up a competing merger deal for Inco with an all-cash offer in 2006.[24]

How did evolving EEs influence Vale's ability to acquire and integrate Inco? Brazil's drive to privatize enabled Vale to shift its corporate governance model to one focused on rapid shareholder value creation from one that emphasized employment of Brazilian citizens. That shift to a shareholder focus also created a management push to expand globally and diversify its sources of income. Thanks to its goal of tapping more advanced EEs in the United States and Canada, Vale management recognized that it would need to reduce its cost of capital and it set out on a winning campaign to achieve that objective. As a result, Vale was able to offer a competitive bid that captured Inco. And Vale used its skills at harmonizing with communities and workers to integrate the Inco deal effectively.

Although Vale did a good job of integrating Inco, the ultimate outcome of the deal remained in question by mid-2009. For example, a ratings service, Fitch, highlighted the "negative market for many of Vale products, particularly nickel." As a result, Fitch expected "Vale to generate Earnings before Interest, Taxes, Depreciation, and Amortization (EBITDA) and Cash from Operations (CFO) during 2009 at levels substantially below 2008, and possibly lower than half of 2008's figures."[25] Perhaps over the long run—assuming demand revives in Vale's markets, particularly that for nickel in which Inco was a major participant—the deal will look good. By January 2010, Vale was benefiting from rising metal prices and a weaker dollar—enabling its stock to hit a 52-week high.[26]

Siemens Revives Holland, MI Company

Vale, representative of a developing country, used its global strength to profit from the economic weakness within a region of a developed country when it acquired Sudbury, ON's Inco. Similarly, strong companies in developed countries can exploit the weaknesses in regions of another developed country. In such cases, the EEs of both the capital supplier and recipient must be willing to accommodate an investment. And in such cases, concerns about national sovereignty take a backseat to the concerns of local politicians in the recipient region who seek to boost employment and economic activity to increase their electoral prospects. This comes to mind while analyzing how Germany's Siemens turned its acquisition of a Holland, MI wastewater treatment equipment plant into a key element of its strategy to expand by making cost-competitive equipment and expanding its global footprint by selling its products to developing countries. The result was increased profits for Siemens and a revival of a region of Michigan that had been stagnating due to a lack of capital and management's inability to perceive the global opportunities for its products.

This transformation began in 2004 when Siemens paid $954 million to purchase a factory on the edge of Holland, which had suffered from declining revenues leading to layoffs. By April 2008, the factory was shipping wastewater treatment equipment to Asia and the Middle East and had twice as many workers on its payroll as it did in 2004.[27]

This transformation from stagnation to success is a microcosm of the economic challenges that Michigan faces. It has lost 300,000 manufacturing jobs since 2000 due in part to the decline of its automobile industry. And while foreign capital, such as the investment from Siemens, has offset some of those losses, efforts to recover those lost jobs have been only partially successful. As of 2005, for example, roughly 200,000 Michigan residents worked for subsidiaries of foreign companies.[28]

The majority of the foreign capital reviving Michigan comes from developed countries—in 2006 that meant Europe. And between 2004 and April 2008, Siemens had contributed $17 billion of that capital. As we saw above, it paid $954 million for the Holland wastewater treatment equipment company in 2004. And in 2007, it paid $3.6 billion for a business management software company, $2.7 billion for a maker of medical diagnostic technology, and $7 billion for another medical testing company.[29]

Despite Siemens' internal concerns that its corporate bureaucracy could slow down decision making, its massive global marketing presence had the potential to provide access to new markets for the wastewater treatment equipment. According to the former plant manager of the Holland wastewater treatment factory, David J. Spyker, Siemens's reputation for bureaucracy could be more than offset by its presence in 190 countries, which would allow Siemens to gain market share in places such as China where relationships with high-level officials are crucial. According to Spyker, instead of dealing with a low-level purchasing agent "[n]ow, we're dealing at the ministry level."[30]

The results of this global strategy have been positive. Siemens reports that its revenue from the plant has tripled and its work force has grown from 105 to 237. Jeff Whipple, a manufacturing supervisor who has worked at the plant since 1995, said that Siemens had provided a huge boost to employee morale by raising the plant's economic prospects. As Whipple said, "Before, people didn't see where their next paycheck was coming from. Morale has definitely improved. People see the benefit of having a strong parent behind them."[31]

This successful economic outcome highlights how several key elements of the EE, in both Germany and Holland, interacted to make both better off. Holland's EE offered human capital with the skills to make globally competitive wastewater treatment equipment while Germany's EE—via Siemens—offered the financial resources, the global marketing contacts, and the corporate governance vision to see the economic potential of acquiring skills in Michigan for a relatively low price. Moreover, Siemens was able to integrate the acquisition effectively—retaining many key people and using the capital generated from its success to expand its geographic scope and its workforce.

Russian Government Uses Legal System to Shut Down Hermitage Capital

Russia's EE is that of a laggard. It lures foreign capital with the promise that it will be able to earn a high return. Once the check clears, Russia changes the rules. It uses its court system and well-earned reputation for selective prosecution of prominent people who disagree with the regime to force out the Westerners who represent the foreign capital investment. The result is that the

Westerners leave the country, generally choosing to remain alive while paying a hefty ransom—in the form of leaving their capital behind for Russian politicians to enrich themselves. Russia's EE punishes foreign capital by considering them fools for investing there. As a result, the memory of these public examples of rent-seeking must fade before an untainted foreign capital provider is willing to fall for the same trick. We are reminded of this when we analyze what happened with Russia's rough treatment of investments by Hermitage Capital into many Russian companies. Russia initially welcomed the influx of Western investment but it changed its mind after it was clear that it could profit by manipulating its books for a huge tax refund.

Hermitage Capital was a private equity firm that at its peak had $4 billion under management invested in Russian companies. Its CEO, William Browder, lost control of his empire after he appeared to criticize Putin's rule. Russia's court system manufactured a legal basis to kick him out of Russia and take away his ownership stakes. Fortunately, Browder was able to escape to London and get much of his money out of Russia before the government could take it.[32]

Browder's financial fortunes seemed to rise and fall based on his support for Vladimir Putin. After Putin became president in 2000, Browder argued publicly that Russia needed an authoritarian leader to establish order. Browder called Putin his "biggest ally" in Hermitage's effort to reform big business. Hermitage's funds grew significantly and managed to exceed $4 billion.[33]

However, Hermitage's prosperity was too good to last. Although Browder does not know exactly why the Kremlin turned against him, he thinks that the Kremlin was taking over Russia's most valuable companies, such as Gazprom, and it recoiled against criticism from outside shareholders. Then things got difficult for Browder. Russian police took key documents from his lawyer's office in Moscow. Browder discovered that his holding companies had been stolen from him and reregistered in the name of a convicted murderer in a provincial city.[34]

Although this scheme transferred control of Browder's corporate structure to the Russian government, it failed to get at the investors' money. Despite that, in August 2008, Browder discovered that his former holding companies had been used to steal $230 million from the Russian treasury. As Browder said, "If ever there was a definition of legal nihilism, this is it. I was actually fighting to make Russia a better place, and fighting against corruption, which is something that they should have given me a medal for. Instead, they drive me out of the country and tarnish everything that I did there."[35]

Browder's path began with his 1996 arrival in Russia where he was reputed to be a sharp analyst of Russian business with an abrasive and stubborn personal style. Browder started Hermitage with $25 million from Republic National Bank and earned an exceptionally high 850% return in its first 18 months. This success attracted an additional $1 billion from institutional investors and others in the West. Although Hermitage's fund plunged to $125 million in 1998's Russian financial collapse, it recovered during the decade that followed, raising more than $4 billion.[36]

How did Browder achieve such success? He concentrated his investments on the largest Russian companies, mostly in the energy sector and under some Kremlin control. Hermitage conducted forensic audits—uncovering insider trading, theft, and other financial crimes. He often leaked the information to the Russian and international press. For example, Browder discovered that Gazprom sold billions of dollars in gas at deeply discounted prices to shady intermediaries. According to Browder, "It became a matter of desperation, not inspiration. You had to become a shareholder activist if you didn't want everything stolen from you."[37]

By 2005, when Putin had assumed complete control over Gazprom as part of his drive to renationalize central energy assets, the end of Hermitage began. The Kremlin cracked down on Browder when he released a report that criticized mismanagement and corruption at Gazprom. The crackdown assumed many forms—Browder's visa was cancelled and his associates and lawyers and their relatives were made victims of crimes; they had to take severe beatings and their documents were robbed. None of the crimes was solved.[38]

While these tactics were frightening, the ultimate expropriation of Browder's business began when Russia's police pursued a policy known as corporate raiding—the practice of using trumped up legal charges and fake documents to steal a company from its Western owners. How did this unfold for Hermitage? In June 2007, with Browder banned from Russia, Moscow police officers raided Hermitage's office and that of its law firm to take documents and computers. When a member of the law firm protested the illegal search, the police beat him and sent him to the hospital for two weeks.[39]

The same police official—Lt. Col. Artem Kuznetsov of the Department of Tax Crime of the Interior Ministry—who had pulled Browder's visa three and a half months earlier supervised this raid as well. Kuznetsov claimed he was seeking evidence in an inquiry into whether Kameya, an Hermitage company, had underpaid its taxes by $44 million. It is not clear whether Kameya owes taxes, but the Russian system is supposed to handle such disputes not with police raids that seize documents but through routine bureaucratic channels.[40]

Nonetheless, once the police had seized the corporate documents, the corporate raiding could begin. Someone used Hermitage's corporate documents to transfer the ownership of three of Hermitage's holding companies to an entity based in Kazan—city 450 miles east of Moscow—registered to a man convicted of murder.[41]

A bogus lawsuit was filed in July 2007 claiming that Hermitage had defrauded a company named Logos Plus of hundreds of millions of dollars worth of Gazprom stock. Although Browder claims it has never done business with Logos Plus, lawyers whom Browder never met showed up in court and admitted that Hermitage had committed the fraud—leading the judge to rule in favor of Logos Plus. Another 15 such claims ultimately yielded $1.26 billion in judgments against Hermitage. It took three months from those settlement dates for Hermitage to learn of these cases.[42]

Browder somewhat outsmarted his Russian government opponents. After it cancelled his visa, he moved his assets out of Russia and sold most of them—leaving his holding companies as shells. Nevertheless, without costing Browder or his investors, the corporate raiders used the legal judgments to alter the holding companies' financial statements to eliminate their 2006 profits and obtain a $230 million tax refund from the Russian treasury.[43]

Browder's Russian odyssey reveals important weaknesses in Russia's EE. In general, cases like Browder's are likely to repel others who might consider investing in Russia. Investors who might hope to earn attractive profits from investing in Russia's energy companies as demand for oil and gas rise are likely to view these EE weaknesses as deal killers. Vivid examples of Russia's willingness to encourage foreign capital investment, and to expropriate it through corporate raids suggest profound weaknesses in EE components such as Corporate Governance and Financial Markets. These weaknesses could well scare away foreign capital investment.

Conclusions on How Capital Flows Change EE

How has the flow of capital among leaders, loungers, and laggards changed the EE's components and the linkages among them? The case studies above reveal three conclusions.

Investors around the world value growth. If a country loosens the barriers to capital entry and changes its corporate governance and financial markets to spur growth, then loungers can become leaders. These leaders not only attract capital to their shores seeking growth, but also become big capital exporters. Moreover, their relatively strong currency makes them attractive to former leaders who—through economic stagnation—are becoming loungers or laggards. The resulting business opportunities bring capital to the capital recipients and often alter the human capital practices of the company receiving the investment.

Investors seek profit by applying skills honed in a leader country to a low-priced acquisition in a laggard one. Investors with a knack for buying undervalued assets in industries ripe for consolidation can apply that skill around the world. However, in order to do so successfully, such investors must avoid the temptation to apply their success template too rigidly when they invest in new markets. Successful investments of these skills come from building a partnership in the new country that makes it possible to pick the right industries based on deep knowledge of evolving industry structure and familiarity with local regulations. The capital provider alters the corporate governance and human capital practices of the capital recipient. And as the investor earns a successful track record, he encourages the capital recipient to upgrade its financial markets to accommodate future capital flows.

Investors must resist the lure of apparent riches from investing in natural resources in countries with weak EEs. Investors are wise to take a skeptical posture toward the claims of a country that seeks Western capital even as it promises to improve formerly weak corporate governance and financial markets practices. It generally does not pay to be a pioneer in making investments in laggards. The Browder case—and others—illustrates just how costly it can be to make investments based on assurances of reform. The lesson is that if you make a financial bet in the upgrading of a laggard, you must always stand very close to the exit door in case that bet proves to be a losing one.

4

The Impact of the Entrepreneurial Ecosystem on Growing Industries

How does the Entrepreneurial Ecosystem (EE) Framework manifest itself in growing, mature, and rejuvenating industries? As we'll explore in chapters 4 and 5, the answers vary depending on the industry's growth trajectory.

A key theme we'll examine in this chapter is how EEs can shape the emergence of growing industries in a country. More specifically, we explore how EEs attract growing industries if they protect intellectual property (IP) and offer strong human capital. In growing industries such as biotechnology and nanotechnology, capital flows to countries that protect IP and employ the talent needed to come up with innovative products and bring them to market ahead of the competition. Conversely, countries with a reputation for weak entrepreneurial capital markets and inadequate IP protection fail in their efforts to attract venture capital for growing industries.

Growing Industries

As we saw in chapter 3, capital seeks growth. And the best place to seek that growth is in industries that are growing rapidly. Most of these growing industries locate themselves in many different countries. However, the mere fact that a country decides to participate in growing industries does not automatically mean that investors will help achieve that country's goals. A country must shape its EE in such a way that it attracts capital to a growing industry.

What makes the difference between countries that attract capital to growing industries and those that repel capital? As we'll explore, countries that attract capital to their growing industries encourage high standards of corporate governance, craft financial markets that are transparent and robust, offer deep human capital resources, and protect IP. By contrast, countries that repel capital from their growing industries treat minority investors as second class citizens, present opaque financial reporting and shallow capital markets, and offer little, if any, IP protection. In fact, EEs that repel capital have a very difficult time achieving the growth goals they set for themselves as a result of their failure to attract capital.

Why would a capital provider care about these differences? It's fairly simple. The general partner of a venture capital firm gets paid a fixed percentage of the assets under management, say 2%, coupled with a share of the profits, usually 20%, that the partnership earns when it sells the companies in which it invests. Such sales can come through initial public offering of a company's shares or through its acquisition by a larger firm.

The VC's odds of achieving those profits are greater if the companies in which they invest have good corporate governance, there are skilled employees working to develop the companies, and their IP is well protected. Moreover, a profitable sale of the companies depends on whether there are many potential buyers—both from IPO investors and corporate acquirers. And such capital markets tend to be transparent and deep. This is why a VC is more likely to place capital in a growing industry whose EE is more like a leader's than a laggard's.

Case Studies of How the Entrepreneurial Ecosystem Changes Management of Growing Industries

Through the exploration of the interplay between growing industries, EEs, and capital providers we will see how capital inflows shape global value chains in growing industries. To do that, we examine the following case studies.

Biocon. the first Indian company to be approved by the FDA to manufacture the cholesterol-lowering molecule lovastatin, has built a 2,000-person "human capital portfolio" whose skills it leverages globally. Such a global effort by a nascent company was feasible mainly because of international flow of capital. Biocon was among the first Indian biotech companies to get access to venture capital and to conduct a successful IPO.[1]

Nicholas Piramal. India's second largest pharmaceutical company, which has grown by acquiring the Indian operations of European and U.S. pharmaceutical companies, setting up joint ventures, and selling the resulting products through its 1,700-person sales force. Again, it has benefited from international capital providers' willingness to support it.

Chinese biotechnology industry. While China has aspirations to build a biotechnology industry, it is failing to attract foreign capital to fuel its growth. The reason for the failure is that foreign investors are convinced that such an investment would be wasted due to China's weak IP protection. Given the risk of biotechnology start-up failure even in countries with strong IP protection, China puts itself at an insurmountable competitive disadvantage in attempting to attract foreign capital due to its unwillingness to strengthen IP protection.

Indian nanotechnology industry. Nanotechnology has yet to emerge from the science project phase into an industry with significant revenues. As a result, despite India's efforts to attract foreign capital, it has not been able to build a strong cadre of strong nanotechnology start-ups. Instead, India has attracted partner-ships with Western companies seeking to tap India's talent to experiment in an effort to create saleable products. If nanotechnology indeed becomes an industry with a solid record of product sales, it may have an edge in attracting venture capital to fund future start-ups.

Biocon

Biocon is an Indian biotechnology company founded in 1978 whose ability to adapt to scarcity and overcome cultural resistance has helped it achieve a market capitalization of over a billion dollars. Its founder Kiran Mazumdar-Shaw was trained as a brewer but her father's brewery was culturally unable to accept her as its CEO. So Mazumdar-Shaw turned this cultural sow's ear into an entrepreneurial silk purse by founding Biocon. However, India's VC business was small and risk averse and she was unable to obtain financing to get her company off the ground. In response to this capital scarcity, Mazumdar-Shaw offered her expertise in making enzymes to an Irish company—providing consulting services to generate her own capital to finance biotechnology R&D. Moreover, when she faced challenges to growth in European markets, she set out to make small acquisitions that would provide Biocon with access to distribution in those countries.

In overcoming these challenges Mazumdar-Shaw was among the Indian entrepreneurs whose success against daunting odds helped to transform India's EE to one that became increasingly supportive of Biocon's develop-ment. While India did not make it easy for her to obtain capital when she started Biocon, it did not hinder her initiative to sell her expertise in Europe to generate the seed capital she required to take bigger risks in developing new products. However, by 2003 her company—and the Indian venture capital industry—had reached the point where it was able to attract venture capital. That year, Biocon's profits rose 76% followed by a 247% leap in profits between 2003 and 2004—the year that Biocon held a successful initial public offering.[2] Since then, Biocon has grown rapidly—achieving 30% sales growth through the third quarter of 2009.[3]

How exactly did Biocon achieve these business milestones? And what was the role of India's EE in shaping Biocon's strategies? As mentioned earlier, Mazumdar-Shaw founded Biocon in 1978 at the age of 25 after it became clear that despite her graduate degrees in brewery science and her father's ownership of an Indian brewery, the company would not accept her as his successor. She initially persuaded an Irish company to form the joint venture that soon tapped her expertise in enzymes such as papain, a proteolytic enzyme extracted from the papaya fruit, that prevents chilled beer from turning hazy. Biocon continued pro-ducing such innovative products even after Unilever acquired its Irish partner in 1989. Enzymes remain a big part of Biocon's business—in 2005, for example, Biocon supplied 25% of the world's demand for pectinase, an enzyme that breaks down the pectin in fruit juice.[4]

However, it was Biocon's ability to transcend its position as a subsidiary of a British company and use its capital to generate a patented biopharmaceutical that launched a big leap forward in its entrepreneurial success. In the 1990s, Biocon introduced PlaFractor, a process for creating and extracting microorganisms that was much more tightly controllable than previous methods. PlaFractor became a big seller and provided the capital and technology Biocon needed to research an immunosuppressant—a biopharmaceutical that lowers the risk that the body will reject an organ transplant. Biocon succeeded with this new patented product—which helped the company triple in size in 1996—giving it the resources it needed to buy Unilever's interest in 1998 and making Biocon an independent company.[5]

As we discussed above, Biocon's success came in part as a result of its ability to overcome the relatively risk-averse nature of India's capital providers. Rather than being able to raise capital from Indian VCs to finance drug discovery, Indian biotechnology companies generate positive cash flow by providing research services to global partners—and some of these firms are taking the risk of using that cash to invest in drug discovery. According to Mazumdar-Shaw, most Indian biotech firms provided research services, clinical development, and diagnostic services to finance their more capital-intensive product development efforts—emulating the outsourcing approach of India's software services sector.[6]

Biocon is among the few firms taking the risk of using the money from their research services to bet on new drugs—what Mazumdar-Shaw refers to as a "hybrid model." In short, Indian biotechnology companies such as Biocon are their own venture capitalists. While this self-funding approach tends to delay the development of new drugs and limits the number that can be financed, it also avoids the problem of ceding control to the VCs. Furthermore, this approach has enabled Indian biotechnology companies to develop many of the capabilities required for a fully integrated biopharmaceutical firm—including drug development and manufacturing. Mazumdar-Shaw believes that more Indian firms will find ways to overcome the risk-aversion of the Indian VC industry to fund drug discovery.[7]

Biocon pursued many different methods to raise the capital for such expansion. Specifically, in July 2007, it sold its enzymes unit for $115 million. It planned to raise more cash through the initial public offering of its contract research unit—Syngene by April 2009. Moreover, Biocon planned to raise between $100 million and $300 million by licensing its oral insulin product.[8]

Biocon has grown by overcoming the obstacles of India's EE. When India's cultural norms—a kind of human capital impediment—prevented Mazumdar-Shaw from taking over her father's brewery, she did not retreat into her shell. Instead, she used her brewery knowledge to start her own company. When India's capital providers shunned risky biotechnology drug development, Biocon generated its own capital by providing pharmaceutical services. But as Biocon was becoming more successful, India's capital markets also became more robust—making it possible for Biocon to finance its acquisition spree through a combination of licensing deals and selling subsidiaries either to a corporate acquirer or to public shareholders.

Nicholas Piramal

Nicholas Piramal has tapped global credit markets to fuel a global expansion through acquisitions. Having refined its skills at manufacturing generic pharmaceuticals, it is attempting to profit by placing bets on its ability to lever those skills into profitable stakes in U.S. and European markets. And thanks to its access to global capital, Nicholas Piramal is accelerating that global expansion through acquisition rather than pursuing the slower green-field approach. In order to capture the profit potential of this strategy, Nicholas Piramal will need to develop the skill of integrating global acquisitions effectively. If it can stretch its skills into this new area, its growing profits will enable it to tap global capital markets to apply this expansion strategy well into the future.

How did Nicholas Piramal accomplish this? After its June 2006 acquisition of Pfizer's UK facility, Piramal's executives obtained board permission to raise $1 billion by issuing foreign currency convertible bonds—either from Indian markets or through other global financial sources. And in so doing, Piramal reshuffled its executive ranks to appoint Nandini Piramal, the daughter of company founders Ajay Piramal and Swati Piramal, as general manager, strategy, in the company's U.S. operations. This move was intended to provide Nandini with an important career development opportunity while keeping the key skill of acquisition integration in the family.[9]

Piramal's UK acquisition marked a major move that strengthened its position as a pharmaceutical contract manufacturer operating in 100 countries. Piramal estimated that the acquisition had 2011 revenue potential of $350 million. Moreover, the deal would enable Piramal to manufacture higher-priced niche products in higher cost, highly skilled countries such as the UK—while continuing to operate its more mass market commodity products in lower cost locations such as India. The UK facility in Morpeth employed workers who were skilled at such niche manufacturing and were fully transferred to Piramal. Specifically, Morepeth's 450 people were experienced in new product launch, site technical transfer, and operational improvement techniques such as Just in Time (JIT) & Right-First-Time. According to Piramal Chair, Ajay Piramal, "We plan to use our European assets to manufacture niche high-value drugs such as cytotoxic products, while keeping lower cost manufacturing in India."[10]

Moreover, Piramal's success in the UK spurred it to make capital available to expand into the market for the contract manufacture of prescription drugs. In so doing, Piramal hoped to expand its presence in pharmaceutical industry contract manufacturing and research services which were expected to grow at an average annual rate of 10% to reach $168 billion by 2009. And within that total, Piramal anticipated that it could grab a share of the global market for contract manufacturing of prescription drugs that was estimated to increase from a value of 2006's $26 billion to $44 billion in 2009. To do that, however, Piramal targeted the U.S. market by making available as much as $200 million to acquire U.S. manufacturing facilities. Michael Fernandes, then head of Piramal's custom manufacturing, outlined the strategic intent: "Our strategy is to buy a more 'niche' capability in the United States, which would be more focused on early phase production. The objective is to have a more technology driven asset in the US." Piramal's ultimate goal was for custom manufacturing to account for half of its 2010 revenues.[11]

Nicholas Piramal's development reflects the complex interplay between India's EE and Piramal's evolving capabilities and business objectives. While India's low labor costs and skilled workers provided the basis for contract manufacturing of lower priced generic drugs, Nicholas Piramal's access to global capital sources opened up new business opportunities. Specifically, its new capital created the chance for Piramal to conduct a global acquisition strategy in Europe and the United States that would enable the company to manufacture higher margin products while challenging it to enhance its ability to target the right deals and integrate its targets effectively.

Chinese Biotechnology Industry

China has made enormous strides in developing its economy over the past several decades. However, success has so far eluded its biotechnology sector. Although China has many scientists with technical expertise its EE lacks critical conditions for attracting the capital needed to build a biotechnology industry. To overcome these EE weaknesses, China must be willing to make some major cultural changes. China deters Western VCs due to its lack of IP protection, its shallow capital markets that preclude exit opportunities, and significant differences in corporate governance.

Despite these obstacles, some elements of a biotechnology-friendly EE are sprouting in China. For example, BioVeda Capital raised $30 million for its BioVeda China Fund. Though this is a tiny amount, it shows that investors recognize that China has significant human capital—including 20,000 life-science researchers, and more than 300 public laboratories nationwide.[12]

However, China's deterrents to significant biotechnology venture investing remain significant. These barriers to U.S. firms investing in China include IP issues, lack of management talent, inability to sell the venture either through IPOs or acquisition, currency exchange issues, lack of innovation, absence of good manufacturing process (GMP) certified plants, and corporate governance difficulties, says Dr. Jonathan Wang, general manager for Burrill Greater China Group (BGCG), a San Francisco based life sciences merchant bank.[13]

Numerous industry participants confirm the details of these barriers to VC investment. For starters, the barriers are perceived to be significant not just to U.S. investors but to Asian VCs as well. For example, an estimated 81% of the $325 million raised by Asian VCs between June 1999 and June 2003 for biotechnology was invested in United States, rather than Asian, firms. Kathleen Ng, editor and publisher of *Asia Private Equity Review*, considered China to have an "anemic" venture capital pool of about $100 million for biotechnology.[14]

One of the most basic reasons that a VC would avoid a market is the difficulty of getting their money out through an exit. But what exactly is it about China's financial markets that makes it difficult for VCs to exit a potential investment there? Jonathan Wang, the former vice president of WI Harper, a San Francisco, CA, based VC firm that has invested in biotechnology start-ups in both the United States and Asia, said, "There is not a clear exit, and being a venture capital firm, we care about how we exit." One reason for the absence of exits is the immaturity of Chinese exchanges. In 1990, the Shanghai exchange opened up; however, it lacks the transparency and disclosure of Western exchanges such as the Nasdaq and NYSE. While some investors in Chinese biotechnology firms exit by listing on the Stock Exchange of Hong Kong, plans to open alternative exchanges, such as a technology-focused board in Shenzhen, a city neighboring Hong Kong, were suspended because of recent banking scandals.[15]

Also, IP protection in China is weak. But in what ways is it weak? China joined the World Trade Organization (WTO) in 2001, which theoretically gives it the obligation to protect IP. However, according to Nancy T. Chang, then-president and CEO of Houston, TX based, Tanox, "there is not a concerted effort in IP protection." This was one reason Chang decided not to invest in mainland China start-ups; it instead funded U.S. start-ups staffed with Chinese scientists.[16]

China also offers investors an array of corporate governance challenges. Chinese law forbids a foreign investor from owning more than half of a company—a discouragement to VCs who typically own the majority of private biotechnology companies. Language and cultural barriers also make it difficult for foreign VCs to comprehend the intricacies of doing business in China where the importance of "guanxi," or connections, remains critical to doing business. Kien Leong, former senior partner with Shanghai's Pacific Venture Design, says domestic VCs may, by comparison, be more comfortable dealing with these grey areas of business conduct linked to the local culture.[17] Other barriers to international partnerships involve language, travel, culture, and differences in project management styles.[18]

Overcoming these barriers may be a challenging task for China. For instance, to fix IP protection problems, China will need to refine civil procedures, developing a body of jurists, and accumulating a body of precedent and custom for assessment of damages. And China has significant problems in distributing the products that biopharmaceutical start-ups might produce. Its health system is weak and in many cases clinicians, facilities, and products do not reach rural or isolated regions. Moreover, while the cost of developing an innovative drug is high, the price that Chinese consumers pay is likely to be very low. This makes it quite difficult for these start-ups to earn a profit.[19]

It's true that China has come a long way in the past several decades, yet its EE is not ideally suited to attracting VC investment and nurturing technology-based start-ups. It is possible that China could adapt its EE to make its biotechnology companies more attractive to these VC funds. However, in order to do that it would need to change opaque and shallow financial markets for transparent and deep ones that provide robust exit opportunities; scrap its weak IP protection for one based on a tight regulatory scheme; and find a way to adapt its corporate governance to create confidence that VCs will be able to manage the firms in which they aspire to invest.

Indian Nanotechnology Industry

The Indian nanotechnology industry is struggling to get off the ground. While there is considerable excitement about the potential for nanotechnology, so far there are few start-ups that have been able to generate sufficient revenues to attract IPO investors. As a result, much nanotechnology financing has come from relatively small investments by government entities and corporate venture capital. Though India clearly has technical skill in this field, much of this ability has been channeled into providing technical services rather than generating products.

The corporate interest in Indian nanotechnology is heartening. Reliance, Tata Group, Mahindra & Mahindra, and Intel India have invested roughly $250 million in nanotechnology both to improve existing products and to explore new ones. For example, Tata Chemical's Hyderabad R&D lab is developing high value fertilizers; Reliance created a nanotechnology R&D center; and Mahindra & Mahindra is investing in technologies such as wiper free windscreen and nanoceramic window films for the automobile industry.[20]

India has a few nanotechnology start-ups; they lack VC backing thanks to the perception that a profitable exit for investors is unlikely. Of the 12 start-ups founded since 2002, half deliver services such as market research and training, and the rest conduct semiconductor product development using nanomanipulation, nanomedicine, and nanomaterials such as carbon nanotubes, silica, and alumina. These start-ups lack significant revenues, which reinforces VCs' fear of not getting a return on their investment. The result is they are unable to attract the very capital that might help them achieve higher revenue targets. In short, these start-ups are stuck.[21]

Although the Indian government has invested some money in nanotechnology, it has been unable to jump start a virtuous cycle that would help the industry reach critical mass. Several Indian government agencies, most prominently the Department of Science and Technology (DST), have helped fund Indian nanotechnology initiatives. DST launched the Nano Science and Technology Initiative (NSTI) in 2001—providing $15 million for nanotechnology over the subsequent five years. The NSTI funded 100 research projects, 10 core groups in nano science, 6 centers of nanotechnology, and 1 computational materials science at different institutions across India. However India's $20 million total nanotechnology funding for 2003/2004 was a mere 0.7% of its total $3.03 billion total R&D expenditures.[22]

As a result of the inadequate financing India's nanotechnology start-ups have trouble building the capabilities they need to operate as profitable stand-alone businesses. These nanotechnology start-ups can't compete for the best talent with cash rich industries that are scrambling for experienced professionals with business skills. Nanotechnology start-ups are also perceived as riskier than IT or services companies due to nanotechnology's inherently high risk resulting from its unproven technologies and long lead time between product development and commercialization.[23] India is able to provide nanotechnology research services for Western multinationals but can't use those skills to develop products that would give it independence. For example, General Electric, General Motors, and IBM have set up captive R&D bases in India. But the service providers have run into trouble leaping across the capability synapse from consulting to product development. According to Hilaal Alam, CEO of Qtech Nanosystem, "India has got (the) potential to become a service provider for (the global) nanotechnology industry; but not a pipeline for new products. The majority of investment in India up (until) now has gone (into the) services sector and into building a testing and characterization infrastructure." Alam regrets that Indian nanotechnology companies have yet to build product development capabilities.[24]

How the Globalization of Growing Industries Is Changing Their Economic Performance

Globalization of growing industries such as biotechnology certainly changes their economic performance. The particular forces shaping a host country's EE influence the extent of that growth. For example, as we've seen, India's EE has accelerated the growth of its biopharmaceuticals industry although those growth-favoring factors have been partially offset by growth-impeding ones. In this case, India's relatively low cost and highly skilled human capital and its openness to foreign capital flows have attracted many Western partners eager to tap its talent. However, India's relatively risk-averse venture capital firms have been unwilling to invest in start-ups that would apply that human capital to building profitable companies selling innovative products.

Before delving into some of these factors, we examine the relatively rapid growth of India's biotechnology industry. Indian biotech revenues grew 31% to $2.08 billion between 2006 and 2007—twice the industry's size in 2005. The majority of revenues, almost 58%, came from exports. And almost 66% of those revenues came from biopharmaceuticals such as generic vaccines, which grew 27% between 2006 and 2007. Moreover, 27% of total biotech industry revenue was taken by the top three Indian biopharmaceutical companies, Serum Institute of India, Biocon, and Panacea Biotec.[25]

India's EE has helped to spur this growth. How? Its relative openness to investment—particularly in the form of Foreign Direct Investment (FDI)—has made it relatively easy for Western pharmaceuticals manufacturers to tap into India's skilled labor and high quality manufacturing facilities. For example, India is second only to the United States in the number of FDA approvals—which illustrates both the strength of U.S. demand for Indian manufactured biopharmaceuticals as well as their adherence to world-class quality standards.[26]

These competitive strengths have attracted significant FDI—$216 million in 2005 alone. The result has been rapid growth in biotech sectors that tap these strengths. For instance, biopharma revenues climbed 30% between 2004 and 2005; bioservices grew 55%; contract research services were up 55%; and bioinformatics rose 25%. Biopharma's relatively large share and growth was driven primarily by the vaccine business. Indian firms such as Biocon, Dr. Reddy's Laboratories, Panacea Biotech, Natco Pharma, Wockhardt, Ranbaxy are tapping that growth thanks to their skills at making generic equivalents of biodrugs.[27]

To build on this excellent performance, India could take further steps to shape its EE to attract VC investment—which would increase the chances that India could build companies that discover, manufacture, and distribute patented biotechnology. To do this, India would need to provide better protection for IP. But such a change would be difficult given India's history that provided very strong protection for IP created by Western pharmaceutical companies up until 1970 when it passed a new law that helped grow the very successful Indian generic manufacturing business by allowing Indian companies to use Western IP with very little modification.

If India went back to a model that protected IP from generic manufacturers, it could help spur the development of new products by Indian biotech companies. Such IP protection might unleash a flood of VC into these companies—lured by the prospect of capturing a share of the profits from patented products manufactured efficiently and available for distribution to markets around the world. The political issue for India is whether the benefits of such a change in IP protection would offset the costs—in terms of lost revenue potential for India's generic manufacturing sector.

How the Changing Entrepreneurial Ecosystem for Growing Industries Is Likely to Influence Their Evolution

As the foregoing example suggests, an evolving EE can indeed attract foreign capital flows to countries with growing industries. However easy it might be to imagine the way such changes might benefit the country, those changes are unlikely to happen instantaneously in a country ruled by democratic principles. The reason is that the current EE has very strong constituents who have a vested interest in keeping things just the way they are. If a leader of a democratic society wishes to change the EE, he or she must mobilize forces for change that are strong enough to oppose interests seeking to keep things as they are.

If the change in EE does not threaten an existing industry or other interest group, then it is much easier for the leader to change the EE to favor the interests of private capital providers. However, if that growing industry is likely to take market share away from incumbents, then it's likely that the incumbents will resist the change. For example, when the Internet first became popular in the 1990s, it was not obvious that it would take market share away from existing industries and thus there was not much resistance to starting and funding Internet-related ventures. By contrast, alternative energy companies would be likely to face significant resistance from incumbent energy providers selling oil, gas, and/or coal. Similarly, as we discussed above, a change in IP protection in India would likely sacrifice the growth and profits of the generic manufacturing sector on the altar of creating a vibrant Indian industry focused on patenting new biotech products.

In short, a leader can envision changes in a country's EE that will attract capital to its growing industries. The difficult part is making that vision a reality. In order to accomplish the change, the leader must craft a solution that minimizes the losses to those who are comfortable with the status quo while maximizing the benefit of the change to the most powerful constituents. Such a solution has the potential to make the change a reality—thus leading to better economic performance for the country that hosts such a change in its EE.

Conclusion

The evolving EE shapes the evolution of industries at different stages of growth in different ways. In a growing industry, capital flows to countries whose EEs protect the IP on which such growth is based. If a country's EE does not protect such IP, then its companies may be able to provide complementary services to companies operating in countries that do protect IP. However, those companies will not get the lion's share of the private capital flows. Therefore, a country seeking capital to support its growing industries must align its EE to support the interests of those capital providers to the extent it can within its political constraints.

The Impact of the Entrepreneurial Ecosystem on Maturing and Rejuvenating Industries

The EE manifests itself powerfully in mature and rejuvenating industries—although in different ways. That makes sense because such industries—while starting from the same place—have different trajectories. Mature industries have been growing slowly in recent years and are likely to continue to do so. By contrast, rejuvenating industries have been growing slowly but thanks to an unexpected change—such as emerging market demand growth—they are likely to enjoy a significant boost to their growth.

This chapter explores how the EE manifests itself in these two kinds of industries as follows. EEs attract maturing industries through flexible financial markets and corporate governance that encourage optimized global value chains. In maturing industries such as systems integration and personal computers, capital flows to companies that excel in crafting global value chains. While such companies must locate activities where they will be the most competitive, they must also excel at coordinating these activities around the world. And such global coordination demands a CEO who travels almost constantly to set global operating standards and resolve the numerous problems that inevitably arise as these activities attempt to work together.

EEs attract rejuvenating industries by providing access to capital and by encouraging acquisitions of declining players by expanding ones. Capital flows to rejuvenating industries such as automobiles and aircraft when the EE in which they operate have financial markets that are willing to finance acquisitions by emerging industry leaders and corporate governance that sees global opportunities and is willing to push the boundaries of existing EEs in order to achieve their ambitious growth goals.

As an industry matures, so do the needs of its customers and employees. Moreover, competitors in maturing industries behave differently than those in growing ones. How? Customers of maturing industries tend to become comfortable with a single supplier and want to assure themselves that their supplier becomes an acquirer rather than a target as suppliers consolidate. Unlike start-up employees who look for rapid growth and rising stock options, those in maturing industries seek job security with the potential for long-term career development. And competitors in maturing industries compete to gain the scale they need to become acquirers or throw up their hands and seek out a partner to fund their exit from the industry.

Why would a country want to host a maturing industry? A maturing industry will seek to locate itself where the EE rewards acquisitions and their related efficiency gains. While a country hosting such industries might run the risk of citizens losing their jobs as acquirers seek efficiencies, they may also get the benefit of higher tax payments that result from hosting companies that lead the industry consolidation process. The profitable growth that results from effective industry consolidation could create a growing stream of tax payments to government and spark the growth of complementary industries.

But what kinds of changes in a country's EE would be required to attract maturing industries? Most importantly a country must lower barriers to global acquisitions and make available the capital required to fuel such deals. Moreover, it must reduce restrictions to achieving efficiencies that acquirers typically seek to achieve in the wake of such deals. Finally, it must encourage the efficient construction and operation of a global logistics and communications network that can support the evolving global expansion of companies seeking to lead the consolidation of maturing industries.

Case Studies of How the Entrepreneurial Ecosystem Changes Management of Maturing Industries

Through the exploration of the interplay between maturing industries, EEs, and capital providers we will see how capital inflows shape global value chains in growing industries. To do that, we examine the following case studies.

Lenovo. Lenovo of China has become a global player through internal growth and foreign acquisitions (from IBM, for example) by using its access to global capital markets as a result of foreign banks' full participation in the Chinese economy—a stipulation under World Trade Organization (WTO) rules.[1] And in so doing, it has changed its corporate governance—encountering opportunities and challenges—as a result of the falling of barriers to the flow of Western capital into China.

Computer services. Computer services firms such as IBM, Accenture, and EDS compete with firms such as Infosys, TCS, Wipro, Cognizant, and Satyam of India. The globalization of the maturing computer services industry has been made possible by the access to foreign capital that the Indian firms enjoyed. The IPOs of these Indian firms have strengthened them and forced American computer services providers such as IBM, Accenture, and EDS to change their global operations. For example, Accenture hired 8,000 people in India—and by August

2007 its Indian operations employed 35,000—making its Indian unit Accenture's biggest in the world.[2]

Lenovo

Lenovo's access to global capital markets brings into focus the challenges facing Western managers seeking to build bridges to their Asian workers. While the management challenge of building an efficient global logistics network is quite considerable, Lenovo's experience trying to meld Western and Asian business cultures appears to be even more formidable. China's decision to join the WTO had the effect of changing its EE to become more open to capital flows from Western financial markets and their approach to corporate governance, bringing Western and Asian management cultures into far closer proximity. In so doing, Lenovo's founders were willing to step aside in order to gain the benefits of Western management. But the costs of trying to meld two cultures raise questions about whether such a corporate transformation will ultimately result in a more efficient PC company.

In late 2008, it was clear that the challenges of managing Lenovo were putting the company at a competitive disadvantage. Lenovo's computer shipments rose 8% in the third quarter of 2008; however, the overall market grew at almost 16% that led Lenovo to suffer a drop in market share from 7.8% in 2007 to 7.3% in 2008. The lost market share led analysts to forecast a 20% decline in Lenovo's net income for 2008—the first year of decline since it acquired IBM's PC business in May 2005.[3]

Lenovo's efforts to change its culture began when it spent $1.25 billion to buy IBM's PC unit. This deal gave Lenovo brand credibility, a global sales force and access to Western management skills. Investors hoped Lenovo's low-cost structure in China would lower the cost to build an IBM PC and make the business profitable for the first time in years. However, along with these came big challenges—including differences in pay levels; handling disagreements; and even the topics of casual office conversations.

One of Lenovo's cofounders believed that its acquisition of IBM's PC business put Lenovo in China's spotlight. Specifically, China viewed Lenovo as a test case for its brand of global capitalism. Lenovo responded to the heightened pressure with a willingness to institute radical change in its approach to corporate governance. Mary Ma, a Lenovo director and former chief financial officer, argued, "We knew we could not fail. Not just for us, but for all of China. They viewed us as a symbol of a Chinese company going global, and we felt a great responsibility."[4]

Lenovo embarked on a significant change in its corporate governance approach by changing from a Chinese executive to an American one. Before the IBM PC acquisition, Lenovo managed in a militaristic style. Lenovo broadcast calisthenics twice daily over its headquarters public-address system. Lenovo humiliated employees who arrived late to meetings by forcing them to stand in front of the room while other executives went silent and bowed their heads for a full minute. Following the IBM PC deal, Lenovo Chairman Yang Yuanqing gave up his CEO title to a Western executive—for about three years—and switched Lenovo's official language from Chinese to English.[5]

Not surprisingly, the change led to conflict. For instance, Bill Amelio, a former Dell executive who became Lenovo's CEO in late 2005, was unhappy that his Chinese colleagues were reluctant to express their opinions. Since he believed that such intellectual debate resulted in better strategies, he was frustrated that his Chinese colleagues did not immediately grasp his desire to replicate that culture at Lenovo. As Amelio put it, "You don't want everyone saying 'Yes, Yes, Yes' all the time. You want them to be able to smack you upside the head and say 'Hey, I've got a better idea.'"[6] However, given the top-down, militaristic style of Lenovo prior to its IBM PC acquisition, he should not have been surprised at Lenovo employees' discomfort with speaking up.

Other cultural differences related to the American propensity to talk while Chinese workers remained silent. For example, during conference calls Americans hogged the airtime. Qiao Jian, a Lenovo vice president of human resources, said, "The Americans would just talk and talk. Then they'd say 'How come you don't want to add value to this meeting?'" And bridging the cultural gap between the American and Chinese workers took other forms as well. Lenovo removed silkworms from its Beijing cafeteria menu. And sports metaphors offered by Americans confused the Chinese workers and were banned from conference calls.[7]

One of the most basic cultural differences between the Asian and Western management styles was confusion over the meaning of silence. According to Chen Shaopeng, former president of Lenovo's China operations, "When we disagreed in meetings we would keep silent. But the Americans assumed we were agreeing." When the silent Chinese meeting participants disagreed, they took their complaints directly to Yang or Amelio. This created a feeling among the American workers that their Chinese peers could not be trusted due to what the Americans called "end runs."[8]

One example of this occurred when a Chinese colleague took a report of a minor quality problem to the CEO rather than to the head of the product division, angering him. Specifically, Peter Hortensius, formerly senior vice president of Lenovo's notebook business, was furious when he found out a Chinese colleague had reported a minor quality problem with a computer shipment directly to the CEO, without informing him first. Hortensius recalled, "I was going, Why the heck did he go behind my back on this one?" However, Hortensius's colleague was trying to be polite. That's because in Chinese companies, executives often take problems to a boss instead of a colleague of similar rank to maintain harmony.[9]

Not all the differences were cultural. In some areas, related to strategy, the Chinese Lenovo founders deferred to Amelio and in others they ended up disagreeing. For example, Yang worked closely with Amelio to cut costs. Yang agreed with Amelio's decision to undertake two major restructurings that cut 10% of its workforce, or 2,400 jobs. Yang also went along with Amelio's push to shift jobs to lower-cost areas. In particular, Lenovo shifted its development of desktop computers to Beijing, while moving its marketing headquarters to Bangalore.[10]

One area of disagreement was Amelio's decision to replace the popular Chinese manager in charge of Lenovo's supply chain repair effort. Amelio felt the Chinese executive, Liu Jun, was not pushing the effort fast enough, so in 2006, he replaced Liu with an executive from Dell. However, Liu was very popular and his removal from a senior position created additional tension that contributed to the departure of two other Chinese executives who quit shortly after Liu lost his position. According to Yang, "The Chinese staff wondered if they were needed anymore at this company."[11]

And this sense that the Chinese workers were second-class citizens under Amelio had a quantitative basis—they got paid less than the non-Asian employees. After the IBM acquisition, many Americans earned far more than their Chinese peers, even though the Chinese unit was profitable and the American one lost money. At IBM, base pay accounted for 80% of salary, and performance-based bonuses about 20%. That meant Americans could miss targets and still get paid decently. For the Chinese managers, pay was almost entirely performance-based. Ma found this frustrating, as she said, "I was the CFO and my subordinates were making far more than me."[12]

Ultimately, Lenovo's diverse, global shareholders demand a more collegial approach to corporate governance. As a result of the IBM PC acquisition, Lenovo took on a shareholder group that included a government, a corporation, and private equity firms. Specifically, the Chinese government, through the Academy of Sciences, holds 15% of the shares and a Lenovo employee shareholder group controls 28%. Other shareholders include IBM and private equity groups Newbridge Capital, General Atlantic, and Texas Pacific Group.[13]

The result of this shareholding structure is a diverse board and a more collegial approach to managing. Specifically, the Lenovo board includes seven American citizens, a British citizen, and four Chinese founders. Amelio runs Lenovo differently than IBM or Dell. He wants each region of Lenovo responsible for its own profits and losses making Lenovo "collegial rather than dictatorial." Amelio added, "The days have gone of a command-and-control strategy. It is difficult to run a far-flung organization that is global in that way. Unfortunately it creates a travel burden—I don't travel with an entourage—but I make sure I do a lot of face time."[14]

China's evolving EE has altered Lenovo's strategy for competing in a mature industry. Specifically, by joining the WTO, China opened itself to global capital flows. This made it possible for Lenovo to purchase IBM's PC business that in turn led Lenovo to take on diverse shareholders—including IBM and Western private equity firms. Lenovo changed its board to reflect the new shareholders. And it then replaced its Chinese executives with a Western CEO who brought in strategies for cost reduction and improved operating efficiencies. Yet Lenovo's efforts to meld a Western management style—characterized by intellectual debate and decentralization—with a more top-down, militaristic

Chinese operating culture created conflicts that have taken a long time to be acknowledged and addressed. And those conflicts—coupled with a $97 million Lenovo quarterly operating loss—led company directors to replace Amelio in February 2009 with Chairman Yang.[15]

Computer Services

Corporate demand for services to build computer systems grew rapidly during the 1990s but slowed down from its torrid pace in the 2000s. Although corporate budgets for computer services grew slowly, if at all, demand remained strong. What changed was the corporate attitude toward IT spending—rather than viewing IT as a way to achieve competitive advantage with a correspondingly low concern about limiting expense, following the dot-com crash, companies began to realize that IT spending was important but that CFOs would scrutinize IT budgets more closely.

One of the corporate IT budget items that received the tightest scrutiny was computer services. And this tight scrutiny played into the hands of companies that could deliver such systems at a lower cost than companies had done in the past. Even as computer services matured as an industry, providers that could deliver these services more cheaply than their higher cost competitors were in a strong position to grow rapidly at the expense of those incumbents.

And it turns out that the upstarts were largely based in India while the incumbents were American. What changed to enable the Indian firms to capture a bigger share of a more slowly growing pie were three key elements of India's EE. First, India's *human capital* was highly skilled at writing software—yet was willing to sell those skills at a much lower price. Second, India's ability to *access global capital markets* enabled its computer services providers to build the global networks of application developers that its customers required. And finally, the high standards of *corporate governance*—in the form of transparent financial reporting and skilled corporate executives—gave investors confidence that their investments would be well guarded.

The leadership skills required to run a global IT services provider are unique. And the ability of some of the most successful Indian providers to adapt their leadership approach to the requirements of global customers suggests that corporate governance may be a critical source of competitive advantage as the industry matures. Corporate governance is so critical because companies will continue to demand ever higher levels of responsiveness to their needs coupled with timely and cost-effective completion of projects. To examine how this corporate governance works, we examine two leading Indian computer services providers—Cognizant Technology and Wipro.

Cognizant was spun off from a U.S. company, Dun & Bradstreet, in a 1998 initial public offering. Historically, it split the development of computer systems into two stages: application development and software writing and testing. Cognizant performed the application development, which required understanding the details of how a client's business operated and how the new system would improve those operations, in the United States. And it turned those applications into software in Bangalore. The key to Cognizant's success was its ability to communicate effectively between its American applications engineers and its Indian coders.

While this approach worked effectively for many years, changing customer needs put significant pressure on Cognizant. Cognizant began to get more sophisticated and more complex requests from customers. To be sure of meeting their needs, CEO Francisco D'Souza, then chief operating officer, decided to change Cognizant's organization structure. The purpose of the change was to allow Cognizant to respond quickly to these customer requests. To achieve this purpose, D'Souza put the power to respond to customers in the hands of the managers who worked most closely with them. As D'Souza said, "We had to find a new way of organizing the company along the customer axis."[16]

While the new approach worked well for customers, it put tremendous strain on managers. That's because the managers spent most of their day at customers' locations in the United States only to stay up late at night communicating with software engineers in India working on projects for these customers and managing their careers. This arrangement put tremendous stress on the managers and Indian workers felt there was too much distance between them and their bosses. As D'Souza said, "It was a little bit like Charlie's Angels. You wake up in the morning; a voice on the phone tells [you] what to do. It's very impersonal." After one manager who worked closely with clients threatened to quit since he almost never slept, Cognizant had to change its approach. But as D'Souza recalled, "Frankly, we were out of ideas."[17]

Cognizant decided that the best way to come up with ideas was to study which of its teams performed the most effectively and find out how. When Cognizant studied its global teams that worked well with solid delivery and quality performance and close professional relationships, it discovered that these teams had informally put two people in charge. A manager on the ground in India managed people there and the other in the United States managed the client. According to D'Souza, "They jointly felt accountable for the outcome of that team. We said: Perhaps there's an organizational model that makes sense here that we can learn from." In response, Cognizant decided to apply this comanager concept throughout the company, assigning two equally responsible managers to each project team and business unit, with one close to employees and one close to customers. In so doing, Cognizant required managers to resolve issues jointly and take equal responsibility for customer satisfaction, project deadlines, and group revenues.[18]

The novelty of Cognizant's approach was that it broke from the traditional idea that a business needs to put a single person in charge who is responsible for results and can handle problems. However, thanks to the vigorous debate within Cognizant about the change, other senior managers were alert to identifying and overcoming negative outcomes they had anticipated— that decisions were not being made by comanagers together or disagreements between the comanagers. The result was a management solution that helped make Cognizant operate more effectively for its customers, managers, and employees.[19]

CEO D'Souza's eclectic upbringing seems to have contributed to his, and by extension, Cognizant's ability to adapt to the unexpected in a changing global economy. This openness to change and willingness to tackle new challenges is a critical success factor for a company competing in a mature industry. This human capital element enables a CEO to see opportunities for growth where others might see a need to cut costs.

D'Souza was able to develop this open-mindedness through his Cognizant mentors and through his childhood experiences. At Cognizant, he experienced various management styles. During his career, he worked with three bosses—each of whom had unique attributes—including Srini Raju, "the consummate entrepreneur"; Kumar Mahadeva, a "brilliant strategist"; and Lakshmi Narayanan, a "phenomenal people's person."[20]

D'Souza's childhood shaped his desire to seize new opportunities. That is when he learned to live in unfamiliar settings. His father was with the Indian Foreign Service (he was India's ambassador to, among other countries, Kenya and Panama), and this meant his family lived in a new country every three years or so. "The first time I went to school, we had just been to Panama. I was probably four-years-old. My parents had this idea that we should go to local schools. Panama is Spanish speaking, so they threw us (sisters and I) into Spanish speaking schools. The first couple of months were very tough. By the end of the three years, when we left Panama, my sisters and I spoke Spanish at home."[21]

D'Souza's ability to adapt to changing surroundings was quite useful in his work at Cognizant. As he said, "To work in Cognizant, you have to be very versatile. I learnt that in childhood." This is because it is typical for D'Souza to spend a week in Chennai, preceded by a week meeting with customers across Europe, which itself preceded a week at Cognizant's development center in China. And from Chennai, he planned to fly back home to New Jersey. "Cognizant is a multicultural place, where people from all over the world work together and recognise each other for what they are, and treat them as individuals. That clearly came from my background. You implicitly learn when you travel, and I consider myself incredibly fortunate to have been able to do it."[22]

Cognizant competitor Wipro invested heavily in U.S. human capital despite being founded and based in India. Wipro has 8,000 people in the United States and opened its first American software development center in Atlanta, GA in 2008. By 2009, Wipro planned to hire 200 employees for its Atlanta office. That number is estimated to jump to 500 by 2011 as Wipro recruits IT graduates from local schools, trains them, and employs them. Former CEO Azim Premji explains, "Your business will have a base wherever it can find the best value of talent and cost. Our biggest challenge is scaling and maintaining uniformity of culture. The uniformity of customer experience has to be the same. It has to be consistent."[23]

For Wipro, delivering systems depended on creating a global value chain. In Premji's view roughly 25%–30% of Wipro's teams should be working on or near customer sites. Moreover, he thought that while 10% of these individuals are currently living near the customer, that proportion will rise significantly. Moreover 40% of Wipro employees in Europe were locals, excluding the local engineering company Wipro acquired. Wipro believed that if it could train local employees to understand its global systems development approach, this value chain configuration could work for Wipro and its customers.[24]

Acquisitions were an important part of Wipro's growth strategy. And access to global capital markets made it possible for Wipro to complete these acquisitions. But Wipro believed strongly in the importance of organic growth and used acquisitions as a way to accelerate that growth slightly. For example, according to Premji, if Wipro grew at 30% or 32%, the acquisitions should add another 3% or 3.5% worth of revenue growth.

Wipro identified areas where it needed expertise that would be faster to acquire than to build through hiring. Wipro targeted candidates in a particular country. For example, Wipro made a $600 million acquisition in Germany. Though Germany and the UK were equally large markets, Wipro had a relatively large presence in the UK and a small one in Germany. Wipro estimated it would take years to grow organically in Germany and concluded that a good German acquisition would enable Wipro to scale in two or three years. Customers told Wipro that they needed local data centers to support large, complex projects. In Germany, customers wanted the local data centers for security and because they wanted to be able to visit the computers on which their systems operated. These customer demands spurred Wipro's German acquisition strategy.[25]

How the Globalization of Maturing Industries Is Changing Their Economic Performance

The globalization of maturing industries has contributed to their strong profitability in the two cases we discussed. For example, the personal computer industry's return on equity between 2003 and 2008 averaged 30.7%—almost 10 percentage points higher than the ROE for the average S&P 500 company during that period, which was 21%.[26] The PC industry's 2008 ROE of 31.7% was above its five-year average—suggesting the possibility that globalization may have improved its most recent performance. And for the management services industry—in which Accenture and Cognizant compete—return on equity between 2003 and 2008 averaged 39.9%— almost 19 percentage points higher than the S&P 500 average. Similarly, the Management Services industry's 2008 ROE of 75.2% was well above its five-year average—again suggesting the possibility that globalization may have improved its most recent performance.[27]

We can't quantify how much of the superior performance of these industries is specifically attributable to their increased globalization. However, we can make two guesses as to how globalization might help increase industry profitability:

- *Costs declining more than prices.* ROE for these industries could rise if by globalizing, firms were able to lower their costs more than their prices fell.

This could be achieved largely by continuing to sell products and services to customers who were willing to pay prices that declined less rapidly than the maturing industries were able to lower their costs by globalizing.

- *Better management skills lead to differentiated services.* While this hypothesis is not likely to apply to all maturing industries, it might work for some. For example, as the complexity of corporate systems building projects increases, only a small number of well-managed global services providers may be in a position to do the work. Simply put, if only a handful of well-managed global suppliers can satisfy the difficult demands of these clients, then those suppliers could be in a position to charge higher prices. And if the cost of delivering those complex services was as low as practical, the industry margins would rise.

It remains to be seen whether these hypotheses are valid. However, the future evolution of these and other maturing industries could well provide a test for them.

How the Changing Entrepreneurial Ecosystem for Maturing Industries Is Likely to Influence Their Evolution

The EE for maturing industries may not need to change in order to attract more global capital. However, these capital flows are likely to decline despite the efforts to attract the capital. The reason is that global capital providers are likely to be unable to borrow money to finance acquisitions—as they did when they helped Lenovo purchase IBM's PC business. And as the economic prospects of their U.S. financial services clients dim, Indian computer services firms are retrenching. No fundamental changes in the EEs in countries such as China or India appear likely to overturn these trends.

By the end of 2008, it appeared as though the lack of fundamental change in India's EE was not going to prevent natural economic forces from damaging the business prospects of India's computer services firms. For example, in November 2008, Infosys told investors that it had lowered its growth expectations from between 19% and 21% to a lower 13–15%—less than half its traditional 30% growth rate. Given the dependence on the banking sector (roughly 33% of revenue)—including clients such as Bank of America and Citigroup—and on business from the United States (about 66% of revenue), Infosys's prospects could deteriorate further. Siddharth Pai, a partner at Technology Partners International, a consulting firm that publishes an index of global outsourcing deals, says its index is at a 10-year low. "People think that outsourcing is a recession-proof industry. It is not."[28]

The business prospects for aspiring workers for India's computer services providers look grim. The Indian National Association of Software and Service Companies (NASSCOM) estimated that India's technology sector would create 50,000 fewer jobs in 2008. And since parents arrange marriages, the downturn has even poisoned the marriage prospects of those in technology outsourcing.

Jagadeesh Angadi, a matchmaker in Bangalore, said "Because there are no job guarantees for IT people, for the last six months brides' families have not been accepting grooms from this background."[29]

The history and prospects of India's computer services industry reveal the benefits and risks of a changing EE in a mature industry. The benefits to a maturing industry are that making high quality, lower priced human capital available to clients in developed countries thanks to more open financial markets can revive its growth. The risks are that if the developed country's demand dips, the maturing industry may be unable to find new sources of growth quickly enough to offset the lost revenues. In this case, the evolving EE is not likely to protect India's computer services industry from the Schumpeterian forces that helped it rise and could challenge its prospects. However, if a country is willing to accept the benefits of these forces, it should also anticipate their costs.

Rejuvenating Industries

Thanks to changing EEs, capital has been flowing into industries—such as steel or automobiles—that had historically been in decline. But thanks to that capital influx and a rise in demand, these industries have become new again—we call them rejuvenating industries.

These twin changes—rising demand and capital influx—are critical conditions for reviving a formerly declining industry. In the case of steel, for example, rising demand—particularly in developing countries such as China and India—created an investment opportunity for private capital providers. Of course, the opportunity had significant risk associated with it since the steel industry is so capital-intensive. However, due to the near-bankrupt condition of many U.S. steel makers, the assets were available at a relatively low price for a private capital provider willing to buy them.

This is what Wilbur Ross did and it made him a billionaire. On April 1, 2000, the 62-year-old banker raised $450 million to invest in bankrupt companies. This was not long before the U.S. economy went into a tailspin that threw many companies into bankruptcy. For instance, in 2001, when LTV, a bankrupt steel company based in Cleveland, decided to liquidate, Ross was the only bidder. Ross anticipated that then president Bush, a free trader, would raise tariffs on foreign steel to win over prospective voters in midwestern swing states. So in February 2002, Ross organized International Steel Group (ISG) and agreed to buy LTV's assets for $325 million.[30]

A few weeks later, Bush raised imported steel tariffs by 30%—which gave LTV a price advantage that it used to increase sales. Workers returned to LTV under more efficient work rules replacing pensions with less costly 401(k)s. In 2002, Ross repeated this process with the defunct Bethlehem Steel. Meanwhile, between the tariffs, China's enormous increase in demand for steel, and the U.S. automakers' 0% financing push, American steel was suddenly in great demand. The price per ton of rolled steel increased and Ross took ISG public in December 2003.[31]

Due to his obsession with maximizing internal rate of return, Ross did not hang on to his ISG shares for long. Instead, on October 25, 2004 Ross got an opportunity to maximize his IRR and he agreed to sell ISG to Lakshmi Mittal for $4.5 billion in cash and stock. This deal netted Ross 14 times his initial investment in just two years.[32]

U.S. capital providers are not the only ones to profit from rejuvenating industries. The most well-known Indian examples in recent years have been Tata and Birla groups in India who have leveraged their access to international capital to go on international acquisition sprees. In the process, they have changed the face of international competition in the steel and aluminium industries respectively.

One example of a rejuvenated company is Transport Corporation of India (TCI), a logistics company whose 1997 joint venture with Mitsui delivers parts to Toyota's Bangalore factory on 6,000 trucks that began after TCI won a Toyota-led competition due to TCI's superior geographic coverage, experience, and professionalism. The human capital TCI acquired through its adherence to Japanese principles of *Kaizen: continuous improvement* has aided TCI in its global expansion.[33]

Case Studies of How Entrepreneurial Ecosystem Changes Management of Rejuvenating Industries

Through the exploration of the interplay between maturing industries, EEs, and capital providers we will see how capital inflows shape global value chains in growing industries. To do that, we examine the following case studies.

Tata Motors. Tata Motors' small car—called the Nano and priced at $2,500—could transform and energize the global transportation industry. Thanks to India's culture of scarcity and iconoclasm, the idea for such a car could emerge from the mind of Tata's founder and be built in India. Though the car did not meet Western safety and emissions standards, the Nano had the potential to be upgraded to meet them following its initial success in India. But Tata's best laid plans were sidetracked by protests from Indian citizens who lived near the proposed Nano plant. Ultimately Tata was forced to scrap its investment and build a new plant in a different part of India. But the Nano did ship from a different plant in Pune by March 2009.

Embraer. The Embraer case reveals important insights into the role of a country's EE in a rejuvenating industry. Brazil's EE featured small cities, long distances, a limited airline market, and scarce capital. Embraer circumvented all these EE barriers by inventing smaller aircraft that suited the demands of the Brazilian market. And since its competitors made aircraft for larger aircraft markets, Embraer was well positioned to tap the smaller markets in these countries with its regional jets.

Haier. The weaknesses in China's EE helped Haier rejuvenate the appliance industry. Zhang's ambition to create a world-class competitor enabled him to work around the impediments that China's Communist approach to running the Haier plant put in his way. Zhang's desire to escape those barriers to creating a competitive product led him to seek financing from private sources. To get that money, Zhang needed to build a product with the quality to compete in a big, sophisticated market. To do this, Zhang convinced his work force to care about product quality—a major cultural leap given Communist China's egalitarian approach to treating people. Once Zhang got private capital, he began to diversify by product category and to expand globally. Now he is trying to harmonize the aspects of Chinese culture he finds worthwhile with the positive traits of the non-Chinese cultures in which Haier operates.

Tata Motors

Indian automobile manufacturer Tata Motors came up with an idea for a small automobile that could solve a problem faced by Indian commuters. And given its anticipated small size and low price, it could revive a shrinking industry. How? With the globe in economic retrenchment and credit unavailable to finance the purchase of new automobiles, consumers who need vehicles must try either to keep their existing ones running or use other means of transportation such as trains and buses.

However, thanks to Tata Motors' idea for a $2,500 small car, the market for automobiles could enjoy a strong revival. That's for two reasons: first, people who never purchased an automobile in the past might now be able to afford one and second, people who could previously borrow money to purchase an automobile and now cannot access that credit would view the small car as a viable way to buy a new car.

To achieve this vision, however, Tata still must overcome some significant practical challenges. First, it must build the vehicles in a region of India that does not protest their manufacture. And second, if it hopes to reach the market for its small car outside of India—the second market alluded to above—it must modify them to conform to the local safety and emissions standards. Neither challenge is insurmountable. Tata has already selected a new site to manufacture the vehicle. And if it sells a sufficient number of them in India, it may generate the profit it needs to upgrade it to satisfy safety and emissions standards in other countries.

The idea for Tata's small car, dubbed the Nano, came from the Tata Motors then-CEO, Ratan Tata, who was appalled by the death rates of those riding on scooters. This gave him the idea of creating an inexpensive automobile that these families could afford and would provide a safer means of transportation. As Tata said, "I saw families of three or four riding on scooters." He then learned that traffic deaths on two-wheelers were three or four times that of cars.[34]

Tata's ideas for how to solve this problem went through several iterations. His first idea for a cheap people's car began as little more than a glorified tricycle, a sort of three-wheeler with a basic canopy. The next step was what Tata calls "a very basic vehicle with no doors." The final four-door hatchback version can seat up to five people and is powered by a rear-mounted 33-horsepower 623cc two-cylinder engine. The car is just over 10 feet long (nearly two feet shorter than the Mini Cooper) and less than five feet wide.[35]

Some of the few people who have seen the Nano describe a tiny, charming, four-door, five-seater hatchback shaped like a jelly bean, small in the front and broad in the back, the better to reduce wind resistance and permit a cheaper engine. A.K. Chaturvedi, senior vice president of business development at Lumax Industries, a supplier in Delhi that developed the car's headlights and interior lamps said, "It's a nice car—cute."[36]

It's possible that the Nano represents an original product of a new brand of engineering that some have dubbed "Gandhian" that combines irreverence for conventional approaches with cheapness resulting from scarcity. Indian auto executive Ashok K. Taneja described the philosophy thus: "When I need silver, why am I investing in gold?"[37]

Tata's engineers applied a cost cutting philosophy in building the Nano—which Tata planned to sell for roughly half the price of the next-cheapest Indian alternative. In so doing their guiding principle was: Do we really need that? Consistent with this Gandhian philosophy, the Nano prototype introduced in January 2008 had no radio, no power steering, no power windows, no air-conditioning and one windshield wiper instead of two. It also lacked a tachometer and used an analog rather than digital speedometer.[38]

Tata's Gandhian engineering also altered its internal machinery—reducing the Nano's safety and shortening its life. For example, to save $10, Tata engineers redesigned the Nano's suspension to eliminate actuators in the headlights, the levelers that adjust the angle of the beam depending on how the car is loaded. Kiran Deshmukh, the former chief operating officer of Nano supplier Sona Koyo Steering Systems, said that Sona used a hollow tube instead of the solid steel beam that typically connects steering wheels to axles. Tata also chose weaker wheel bearings—they work as long as the car runs at less than 45 miles an hour, but wear down quickly above that speed. The car will wear down soon for people driving it at between 45 MPH and 75 MPH, the Nano's top speed.[39]

The Nano may be sufficiently sturdy to satisfy Indian safety standards. However, if Tata hopes to sell the vehicle in Western countries such as the United States and Europe, it will need to make the vehicle more crash proof. While this added safety is likely to add to the Nano's cost, there is likely to be sufficient demand at a higher price to make those markets profitable for Tata. During the Nano's unveiling, Ratan Tata stated that the Nano has met Indian frontal-impact crash tests. As for other markets with more stringent crash criteria, he said that his company "would and could address foreign markets." He claimed that the Nano had been engineered to pass "international" offset frontal and side-impact crash tests. Moreover, while Airbags were unavailable in early 2008, Tata could easily add them.[40]

The Nano will also get excellent gas mileage; however, it does produce significant air pollution. However, the Nano's emissions are likely to decline thanks to Tata's plans to design future versions of the vehicle to conform to higher emissions standards. The Nano is capable of achieving 50 miles per gallon. According to Tata, in early 2008, "emissions [were] applicable to Euro III and will be up to Euro IV standards in a few years." Although the Nano's emissions are pretty high, they are equal to or cleaner than many of the scooters and motorcycles that it is designed to replace.[41]

Despite the Nano's market potential, Tata faced a costly political problem that impeded its ability to satisfy that demand. The result of this problem was that Tata had to scrap a $350 million plant in one part of India and build a new plant in a different region. The problem was that landowners were opposed to a move by the local Communist Party to force them to give up their land for the plant. Tata, which already had invested more than $350 million in the plant to build 250,000 Nanos in Singur, in India's eastern state of West Bengal, said demonstrations had disrupted its efforts to get the plant ready to begin production. The demonstrations were the joint result of West Bengal state's main opposition party, Trinamool Congress, and farmers' lobbies that opposed Tata's Nano project, contending that West Bengal state's ruling Communist government had forcibly acquired prime agricultural land for the factory.[42]

By October 2008, Tata had had enough. It decided to scrap the Singur plant and move the production facility to Sanand in the western state of Gujarat. The new Sanand facility was located on 1,100 acres of government-owned land—yielding what Tata anticipated would be "the shortest possible time lag and least possible incremental project cost." Since Tata was continuing Nano production at two of its other facilities in Pune and Pantnagar, it ultimately launched the Nano from its Pune plant by March 15, 2009.[43]

The Tata Motors Nano case reveals important insights into the role of a country's EE in a rejuvenating industry. India's high population density and poverty, relatively weak safety and environmental standards, and tense government policies toward business expansion created a largely favorable environment for Tata Motors to rejuvenate the automobile industry. India's EE has helped Tata to realize his inspiration to build a very low priced car to help improve the lives of families risking their lives on scooters. And as demand grows, Tata is likely to get access to the capital it needs to improve the Nano to meet European and American safety and environmental standards.

Embraer

The aircraft industry has enormous entry barriers; yet one Brazilian manufacturer, Embraer, surmounted them to start the first successful new entrant since 1960. Thanks to support from the Brazilian government, Embraer grew from its 1969 founding into the country's biggest exporter. The key to Embraer's strategy was to make aircraft that suited its geography—they were smaller and less costly for airlines. And Embraer built these aircraft through partnerships because it lacked the capital to do everything itself.

Embraer is Brazil's biggest exporter—with 98% of its sales to foreign customers. To drive those foreign sales, Embraer has offices in Australia, China, France,

Singapore, and the United States. Partnerships have allowed Embraer to boost its production rate on its best-established, 30–50-passenger ERJ-145 family from 7 aircraft per month at the end of 1999 to 17 per month by 2001. And Embraer planned to expand the role of partners for its larger aircraft. For example, with the larger ERJ 190 model, Mauricio Botelho, Embraer's former CEO said, "we expanded the concept of partnership—making these partners more responsible for systems rather than parts."[44]

The key to Embraer's ability to rejuvenate the aircraft industry is its products that make it profitable for airlines to serve smaller cities. By opening up previously underserved airline markets, it has created a new growth opportunity it is well positioned to capture. How? On many secondary routes, a 150-seat aircraft, such as an A-320 or Boeing 737, might be too expensive to fly more than once or twice a day or it might leave the ground with empty seats. Neither option would be profitable. However, Embraer's 70- and 90-seat models make it profitable for U.S. airlines to serve smaller markets such as Shreveport, LA and Montgomery, AL more frequently. This pleases customers and produces revenue growth for the airlines.[45]

However, the cost of developing these new models was more than Embraer could afford so it expanded its partnerships. Specifically, the project cost almost $1 billion to develop so Embraer recruited 16 cost-sharing partners—4 times as many as worked on its earlier ERJ-145 model. These partners included General Electric, which produces the jet's engines, and Honeywell, which makes the cockpit information system. Embraer's partners took on roughly 33% of its development cost and shortened the time from plane launch to first delivery to less than five years.[46]

As with most aircraft manufacturers, Embraer's dependence on exports makes it vulnerable to slowing global economies. By the fall of 2008, Embraer was being affected by the financing challenges resulting from the credit crisis. Although none of its airline clients had cancelled orders, their inability to get financing made it likely that orders might peak. According to Botelho's successor as CEO, Frederico Fleury Curado, "We see signals that the customers' financing options are getting scarce. But so far we have had no direct impact."[47]

However, airlines were expected to lose $5.2 billion in 2008 as a result of high oil prices and a global economy stymied by the ongoing financial crisis. As Fleury Curado said, "If this crisis goes on longer and deeper, then everyone will be affected. But we will have to wait and see." He expected Embraer to sell the forecasted 195–200 regional jets in 2008. And he also expected less of a fall off in demand from its customers who purchased business jets thanks to their relative ease of getting access to credit (compared to airlines). As Fleury Curado said, "We're seeing less impact on our business jets as those individuals and corporations that we target have easier access to credit, unlike the airlines."[48]

The Embraer case reveals important insights into the role of a country's EE in a rejuvenating industry. Brazil's EE featured small cities, long distances, a limited airline market, and scarce capital. Embraer innovated around all these EE barriers by inventing smaller aircraft that suited the demands of the Brazilian market. And since its competitors made aircraft for larger aircraft markets,

Embraer was well positioned to tap the smaller markets in these countries with its regional jets.

As a result, airlines seeking to make money in these smaller markets were happy to buy Embraer's smaller, less costly aircraft to fly with sufficient frequency to attract enough passengers to make those markets profitable for the airlines to serve. Moreover, since it was unable to get sufficient capital to finance the development of new, smaller aircraft, Embraer benefited from a global EE that was willing to partner with Embraer because those partners believed that airlines would buy enough of the new aircraft to earn the partners a return on their investment.

Haier

Haier is a formerly Chinese state-owned appliance maker that has cleverly tapped the Chinese EE to rejuvenate the global appliance industry. Haier's CEO took over the company when it suffered from all the competitive disadvantages of a Communist Party run enterprise. Haier produced far more inventory than people would purchase because that production kept people employed. Moreover, no government financing was available to run the business efficiently. In order to get access to private capital, Haier needed to develop a better quality product that would be able to compete in a free market economy. Haier's ability to make this transition was the key to its global success.

Haier was originally a state-owned enterprise in China's Shangdong province when Zhang Ruimin took over its original Qingdao factory in 1984. Zhang decided that Haier could survive as a business only if it became independent of state funding. As he said, "The way of the government in factories was to have reservoirs. Reservoirs hold a lot of inventory, hoping that some day someone will want it. Our idea was to have a river, with goods flowing out, and very little, if any, inventory."[49]

To get that river, Zhang sought funding outside the traditional government-oriented system. And in order to get that funding, he needed to prove that his factory could not only produce refrigerators but also get customers to buy them. Zhang realized that the only way he could accomplish this would be to start making better refrigerators. But workers had little incentive to do so. According to Zhang, "You couldn't be fired. My first rule in the factory was that no one could urinate on the floor. So you see how hard it was going to be. Since I couldn't even fire anyone for urinating on the floor, I put them on two years' probation."[50]

Probation and the practice of smashing defective refrigerators were both symbolic gestures. However, these gestures sent workers an effective signal that Zhang wanted to change how Haier operated. Eventually, he persuaded workers to follow his way of operating and the Qingdao factory started producing better refrigerators. Zhang began selling them in Shanghai, which was a bigger and more sophisticated market that demanded better quality. Zhang's new strategy convinced investors from Shanghai to put money into Haier.[51]

By expanding into other product lines and selling into new countries, Haier grew from $400,000 in sales in 1984 to over $2 billion in 1999. Specifically, Haier accomplished this by starting factories that made washing machines, micro-waves, dishwashers, vacuum cleaners, freezers, air conditioners, TVs, electric irons, air purifiers, gas cookers, and mobile phones.[52]

Zhang had three seven-year plans. As he said, "We had a three-step goal, each one taking about seven years. The first was to establish a brand name. It was new in China to have quality design in appliances. In 1984, there were 300 refrigerator factories, most of them making bad products. We wanted to distinguish our-selves and eventually we did."[53]

His second seven-year plan was to diversify, but only within his sector. According to Zhang, "In China, the idea is to make what you make and put out volume. But since we were basing ourselves on quality instead of quantity, we decided that if someone bought a Haier Group refrigerator, then maybe they would look to buy something else from us." He spent the next seven years buying or establishing factories in other appliances and electronic consumer goods.[54]

Between 1994 and 2001, Zhang focused on his third seven-year plan—globalization. As Zhang said, "We feel it is time we push into the global market-place. And our feeling is that we have to tackle the hard markets first [like the United States and Europe] and then later go onto the easy markets."[55]

A key element of Haier's globalization strategy is to meld the Chinese culture with that of the country in which its global plants operate. For example, although Haier's South Carolina factory is run by local executives, Zhang brings Chinese culture to that American factory. According to Zhang, "We can talk about our culture, about the ways Chinese do things, but in the end, we have to respect Western ways in their market or we will fail."[56]

Now that China has slowly begun to open up its business climate, Zhang will be focusing on melding Western business practices with the traditional Chinese. He likes the idea of having a spiritual core—a particularly Eastern concept—in which managers push workers to make all products better. Yet he resists the Chinese idea of egalitarianism. Zhang calls this "the rice bowl approach" and he prefers to reward those who contribute more rather than to treat everyone equally. As Zhang said, "Everyone should be encouraged to innovate, and those who contribute more to the product should benefit more." Haier does this in many ways—for example, it names products, parts, or even manufacturing prac-tices after the employee who is responsible for the innovation. That way, Zhang said, everyone knows they have a chance to become someone special in the organization.[57]

How the Globalization of Rejuvenating Industries Is Changing Their Economic Performance

The globalization of rejuvenating industries is slashing the sales and profits of some incumbents while providing attractive growth opportunities for challeng-ers. The U.S. automobile industry has lost billions of dollars in the past several years as its market share declined. Yet Japanese firms have steadily gained mar-ket share and earned attractive returns over the past 30 years thanks to superior product development, manufacturing, and customer service capabilities. And upstart competitors, such as Tata Motors, have the potential to create entirely new categories of automobiles thanks to their Gandhian approach to product development.

In the aircraft industry, the barriers to entry are so high that very few new entrants can gain a profitable foothold. As a result, the new entrants who have succeeded are not able to damage significantly the positions of the incumbents. Embraer (whose profit was $5.2 billion in 2007) and more recently China's state-backed aircraft industry are two recent entrants. As we explored earlier, such new entrants remain relatively small—occupying niches of the market that do not warrant the attention of the larger players such as Boeing (whose sales totaled $66 billion in 2007) and Airbus.

China could also prove to be a formidable competitor—although that threat could be years off. For example, a government-funded company, China Aviation Industry Corporation I Commercial Aircraft Co. Ltd. (ACAC), has gotten a lift by building an aircraft—the Advanced Regional Jet for the 21st Century (ARJ21)—that could take off at very high altitudes, such as Bangda airport in Tibet (at 14,000 ft, the world's highest runway). And ACAC is targeting a big market—China is expected to spend $340 billion for 3,400 new aircraft—nearly quadrupling its 2007 fleet of about 1,000—by 2026. Moreover, ACAC could tap a global market of 1,600 regional jets that could be purchased between 2007 and 2025.[58]

Such new entrants could alter the dynamics of the industry by taking market share from the current leaders—Boeing and Airbus. For example, while Embraer is far smaller than Boeing, it is growing much faster. For example, between 2006 and 2007, Embraer sales grew 40% whereas Boeing's sales were up a relatively paltry 8%. Nevertheless, despite its faster growth, Boeing was far more profitable—for instance, in the quarter ending September 2008 Boeing's return on average equity was 31.7% compared to 10.8% for Embraer.[59] Nevertheless, as long as Embraer and ACAC do not take share from the segments in which incumbents currently compete, these upstarts are not likely to damage the attractiveness of the industry. In fact, by adding new markets they are enhancing its opportunities for all participants.

How the Changing Entrepreneurial Ecosystem for Rejuvenating Industries Is Likely to Influence Their Evolution

The changing EE in rejuvenating industries will almost certainly increase the level of creative destruction. However, that creative destruction is likely to be good for customers since it will encourage the creation of new products that satisfy previously unmet needs. If these new products then evolve to disrupt the markets that incumbent firms currently dominate then incumbents will face a choice. They can either adapt to the upstart competitors—or they can slowly lose market share and eventually fold. Meanwhile, the upstarts will also need to adapt and expand—as Haier has done—in order to maintain their growth.

The evolving EE plays a significant role in all this creative destruction. By upgrading corporate governance in developing countries, firms in those countries are able to attract private capital which can tap the growth potential and relatively inexpensive, yet-high quality human capital. This human capital can design and build products that capture market share globally and provide more robust financial markets which can finance acquisitions to boost these new firms. While IP protection in some of these developing countries may be the last EE element to evolve, over the long run it too will need to improve. The reason is that as companies in developing countries move up the value-added chain, they will ultimately need to compete on the basis of IP. And IP will only attract capital investment if investors believe they'll be protected.

Conclusion

The evolving EE shapes the growth of industries at different stages in different ways. In a maturing industry, capital flows to countries whose EE provides a nurturing environment for consolidation and which houses the human capital required to manage effectively a global enterprise. And in a rejuvenating industry, capital will flow to countries that have the human capital that can innovate in ways that create markets where none previously existed. Such innovation can spark new revenue sources that can upend incumbents and challenge all participants to adapt.

Part III

The Implications of the Entrepreneurial Ecosystem and Recommendations for Policymakers, Capital Providers, and Managers

Implications for Policymakers

Policymakers play a critical role in attracting capital. They have the power to encourage capital to flow into their countries and the power to block it. And in a general sense they can exercise that power by changing the shape of their country's EE. Given the importance that such capital flows play in creating new jobs, policymakers seeking reelection can sustain their power by reshaping their country's EE to switch on the capital flow spigot.

To help such policymakers, this chapter addresses the following critical questions:

- What can policymakers do to shape the EE to attract global capital flows?
- What useful lessons are available to policymakers based on the experiences of other countries in trying to make the key trade-offs involved in creating a vital EE within their countries?
- How do these choices affect the economic performance of their countries?
- What tools are available to help a policymaker assess what changes, if any, the country must undertake to attract global capital flows?
- How should a policymaker use such tools to decide whether to make a country more receptive to such flows?
- And if so, what changes should a policymaker endeavor to institute?

In considering these questions, here are five key principles that can guide policymakers:

- *Policymakers should build off of their strongest EE elements to offset their weakest ones.* Modern Israel was founded in 1948 with its economic and political back up against the wall. It lacked the means to feed its people or defend them from enemies. And, unlike some of its geographically proximate enemies, Israel lacked oil reserves, which could have provided it with capital. It did have one very strong EE element—human capital. And by managing that human capital in the right way, it was able to offset the weaknesses in the others. How so? Israel's technically innovative entrepreneurs created intellectual property that attracted venture capital whose pressure to issue IPOs on Nasdaq set very high corporate governance standards for the start-ups—dozens of whose shares now trade on that exchange.

- *Policymakers should encourage global capital flows that later lead to transfer of valuable know-how.* The partnership between Wal-Mart and Bharti illustrates an effective strategy for transferring know-how from a capital provider to a capital recipient. Due to Indian laws that prevent a foreign company from owning a storefront in India, Wal-Mart cannot open a regular store there. However, Indian rules allowed Wal-Mart to provide supply chain services to Bharti and in so doing, policymakers expect that Wal-Mart will transfer its operating know-how to Bharti. This will benefit both companies in the short term; however, over the longer term Wal-Mart risks making itself obsolete as a supply chain partner for Bharti.
- *Policymakers in capital-receiving countries must raise their standard of corporate governance to the capital providing countries' level.* In the case of Satyam Computer Services the family founders unilaterally decided to acquire their children's construction company. The outrage of minority shareholders from outside India led the founders to reverse their decision. However, the resulting loss in stock market value and threat to its customers' willingness to continue purchasing Satyam's services made it apparent to Indian policymakers that they must raise India's corporate governance standards if they wish to attract and sustain global capital flows.
- *Policymakers must weigh the political and cultural costs of permitting entry of foreign capital against its economic benefits.* In many countries—particularly those with histories of Communist or Socialist rule—policymakers have chosen to move their countries toward a more capitalist economic model. However significant the economic benefits of encouraging global capital flows, policymakers must also be careful not to push their countries beyond the limits of what makes cultural and political sense. A country such as China—which has a one-country/two systems policy that encourages capitalism but discourages democracy—is one model. In India, trade-offs are often made to find an acceptable center of political gravity between the needs of foreign capital providers to earn an attractive return and the demands of local workers and companies who want the government to protect their interests from these foreign capital providers.
- *Policymakers should avoid decisions that create short-term benefits but higher long-term costs.* Iceland's high deposit rate policy and Russia's creepingly expropriating policies toward foreign investment have shown that these countries chose to take the short-term benefits—such as rapid capital inflows—without considering the potential for long-term damage. While the short-term benefits may help policymakers gain and maintain political power, the long-term costs—in the form of the bankruptcy of the financial system or an inability to attract new capital from singed foreign capital providers—could offset these short-term benefits.

Case Studies of Countries that *Flow with*
and *Fight* the Globalization of
Entrepreneurship

Recent cases in countries around the world—including those who flow with and against the waves of global capital flows—help enliven these themes. Here are seven mini cases that address these different themes.

- *Israel builds a start-up nation on human capital.* Israel was founded without the resources it needed to survive. Lacking significant physical resources, it built an economy based on the only resource it had—the human capital of the immigrants who flowed into its borders. Their spirit of innovation and entrepreneurship yielded a rate of small company formation that rivals that of much larger nations.[1]
- *Iceland's high deposit rate policy backfires.* Iceland rose and fell by trying to attract deposits from around the world by offering high deposit rates. Iceland succeeded in the short run but bankrupted the country and wiped out much of that foreign capital in the process.
- *Sovereign Wealth Funds (SWFs) get burned by investing in U.S. banks.* SWFs raised the hackles of U.S. politicians in early 2008. It turns out that SWFs' investments in U.S. financial institutions were not a threat as much as they were a sign of a market top. After losing significant sums on these investments, SWFs are no longer interested in being played for fools. The result is that the United States ultimately unleashed a $23.7 trillion bailout of its collapsing financial system since SWFs would not step in.
- *India's banking system survives by resisting America's fast-buck culture.* India's banking system has remained relatively intact compared to that of Iceland or the United States. India's culture frowns on going heavily into debt and its banking system scrutinizes borrowers much more closely than does the U.S. banking system. Since so many U.S. loans are sold as bundles, U.S. bankers don't care too much about borrowers' credit-worthiness—at least during a period of economic expansion. India resisted the lure of fast growth by taking on more risk—and it is, therefore, better positioned to weather the downturn.
- *Satyam collapses after governance failure exposed.* Nevertheless, India is far from perfect. Satyam Computer Services created the illusion of good corporate governance while acting quite differently. A failed effort to close the gap between actual and reported cash—in the form of a failed deal to acquire the construction business of the founders' children—exposed a multiyear fraud that Satyam's auditor, PriceWaterhouseCoopers, failed to uncover. This fraud caused investors and customers to flee and raised serious questions about the sufficiency of India's approach to regulating public companies and the financial markets.

- *BP is buffeted by changing political winds in Russia and loses its control over energy joint venture.* British Petroleum (BP) formed an oil and gas venture with Russia, which exposed the danger of investing in Russia. While Russia happily accepted BP's investment, its effort to manage the venture by buying out the holdings of Russian oligarchs completely backfired. In the end, due to threats from the Russian court system, BP's management team decided it was safer to leave Russia. The oligarchs took over control—quite possibly with the secret encouragement of Russia's most powerful political leaders.
- *Wal-Mart/Bharti partnership transfers supply chain know-how to India.* Wal-Mart's decision to enter the Indian market by acting as a wholesaler to Bharti Enterprises created opportunities for both firms. This case study examines the benefits to consumers and farmers of using Wal-Mart's logistics skills to reduce inefficiency in India's produce delivery network and the benefits to Bharti and other Indian companies and industries of accessing Wal-Mart's logistics expertise through daily interaction with Wal-Mart and ultimately by hiring some of its people.[2]

Israel Builds a Start-Up Nation on Human Capital

Israel's ability to spur entrepreneurial innovation vastly exceeds its size. Israel has 7.1 million people but the number of Israeli companies listed on the Nasdaq far exceeds its relative population. For example, India has 3 companies listed; Japan has 6; Canada has 48; Israel has 63. Israel has received as much foreign venture capital as the much larger Britain—$2 billion in foreign venture capital invested there in 2008 alone. And Israel has the highest density of startups in the world 3,850—the equivalent of one start-up for every 1,844 Israelis. Moreover, during the past few decades, Israel's high-tech innovations have spread around the world.[3]

How did Israel accomplish this feat? It was certainly not because its geographical neighbors welcomed it with open arms. Instead Israel took its many physical limitations and overcame them with the spirit of its people. After all, an Arab nation boycott made regional trade impossible and it had very few natural resources. And yet thanks to the way it managed its human capital—a critical element of its EE—Israel became an innovation hub.

Israel's entrepreneurial success depends on the people it attracts and how it harnesses their skills. Since Israel is besieged by enemies, all its citizens serve in the military, which creates social networks and leadership training. Furthermore, Israel's culture of critique, fostered by centuries of Jewish tradition, encourages a spirit of relentless improvement. Moreover, an open immigration policy for Jews restocks Israel's population with motivated people. The result is a business climate that embraces risk and spurs the growth of good ideas.[4]

Many examples of Israel's most successful start-ups spring from the application of its human capital to the gap between demand and supply. For example, drip irrigation was invented when a farmer in the Negev desert noticed one of his trees flourishing despite drought conditions. When he discovered a leaky under-water pipe, he had a moment of creative inspiration, developing a technology that spread around the world.[5]

Many of Israel's greatest innovations were in the area of information technology. They include PC antivirus software, AOL Instant Messenger, and the Intel Pentium microprocessor chip. Israelis also created medical devices such as radiation-free breast cancer diagnostics and the "Gut Cam," an ingestible pill video camera that diagnoses abnormalities.[6]

Isreal's success at building a start-up nation suggests four important implications for policymakers:

- *Focus on policies that close the most important gaps between demand and supply.* Rather than wallow in the misery of being surrounded by enemies with no significant natural resources, Israeli policymakers recognized that with their backs against the wall, they would need to adapt in order to survive. Israel needed food and water to feed its people and healthy industries to provide jobs and tax revenues. And Israel found a way to use the one resource it had—human capital—to close the gap between those needs and its ability to supply them.

- *Manage human capital in a way that rewards innovation.* Israel could have taken a hard line against bringing in new people since they certainly imposed a cost on its scarce resources—particularly before those immigrants could contribute to the economy. Instead Israel chose to welcome the immigrants while requiring them to serve in its military as a way to defend the country and forge a unique culture. Moreover, Israel placed a high value on risk taking and pushing good ideas from all sources. Its valuable human capital attracted the venture capital Israel needed to build these ideas into viable companies.

- *Encourage companies to locate activities where they will yield the greatest corporate advantage.* To maximize local employment, Israel could have required that Israeli companies perform all their activities—such as R&D, manufacturing, marketing, and logistics—in Israel. But Israeli policymakers saw such limitations as short-sighted. Instead, they encouraged entrepreneurs to locate activities where they could generate the most global growth. As a result, many Israeli companies located their R&D in Israel and Silicon Valley while starting marketing and manufacturing outposts in their largest markets—such as the United States or China. Such global value chains enabled Israeli entrepreneurs to develop new products and sell them around the world.

- *Push companies to adopt the corporate governance standards needed to list their shares in the deepest global capital markets.* Finally, Israel's high rate of listings on the Nasdaq illustrates the importance that its policymakers placed on high standards of corporate governance. By encouraging the flow of global venture capital into Israel, its policymakers also realized that the companies receiving that capital would need to meet the governance standards of the securities exchanges where the VCs would aspire to an IPO. Israel's decision to permit such capital flows pushed its start-ups to adopt the highest standards of corporate governance.

Iceland's High Deposit Rate Policy Backfires

In the early 1990s, Iceland decided that it wanted to get a piece of all the liquidity floating around the globe so it raised the rates it paid on bank deposits. The rates were so high that they attracted money from around the world. That flow of capital boosted the value of Iceland's currency, the krona, so high that it became very inexpensive for Icelanders to import goods from around the world. The result was Iceland had the highest standard of living of any country in the world. Then in 2008, the global credit crunch called home all that money deposited in Iceland's banks. And now Iceland has gone from having the world's highest standard of living to bankruptcy.

How did Iceland blow up the bubble? It liberated its banks from state control and those banks raised deposit rates and loosened their lending standards. This change was the result of a decision by a man who rose to become Iceland's prime minister, David Oddsson. In the early 1990s Oddsson decided that what most held Iceland back from increasing its standard of living was government control of banking, which let politicians decide how to allocate capital.[7]

When Oddsson became Iceland's Prime Minister in 1991, he decided to take away the economic roadblocks by selling off government-owned companies— including its banks. Within a few years, Iceland had sold off companies worth $2 billion, which was a significant sum for a small economy in a country with 300,000 people.[8]

The first of those privatizations was Iceland's banks. Soon after becoming private, the banks started to look for growth outside of Iceland because with such a small population there were not enough new accounts in Iceland. To get these foreign accounts, Iceland's central bank raised its interest rates, and its banks, in turn, raised their deposit rates to a relatively high level that kept foreign money flowing into Iceland, strengthening the krona and making imported goods easily affordable. Iceland imported high quality Scandinavian furniture, building materials for new houses and sport-utility vehicles. As evidence of the growth in Iceland's banking system, consider this: in 2000, Kaupthing Bank, Iceland's biggest, had assets of just 208 billion kronur; however, by offering high interest rates—such as 7.15% on one-year deposits—it ended June 2008 with 30 times more assets—or 6.6 trillion kronur.[9]

However, by December 2008, all that prosperity had ended and demonstrators were crowding into a Reykjavik city square protesting Iceland's deteriorating economic condition. The global credit crunch had destroyed Iceland's three main banks, and many businesses had failed, unemployment had risen, prices spiked up, and the krona plummeted.[10]

How did the bubble collapse? Iceland tried to build a global banking center on top of a tiny currency. So when foreign investors tried to pull out—converting kronur back into dollars or euros in large numbers—the kronur fell rapidly, which created a snowballing withdrawal effect. Hedge funds tried to force the krona down but the banks survived and the krona recovered. But Iceland misjudged the banks' resilience.[11]

In a matter of just a few days starting in late September, Iceland's entire banking system failed. In mid-September, Glitnir Bank, one of Iceland's big three, could not come up with the cash to pay back a bond it had issued five years earlier. Glitnir had until October 15 to make a €600 million payment it owed. However, it ran into trouble borrowing the money it would need to make the payment. The mid-September collapse of Lehman Brothers had frozen interbank lending worldwide. Glitnir had hoped that Germany's Bayerische Landesbank would let it be late with a €150-million loan payment so it could repay the bond. However, BL demanded to get its money on time on September 24.[12]

Iceland's central bank could have helped; however, it did not have sufficient euros in its coffers to lend to Glitnir. For instance, while it had plenty of kronur, by mid-2008 it only held €2 billion in foreign currency reserves—a mere 4% of its €49.9 billion in debts to foreign banks. Oddsson negotiated a deal to take a 75% stake in Glitnir for €600 million. And that deal's announcement caused Glitnir's shares to collapse; rating agencies downgraded Glitnir's debt ratings and those of other Icelandic banks as well as Iceland itself. This caused the krona to plunge.[13]

Foreign depositors, such as those from Britain, were spooked by the bad news, so over the weekend they withdrew £200 million from the London branches of Iceland's Landsbanki's Icesave accounts. British banking authorities told Landsbanki that it had until Monday afternoon to replenish the London branch with about the same amount. Iceland decided to solve the problem by seizing its banks—passing a law to that end that very night.[14]

By the next morning, October 7, Landsbanki was nationalized—this protected Iceland's depositors but left UK depositors unable to get access to their funds.

Iceland did not even have sufficient funds to provide depositors with the €20,000 minimum prescribed by European regulations. And anecdotal evidence suggests that foreign depositors are not going to get much of their Icelandic deposits back. As of December 2008, Landsbanki's 2,000 depositors in Guernsey, a British island, had been paid 30% of their £120 million in deposits. But the bank's court-appointed administrator wasn't optimistic that they'll get the rest back. Guernsey has no deposit-guarantee protection.[15]

Prospects for Iceland's future are not bright. Iceland's GDP was forecast to shrink by 8% in 2009. Inflation, at 18% and expected to rise, is slashing the value of the typical Icelanders' assets and squeezing their formerly flush household budgets.[16]

Iceland's economic rise and fall suggest four lessons for policymakers:

- *Set policies that attract global capital and retain it over the long run by raising effective exit barriers.* The ideal form of exit barrier is self-interest in the form of sustained high returns on capital for global investors. Iceland's short-term high deposit rate policy was ineffective in part because it was so easy for depositors to flee when their investment was imperiled. If Iceland had provided better long-term investment opportunities it may have avoided the rapid capital flight.

- *Control the rate of bank asset growth because rapid growth leads to even more rapid collapse.* As a general rule in finance, there is a limit to the growth rate that a bank can manage. If a bank attracts too much capital too quickly, it will feel compelled to lend it out quickly. This will lead to bad loans as bankers hurriedly approve deals that under more normal circumstances they would view as too risky. To avoid overly rapid growth, policymakers must set conservative capital limits and install regulators in bank credit committees to monitor their credit decision making.
- *Maintain a cushion of foreign currency reserves sufficient to backstop the banking industry.* In retrospect, Iceland might have avoided the need to nationalize its banks if it had maintained a sufficient level of nonkrona reserves—particularly keeping substantial levels of euros and pounds to help backstop the loan obligations of its banks, which issued debt and borrowed money in these other currencies. Because Iceland's central bank had so much of its reserves in krona, it was caught short when foreign lenders called in their loans.
- *Create an EE that encourages long-term investment rather than short-term capital parking.* Ultimately, Iceland would have been better off if it had created the conditions to attract private capital flows that would seek out long-term investment in developing Iceland's corporate sector and its infrastructure. For example, Iceland might have focused its resources on educating a well-trained group of engineers who could provide computer services for global corporations. Such human capital might have attracted longer-term capital flows that would have had a greater incentive to sustain initial investments from foreign capital providers.

Sovereign Wealth Funds Get Burned by Investing in U.S. Banks

In 2007, the United States began to realize that its financial system was showing cracks. However, it was reluctant to provide the financing to repair them. Its first instinct was to seek out capital from U.S.-based financial institutions—such as banks, insurance companies, hedge funds, and private equity firms. However, these U.S.-based capital providers were suffering enough themselves to realize that such a fiscal rescue would further weaken their balance sheets rather than spur economic recovery.

So the United States—still reluctant to put government money into the system—decided to encourage U.S. bank executives to hop on their corporate jets and fly to foreign capitals to ask them to provide capital. And initially, these ventures yielded success—in the form of multibillion investments from foreign investment pools into U.S. financial institutions.

The only problem with this strategy was that it created a protectionist feeling within the U.S. SWFs—government-controlled pools of capital generated from profits selling oil and gas (Middle East) and/or trade surpluses (Asia)—managed $5 trillion. Some in the United States feared that the SWFs were potentially economic and political Trojan horses. They feared that the United States was being short-sighted in allowing the problems in the credit markets to create an opening for SWFs to buy stakes in U.S. banks for relatively paltry sums.

At the time they made those investments it was unclear whether they were getting in at the bottom or were foolishly buying in way too soon. However, there was a fear that if the SWFs bought sufficiently large stakes in strategic industries in the United States, they would be in a position to influence U.S. policy. For example, if the funds did not like U.S. or Middle East policies, they could threaten to withdraw their capital. If that capital was hard to replace, the United States would find itself needing to choose between imperiling the survival of its banking system and changing its foreign policies.

Many of these SWFs found themselves in the middle of a political tussle between Wall Street money managers who salivated at the chance of extracting fees for helping manage the SWFs—about $1 trillion of SWF capital is externally managed—and politicians seeking to retain power by rattling the sword of American protectionism in the face of the SWFs. However, the SWFs' managers could not understand why they were being treated so shabbily. They expected that since they were willing to do what nobody else in the U.S. private capital or government would—write multibillion checks to recapitalize U.S. banks—they should be welcomed with open arms. Instead, their reward for investing in these financial institutions was to lose their shirts—as Peter noted at Stanford, five major SWF U.S. financial institution stakes had declined an average of 16.6% from their date of inception—and get criticized in Congress.[17] Some Saudi SWF officials felt embarrassed and insulted—they would need to get U.S. Homeland Security department to sign off on a U.S. visa for them to attend the closing dinner for bailing out a U.S. bank.[18]

And in 2007, SWFs did indeed write some big checks to buy stakes in capital-starved Western banks. For instance, in December 2007, Switzerland's UBS AG took a $10 billion write-down in the value of its risky "super senior debt" and collateralized debt obligations (CDOs). As it announced the write-down UBS also gave notice of its $11.5 billion investment from SWFs—including the Singapore Investment Corporation (GIC) and a Middle East investor believed to be the government of Oman. A few weeks before that, Citigroup had received a $7.5 billion capital infusion from another SWF, the Abu Dhabi Investment Authority.[19]

These two examples illustrated a common financial tango in which a Western financial institution that had borrowed heavily to purchase complex securities with relatively high investment yields was forced to write-down the value of those securities while simultaneously announcing a capital injection. In those months, the capital injections came from the part of the world whose economy appeared to be decoupled from the woes of Western financial institutions. That apparent decoupling made it appear that the collapse of the false prosperity of

Western financial institution borrowing was coming face to face with the true prosperity of Asia and the Middle East, which had been enriched by high oil prices and Chinese trade surpluses.

The United States had overborrowed and accounting rules required its banks to recognize that the assets it had borrowed to buy were now worth hundreds of billions less. But that borrowing had created a temporary sense of prosperity. Specifically, the United States's $9 trillion in government debt, $450 billion federal deficit, $2.4 trillion in consumer installment debt, and $1.3 trillion in subprime mortgages made it possible for the United States to grow by giving consumers—who accounted for 67% of its economic growth—the cash they needed to keep buying more goods.

But when it was time to repay that debt, those whose prosperity resulted from business operating profits ended up in the driver's seat. And that's why Asia—with its cheap labor costs—and the Middle East—with its enormous oil resources whose prices have been driven up by U.S. military policy and Chinese and Indian demand—were buying up big chunks of the global banking system for what then appeared to be a song.

However, it was clear from an April 2008 conference at Stanford University at which Peter spoke that the Fed believed the SWFs to be greater fools rather than significant threats. At the conference, an economist from the San Francisco Fed suggested, without officially saying it, that despite their big wallets, SWFs were not the brightest investors on the block.

That economist Reuven Glick made it clear unofficially that he did not view SWFs as having done sufficient due diligence—however, given the United States's need for capital and its belief in the free flow of capital around the world, he seemed to feel that there was no reason to protect the SWFs from taking their chances. Peter suggested that China, which in June 2007 bought a big stake in Blackstone Group, may not have even read the prospectus before buying a $3 billion stake. If China had read the prospectus, it could have saved itself the embarrassment of what was then a 46% drop in the value of its Blackstone stake.[20]

Moreover, the temporary sense that there was a decoupling between the U.S. economy and that of the rest of the world—specifically those that house the SWFs—proved to be quite fleeting. By the end of 2008, for example, the price of oil had fallen from $147 a barrel to about $33—due to the lack of credit for traders who borrowed to buy oil and sell the dollar coupled with a drop in economic activity, which crimped energy demand. The plunge in energy prices put many Middle Eastern countries into a position in which their dwindling SWFs would need to invest in their home economies rather than looking outside for investments. Moreover, many of the Asian countries that depended so heavily for their trade surpluses on robust Western demand for their products also experienced a painful slowdown, which required them to siphon money that had previously been funnelled into U.S. government securities into domestic stimulus plans.

The United States's stance toward SWFs has implications for capital providers and capital recipients.

Capital recipients should consider setting up standard disclosure require-ments for SWFs. Although congressional support never reached the threshold level needed to pass a bill, there was significant and reasonable discussion about transparency regarding SWF investments. Specifically, this discussion suggested that it would be wise for all SWFs to follow the extensive disclosure standards of Norway's SWF that published its investments—many others don't.

Capital recipients should set clear governance rules accompanying SWF invest-ments. When a U.S. investor purchases a stake of sufficient magnitude in a U.S. company, there are often expectations that the investor will receive a board seat. Capital recipient countries should set clear policies regarding whether SWF investors are entitled to similar governance rights. While the United States currently has established a governmental review process to vet such issues on a case-by-case basis, it may make sense to set up a more standard policy—particularly if such SWF investments happen more frequently.

SWFs should conduct intensive due diligence before investing. SWFs should have been far more inquisitive about the reasons the United States was so eager for them to invest in its financial institutions. After Peter read the prospectus for the initial public offering of Blackstone Group, there were many red flags that an investment would be fraught with risk—but this did not stop China from making its May 2007 $3 billion investment in Blackstone that had lost 80% of its value by January 2009. Basic due diligence about that investment would have revealed its perils.

India's Banking System Survives by Resisting America's Fast-Buck Culture

As we'll see in our discussion of Satyam's corporate governance implosion, India is not without its problems. However, it is also clear that by following sound banking practices, India avoided the catastrophic outcomes suffered by U.S. and European financial institutions resulting from policymakers' failure to enforce prudent capital and credit standards. At the core of the relatively strong position of India's banks was their decision to shun high leverage and extend credit only to people who were likely to repay. These policies sound like basic principles for a sound banking system—but India followed them and the U.S. and European banks did not.

Indian bankers—observing the collapse of the U.S. banking system that caused the demise of Bear Stearns, Lehman Brothers, and Merrill Lynch and led to $1 trillion in asset write-offs—were surprised by the United States's lack of regulation and supervision. As Rana Kapoor, CEO of Yes Bank, said, "What has taken a number of us by surprise is the lack of adequate supervision and regulation. This was despite the fact that Enron had happened and you passed Sarbanes-Oxley. We don't understand it. Maybe it's because we sit in a more controlled economy."[21]

Commenting on the problems with the U.S. banking system, Indian bankers asked some basic questions: "How could the United States have brought so much trouble on itself, and the rest of the world, by acting in such an obviously foolhardy manner? Didn't the United States understand that you can't lend money to people who lack the means to pay it back?"[22]

India's banking standards were different. For example, Chandra Kochhar, CEO of India's largest private bank, ICICI, said, "In India, we never had anything close to the subprime loan. All lending to individuals is based on their income. That is a big difference between your banking system and ours. Indian banks are not levered like American banks. Capital ratios are 12 and 13 percent, instead of 7 or 8 percent. All those exotic structures like C.D.O. and securitizations are a very tiny part of our banking system. So a lot of the temptations didn't exist."[23]

Nor does India make the kind of risky consumer mortgages that have blown up in the face of U.S. mortgage originators and their investors. As Deepak Parekh, the retired chief executive of HDFC, said, "We don't do interest-only or subprime loans. When the bubble was going on, we did not change any of our policies. We did not change any of our systems. We did not change our thought process. We never gave more money to a borrower because the value of the house had gone up. Citibank has a few home equity loans, but most banks in India don't make those kinds of loans. Our nonperforming loans are less than 1 percent."[24]

One reason for the lower loan losses is that Indians are simply not as comfortable with credit as Americans. Many Indians believe that if they spend more than they earn they will get into trouble; whereas in the 2000s, many Americans borrowed against the value of their houses to offset their stagnant incomes and used the extra cash to buy consumer goods such as flat screen TVs. By contrast in India, there are joint families in which savings are important because the families use their savings to help all its members—for example, if a son moves out, the family uses some of its savings to help him.   This makes many Indian families reluctant to take financial risk so they can fulfil these joint family obligations. Moreover, even when Indians do take on mortgages, they tend to have 33% downpayments rather than the relatively slim 20% ones typical in the United States.[25]

India did not get sucked into the real estate bubble. In 2006, Dr. Y.V. Reddy, governor of the Reserve Bank of India, began to sense that Indian real estate was a bubble waiting to burst. As a result, he banned the use of bank loans for the purchase of raw land, a practice that was growing rapidly. He changed policies so that banks could offer only construction loans at the point where a developer was about to start building. U.S. private equity and hedge funds were the only capital providers willing to make those land purchases that Reddy thought too risky.[26]

Nor did India get sucked into the securitization and derivatives waves. To protect India from their dangers, the Reserve Bank of India slashed their use in the country. When Reddy saw American banks setting up off-balance-sheet vehicles to hide debt, he banned them in India. As a result, banks in India wound up holding onto the loans they made to customers instead of selling them off to securitizers. The short-term downside was that Indian banks made fewer loans than American ones. On the other hand, it meant that Indian banks had an incentive that American banks lacked to assure that borrowers paid back the loans.[27]

India also decided to put the brakes on the money supply to nip inflation risk in the bud. Reddy took several steps to achieve that: he boosted interest rates to over 20% to stop the Indian housing bubble. He forced banks to double reserves for loans made against commercial buildings and shopping mall construction. And he increased the amount of capital that banks had to set aside for each loan they made. Simply put, Reddy shored up Indian bank balance sheets before the global liquidity crisis hit.[28]

In general, India's conservative bank regulators and executives believed that they might have been missing opportunities that the rest of the financial world seemed to be grabbing to their benefit. As Kochhar said, "For a while we were wondering if we were missing out on something. Banks in the United States seemed to have come up with some magical new formula for making money: make loans that required no down payment and little in the way of verification—and post instant, short-term, profits." Or as Luis Miranda, a private equity runner who invests in India's infrastructure, noted, "We kept wondering if they had figured out something that we were too dense to figure out. It looked like they were smart and we were stupid." However, it turned out that India was smart and we the West was stupid.[29]

Among the most obvious risks India avoided was that of securitization. It appears to be a global principle of sound finance that in order to get a loan repaid, there should be a clear incentive for repayment on the part of the individuals who borrow and lend the money. Securitization severs the link between those individuals and thus creates an incentive for closing the maximum number of loans rather than making loans that get repaid. Kochhar pointed out that the underlying risks of having "a majority of loans not owned by the people who originated them was not apparent during the bubble. Now that those risks have been made painfully clear, every banker in India realizes that Reddy did the right thing by limiting securitizations." While some Indian bankers found Reddy's limitations frustrating at the time, they now realize that he saved the Indian banking system from the catastrophic fate that Western banks suffered at the hands of securitization.[30]

India's policies toward bank regulation reveal important insights for policymakers:

- *Don't securitize loans.* India's banking regulators demonstrated tremendous foresight in limiting exposure to securitization. India recognized that the practice of severing the ties between borrowers and lenders would lead to shoddy lending practices—turning bankers into loan pushers instead of credit extenders and collectors. Banning securitization protected India's financial system from substantial losses.
- *Limit banks from lending against the riskiest assets.* Indian bank regulators wisely banned lending against raw land which absent any cash-generating properties is an extremely risky collateral. India's willingness to limit lending to assets that had a reasonable prospect of generating cash flow turned out to limit banks' repayment risks.

- *Assure that banks maintain conservative capital levels against different classes of loans depending on their risk.* Similarly, India's banking regulators were prudent to require higher down-payments on mortgages and to demand that bankers set aside more capital based on the level of risk in each loan category. Such requirements limited not only asset growth—and the associated profit opportunities—but also the amount that India's banks could lose when the capital tide went out.

India's Satyam Collapses after Governance Failure Exposed

While India's banking regulators and executives were patting themselves on the back for not allowing their banking system to collapse as the United States's did, India faced the painful reality that its corporate governance practices were shoddy. India's publicly traded companies had a long tradition of neglecting the interests of minority shareholders and that neglect came with a price.

And that price was never more dramatically revealed to India than in the case of Satyam Computer Services that was quickly dubbed "India's Enron." Though there were many differences between the two companies, they shared two common attributes. First, up until nearly the day they collapsed both firms were seen as innovative paragons of virtuous corporate governance. Second, without deeply rooted fraud—which was enabled by their willingness to cook their books— neither firm would have reached the tremendous heights from which they both plummeted.

The Satyam problems started relatively quietly but metastasized with stunning speed. There were glimmers of trouble in December 2008 when Satyam's chairman, Ramalinga Raju, unilaterally decided to spend $1.6 billion to buy his son's construction companies—Maytas Properties Ltd. and Maytas Infra Ltd.—but when the stock collapsed after the announcement, he pulled back within 12 hours.[31]

While that was bad enough, the biggest shocker came in the second week of January 2009 when Raju resigned after announcing that he had faked Satyam's numbers for several years. It turns out that the reason he wanted to buy those construction companies was to plug the $1.04 billion gap between the falsely accounted for and real cash and bank loans on Satyam's books.[32]

One irony of the Satyam situation is that the word Satyam means "truth" in Sanskrit. And when the truth came out, Satyam got into a rapidly cascading wave of troubles. First, the World Bank banned Satyam from bidding for orders for eight years, alleging that improper benefits were given to World Bank employees, then shareholders blocked Raju's asset purchases, next four directors quit, and finally, Raju quit the company and announced his fraud.

Another irony is that in September 2008, just months before the scandal broke, the London-based World Council for Corporate Governance gave the Golden Peacock Global Award for Excellence in Corporate Governance to none other than Raju.[33]

Raju's announcement put Satyam in peril. Its clients and 53,000 employees were up for grabs and its stock—which did not open for trading on the New

York Stock Exchange—was down 92% from its previous trade in premarket. In a world of shrinking budgets, Satyam's vulnerability presented a tempting target for competitors who would have every reason to attempt to poach its blue chip clients, which included GE and Cisco Systems.[34]

In the wake of the Satyam scandal, Indian regulators acted swiftly. They sacked Satyam's top executives and replaced its board. Two new directors who were appointed called for an independent audit of its financial statements— clearly its auditor PriceWaterhouseCoopers had failed to compare Satyam's financial statements to its bank account balances. The objective was to find out Satyam's true financial picture so banks could decide whether to lend and if so how much money was needed to keep Satyam operating.[35]

One of the reasons for the problems at Saytam may have been the weak influence of its minority shareholders. However, Satyam's institutional shareholders controlled a majority—over 50%—of its stock and this high proportion may have given them the feeling of power needed to protest Satyam's $1.6 billion construction company purchase that set its final collapse in motion. As Adrian Lim, an investment manager at Aberdeen Asset Management—which was among Satyam's largest foreign shareholders—said, Aberdeen "won't tolerate a change in principal activity without consultation. Minority shareholders should be consulted and given a say." Unfortunately, that say came too late to save investors from an enormous plunge in Satyam's stock value.[36]

While it is too early to tell at this writing how widespread the changes will be to India's corporate governance policies, the Satyam collapse does suggest several important possible policy prescriptions:

- *Require directors to conduct an independent review of strategic decisions.* If Satyam's independent directors had actually conducted an independent review of the decision to acquire the construction companies, they may have objected to the decision. If independent directors can agree on a set of standards to use in evaluating different strategic decisions—such as acquisitions or divestitures— then they can hold management to a higher standard of decision making.
- *Require objective financial reporting of the firm's performance and prospects.* In Satyam's case, it is clear that PriceWaterhouseCoopers had failed to perform very basic independent audit activities. If this is a widespread problem in India, then the Indian government may need to conduct audits itself—or perhaps even create an independent group that produces financial statements for public companies.
- *Assure that independent directors have an opportunity to represent the interests of minority shareholders.* India's policymakers may wish to provide a mechanism for minority shareholders to appoint their own directors who will represent their interests in an independent fashion. Such directors should be selected for their polite aggressiveness, industry knowledge, and financial acumen. Policymakers should assure that such directors can obtain the information they need to make intelligent decisions.
- *Design financial incentives to align the interests of founders, executive management, and minority shareholders.* Policymakers should provide

compensation mechanisms for directors and executives that align the interests of all groups of shareholders. Self-dealing by founders and top executives at the expense of all other shareholders should exact a painful economic price that will eliminate any motivation for such behavior.

BP Is Buffeted by Changing Political Winds in Russia and Loses Its Control Over Energy Joint Venture

BP thought it would be able to handle the political challenges of forming an energy joint venture in Russia. However, when it formed TNK-BP in 2003, it was in a temporarily strong position that eroded a few years thereafter. The result was Russia used its courts to make life miserable for the joint venture's executives. And they ultimately left Russia behind as an implied condition of retaining BP's equity in the venture.

Simply put, cases such as TNK-BP run the risk of keeping foreign capital providers from stepping foot in Russia. They reveal that Russia is happy to extend the welcome mat to capital providers who are willing to invest there. However, once Russia has what it needs from those providers, this case demonstrates Russia's willingness to use its political control to give capital providers a stark choice—leave behind the investment or stick around to protect it and ultimately give up in frustration.

Before examining the TNK-BP case, it is worth spending some time on a few related anecdotes that shed light on how Russian business is perceived. For example, in August 2008, News Corp. CEO Rupert Murdoch, who has been doing business in China for years, made it clear he was nervous about his Russian enterprises. As Murdoch said, "We have great growing business there but just—this is purely me, I'm sorry, I'm—the more I read about investments in Russia, the less I like the feel of it. The more successful we'd be, the more vulnerable we'd be to have it stolen from us, so there we sell now."[37] And it didn't take much to wipe out the stock market value of a Russian company. For example, in August 2008, Mechel, a coal mining and steel company, lost billions in shareholder value following Vladimir Putin's criticism of its CEO.[38]

Then there's TNK-BP, whose Western CEO was denied a Russian visa and whose CFO had just left the country in August 2008.[39] A group of Russian shareholders wanted the BP side out. What is TNK-BP? How did it get started? Why did it go wrong for BP? What are the implications for policymakers?

TNK-BP was the third largest producer of oil and gas and the first 50–50 joint venture with a Western integrated oil company in Russia—the parties were BP and Russian firm Tyumen Oil Co. (TNK) that was owned by three oligarchs—Alfa, Access, and Renova (AAR). But TNK-BP was not BP's first foray into Russia. In the late 1990s, BP nearly lost its $500 million investment when certain oligarchs—a group of politically well-connected Russians who accumulated vast wealth from privatizing Russian energy assets that occurred under the rule of Boris Yeltsin—took advantage of Russia's weak courts to seize the assets of a BP-owned company.[40]

However, after Vladimir Putin came to power in 2000 and began reasserting Kremlin authority, the same oligarchs came to BP looking for a deal they hoped would protect them from rising government pressure—the sort that later led to the partial nationalization of oil giant OAO Yukos. In 2003, BP swallowed its reservations about the oligarchs and it paid $7.6 billion for its 50% share in the new entity, TNK-BP, and installed a former BP executive, Robert Dudley, as CEO.[41]

Putin personally approved the deal, presiding over its signing in February 2003. Still, by 2006 the 50–50 structure looked increasingly out of place as Putin began retaking control of Russia's oil sector. Foreign companies were being forced into minority stakes. Facing a wave of regulatory pressure, for example, in late 2006 Royal Dutch Shell PLC gave up control of a $22 billion gas project to Russia's Gazprom.[42]

It was around that time that TNK-BP got into trouble as Putin quietly backed Gazprom's attempts to wrest control of some of TNK-BP's most valuable assets notably including an enormous gas producing asset—the 1.98 Trillion Cubic Meters (TCM) Kovykta gas field in the east of Russia. BP realized after watching Royal Dutch Shell's problems that it would need to find itself a Kremlin-backed partner.[43]

TNK-BP thought that its best bet was to try to form a partnership with Gazprom—which looked promising when in 2007 it signaled its interest in forming a partnership. Things did not work out as planned—and now BP's position in Russia is more fragile. The Gazprom deal did not happen. And BP was forced to give up management control over TNK-BP and its BP-backed CEO left Russia.[44]

BP thought it was operating according to the Russian government's stated policies. Its understanding was that Russia welcomed foreign investors but only as minority owners with control in the hands of big state companies. Based on that assumption, BP thought that TNK-BP—which was a partnership with a group of oligarchs—would not last. And to survive, BP thought it needed to replace those oligarchs with a state company like Gazprom. As it turns out, BP's assumptions about Russia's implicit rules for foreign investors were wrong. Instead, Gazprom suddenly could not close its deal. And the Kremlin did nothing to stop the oligarchs who took over TNK-BP.[45]

Ultimately, it never became clear why the deal to replace AAR with Gazprom never happened. Gazprom may have lost some influence when Medvedev became president in May 2008 and gave up his post as Gazprom chairman. It's also not clear whether Putin ever really backed the deal. Although BP has lost its management role in the venture, it has been allowed to retain its 50% stake in TNK-BP. Furthermore, BP still has a larger share in the Russian oil industry than its competitors. And if ceding management control to its Russian partners helps it survive a tight period of contracting prices, the outcome may not be so bad for BP.[46]

The TNK-BP case has implications for policymakers in capital recipient and capital provider countries.

To attract significant and patient foreign capital, capital recipient countries must issue and enforce clear policies. Russia's unwillingness to issue and enforce clear policies regarding the treatment of foreign capital providers makes it unlikely that all but the most risk-seeking investors will invest there. While there will always be some traders willing to risk the loss of their investments and even their lives, the fate of such firms as TNK-BP will repel many potential capital providers.

Policymakers in capital provider countries ought to require explicit disclosure of investments in countries that treat foreign capital providers roughly. Since investing in countries like Russia involves significant risk of loss—above and beyond normal investment risks—policymakers in capital providing countries should require that pension funds and mutual funds that invest in such countries have strict disclosure requirements of their investments. Moreover, policymakers should limit the proportion of a fiduciary's total portfolio that can be invested in such a country.

Wal-Mart/Bharti Partnership Transfers Know-How

The partnership between Wal-Mart and Bharti is structured to combine the strengths of both companies to build a venture that can capture significant market share while complying with India's regulations that limit foreign retailers from operating storefronts in India. The venture has run into significant political opposition in India because many small retailers feel threatened by its potential market power. By transferring significant logistical skills, by purchasing products from India's farmers and small manufacturers, and by employing thousands of people in the venture Wal-Mart and Bharti hope to overcome local opposition to their efforts.

Bharti Wal-Mart Private Limited is a joint venture between Bharti Enterprises and Wal-Mart to develop operations in India that will sell to small retailers, manufacturers, and farmers. Bharti Wal-Mart anticipated launching its first store in Northern India in 2009. Each Bharti Wal-Mart store was expected to be between 50,000 and 100,000 square feet and to sell fruits and vegetables, groceries, footwear, clothing, and other general merchandise. Bharti Wal-Mart expected to open 10–15 stores and to employ 5,000 people by 2015.[47]

The Bharti Wal-Mart cash-and-carry stores would serve only business owners, not common consumers. They would offer fixed prices, convenience, choice, quality, and hygiene. Their 50,000–65,000 business customers would include traders, restaurant owners, hoteliers, caterers, fruit and vegetable resellers, and small convenience stores, known as *kiranas*. The stores would sell between 6,000 and 10,000 products 90% of which would be sourced locally to keep costs low and to stimulate the local economy—including employing 170 local people in each store.[48]

Wal-Mart might have tried to enter India without a partner were it not for India's legal system that prohibits multibrand foreign retailers, such as Wal-Mart, to sell directly to consumers, but they can run wholesale operations and provide back-end support to Indian retailers. Indian companies are also allowed to operate stores selling foreign brands under franchise from their producers.

Wal-Mart and Bharti Enterprises worked around those rules, forming a venture that would benefit both companies. It would give Wal-Mart indirect access to India's massive retail market—estimated at $250 billion and growing at a 20% annual rate—while transferring some of Wal-Mart's logistics expertise to Bharti. Under the first agreement, the Bharti and Wal-Mart established a 50–50 venture "for wholesale cash-and-carry and back-end supply chain management operation in India." Wal-Mart clearly saw its logistics expertise as helping to make India's supply chain more efficient that would benefit an important constituent of the venture—India's farmers.[49]

To that point, Wal-Mart's then–Vice Chairman and current CEO Mike Duke said that the joint venture "will help drive efficiencies across the supply chain and work toward the betterment of India's farmers, manufacturers and retailers." Although by 2007 Wal-Mart imported $600 million worth of goods from India, this was a fraction of the $9 billion it bought from China where its joint venture had been operating for a decade.[50]

In order for Bharti to benefit, it signed an IP-sharing agreement with Wal-Mart. This came in the form of a separate franchise agreement signed in August 2007 that would allow Wal-Mart to share its technology and expertise for a chain of retail stores that Bharti would build through its Bharti Retail Ltd. subsidiary.[51]

Despite complying with the letter of Indian law, the deal faced political opposition and scrutiny from the government. Wal-Mart faced competition for its entry into the Indian market from Carrefour of France, Tesco of Britain, and Metro of Germany—all of which had lobbied the Indian government to liberalize retail trade. Opposition from India's left prevented the government from allowing foreign retailers to open their own stores in India. When the venture was first announced in 2006 it ran into opposition from a key ally of India's ruling coalition government, the Communist Party of India (Marxist), on fears it would harm the livelihoods of millions of small shop owners.[52]

One way that the venture sought to overcome political opposition was to offer training to potential employees in Northern India where it intended to open its first store. To that end, in November 2008 it agreed with the government of Punjab to establish a training center in Amritsar to train workers to become floor and sales assistants or supervisors. The training center was intended to solve a basic problem in India—youth unemployment. The training center would accomplish this end by complementing the theoretical curriculum in most schools with vocational training to make India's youth employable. The Bharti Wal-Mart Training Center was expected to train 125 candidates each month. It planned to offer two-week half-day training programs for floor assistants and sales assistant and an additional week-long program for supervisors.[53]

Meanwhile the companies wait for India to permit the venture to operate its first store. The Bharti Wal-Mart case has important implications for policymakers and business leaders. They include the following:

Policymakers must balance the interests of a complex and ever-changing constellation of constituents for such ventures. The venture's stakeholders include small retailers and competing foreign retailers who oppose the venture as well as competing political parties who are inherently opposed to foreign investment in India. Policymakers must balance the interests of opponents against those of the proponents that include the Indian and Western companies, local workers and suppliers, and political parties who stand to benefit.

The joint venture partners must understand these competing constituents and create enough benefits for proponents to overwhelm the opposition. Bharti and Wal-Mart are trying to create so much benefit for those who want their venture to go ahead that their opponents will lose their case to stop it. Achieving this goal requires both companies to identify the key decision makers among the various groups who influence the decision and to give them sufficient benefits to earn their support.

Differences in country-specific economic performance resulting from these countries' choices

Of the countries we addressed in the six mini cases it is clear that there is some correlation between their openness to global capital flows and their rates of economic growth and GDP per capita (as measured by 2007 GDP growth and GDP/capita)—the United States (2% and $45,800), India (9% and $2,600), Iceland (3.8% and $40,400), China (11.9% and $5,400) and Russia (8.1% and $14,800).[54] However, there are many other factors that drive their growth as well.

We hypothesize that the differences in economic performance between these countries is due in part to factors that are not directly related to policymaker choices regarding the shape of the country's EE. Such factors include the following:

- *Energy prices.* In Russia and other countries dependent on oil and gas for their economic growth, a rise in energy prices can boost growth and a drop can cripple the economy. As happened between July 2008 and early 2009, the 70% drop in oil prices caused severe economic problems.
- *Demand for cheap imports.* In countries like China, its ample supply of cheap labor—as evidenced by its extremely low GDP per capita—makes it a very attractive place to manufacture items in demand by Western countries. However, if—as happened in 2008—that demand collapses due to an economic contraction, the ultimate impact can be a growth slowdown in the country with the cheap labor rates.
- *Excessive financial institution borrowing.* In the United States, much of Europe, and Iceland, banks borrowed way too much money to buy risky assets and make loans for deals that had very high risk. While such borrowing created the illusion of prosperity, the drop in asset values that accompanied the freeze up in additional debt extension led to a frenzy of writing off bad loans and writing down overvalued assets. The resulting economic collapse led to numerous bankruptcies and shrinking economies.

However, we believe that there are important policymaker choices related to the contour of their EEs that have influenced differences in the economic performance of these countries. Two of the most fundamental of these choices include the following:

- *Attracting long-term capital boosts economic growth.* India's willingness to allow a partnership between Bharti and Wal-Mart can encourage foreign capital to make long-term investment that leads to economic growth, significant hiring, and the transfer of important know-how in the form of formal and on-the-job-training for workers, managers, and even executives. Such capital flows contribute to long-term economic growth.
- *Attracting short-term capital that can exit quickly leads to unsustainable bubbles.* The cases we examined of Iceland and Russia both illustrate the dangers of encouraging the easy inflow of capital only to make it very difficult to exit in an orderly way. In Iceland's case, many investors fled after the first whiff of trouble as they tried to shore up their declining capital base in a global financial crisis. In the TNK-BP case, Russia happily took the investment from BP but later made it quite painful for BP to capitalize on it—ultimately forcing out its executives and creating a toxic environment for other potential investors. Such capital flows boost short-term economic growth but threaten longer-term prosperity.

On balance, policymakers should consider shaping their country's EE because these factors are far more controllable than the price of commodities—such as oil and gas—and the level of economic growth in a country such as the United States to which a producer of low cost goods, such as China, exports. In a nutshell, policies that make a country's EE more receptive to global capital flows, can—if they properly shape the EE—encourage long-term investment and economic growth.

Can policymakers help foster entrepreneurship? Here we have to acknowledge skeptics who argue that it is not realistic to expect policymakers to promote entrepreneurship in a big way. For example, Harvard Business School professor, Josh Lerner, suggested in a 2009 book, *Boulevard of Broken Dreams: Why Public Efforts to Boost Entrepreneurship and Venture Capital Have Failed—and What to Do About It*—that many government efforts to spur entrepreneurship fail. He concludes that these failures spring from poor design, a lack of understanding for the entrepreneurial process, and implementation problems.[55]

We agree as well as disagree with Lerner's analysis. Our case studies illustrate that some governments are more successful than others at attracting capital flows and spurring entrepreneurship. So, Lerner's assessment that governments are not always successful is valid. Where we disagree with his diagnosis is when we identify the factors that separate the successful from the unsuccessful government interventions. Where Lerner offers vague diagnosis and prescriptions—such as, "Remember that entrepreneurial activity does not exist in a vacuum"—our EE framework provides policymakers with a unified way to think about how they can attract capital and spur entrepreneurial activity in their countries. We conclude that countries that harness these EE factors effectively can achieve positive outcomes while policymakers who ignore them suffer the consequences.[56]

Globalization Receptivity Index

How should policymakers decide whether their country is ready for globalization? To address this question, we present a globalization receptivity index (GRI) to help policymakers rate their country's entrepreneurial ecosystems based on their receptivity to global capital flows. The purpose is to help these policymakers make a choice regarding how to shape their country's EE that will fit best with the country's unique attributes.

The GRI is based on the premise that in order to decide how much globalization a country should embrace, policymakers need to know where they are now and how much they must change their EEs in order to attract global capital flows. To that end, as illustrated in figure 6.1 (which we initially saw in chapter 3) policymakers should assess their country's EEs in

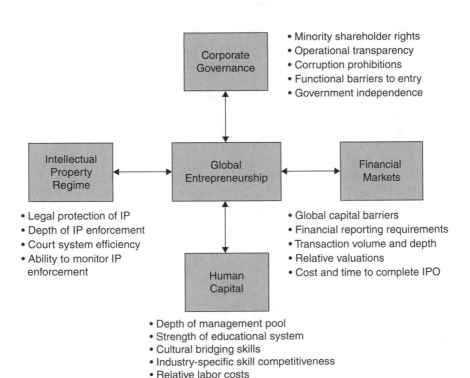

Figure 6.1   Drivers of Globalization Receptivity

four broad areas:

- Corporate governance;
- Financial markets;
- Human capital; and
- Intellectual Property (IP) Regime.

The remainder of this section explores the key questions that policymakers must answer to assess their receptiveness to global capital flows within the four areas. The more often you answer yes to a question, the more receptive your country is to global capital flows. Here are the questions.

Corporate Governance

- *Minority shareholders rights.* How much does your country respect minority shareholder rights? Are examples such as Satyam's shabby treatment of its minority shareholders extremely rare or the norm?
- *Operational transparency.* Does your country require a high level of detailed and objective reporting about a company's financial position to minority shareholders? Does your country require disclosure to minority shareholders of the threats and opportunities facing the business? Does your country require companies to get input from minority shareholders regarding the rationale for key strategic decisions before the decisions are implemented?
- *Corruption prohibitions.* Does your country have strict legal prohibitions against corruption such as bribing government officials to close business deals or ignore legal violations? If so, are these prohibitions tightly enforced?
- *Functional barriers to entry.* Does your country have specific prohibitions against foreign investors performing common business activities—such as India's regulation prohibiting foreign companies from operating retail stores? If so, could such prohibitions be lifted easily?
- *Government independence.* Do business executives operate independently of government officials in your country? Can foreign capital providers make investments only after consulting with executives? Or must foreign capital providers also consider the likely actions of government officials?

Financial Markets

- *Global capital barriers.* Does your country permit the free flow of foreign capital to invest in public and private equity? If there are restrictions on the flow of foreign capital, would it be relatively easy to lift those restrictions?
- *Financial reporting requirements.* Are the financial reporting requirements for companies seeking to sell stock and bonds in your country comprehensive, detailed, frequent, and objective?

- *Transaction volume and depth.* Is there a high volume of securities trading within a broad range of securities such as stocks, bonds, currencies, and initial public offerings? Are there many well-capitalized securities dealers in your country? Are there many institutional investors willing and able to buy and sell such securities on a regular basis?
- *Relative valuations.* Are your country's IPO valuations—as measured by price/earnings ratios and other valuation metrics—high relative to those in other countries' securities markets?
- *Cost and time to complete Initial Public Offering (IPO).* In your country, is the cost—in terms of fees paid to underwriters, regulators, legal and accounting advisors, and others—as well as the time required to complete IPOs competitive with those in other countries?

Human Capital

- *Depth of management pool.* Does your country have a deep pool of skilled managers relative to competing countries that seek to attract private equity and venture capital?
- *Strength of educational system.* Does your country's educational system produce a strong supply of workers needed to perform specific activities—such as general management, computer systems design and development, manufacturing process design, and call center staffing—relative to competing countries that seek to attract private equity, venture capital, or other forms of investment?
- *Cultural bridging skills.* Do your country's workers share a deep cultural link with the country that is seeking to invest there relative to competing countries? For example, many U.S. companies have found that Philippine call centers can serve U.S. customers effectively because Filipinos have a deep cultural knowledge of America and their English-speaking skills are strong;
- *Industry-specific skill competitiveness.* Do your country's workers have deep skills in industry-specific business skills—such as automobile parts manufacturing, accounts receivable collection, or technical service relative to competing countries?
- *Relative labor costs.* Do your country's workers receive relatively low pay compared to those in competing countries for performing the same task? Is the cost of hiring your country's workers and making their product useful to customers—for example, by shipping the products they make to the consuming country—competitive with those of other countries?

Intellectual Property Regime

- *Legal protection of IP.* Does your country have specific regulations that protect IP? If so, are those regulations more stringent than those in countries with which your country competes for venture capital?

- *Depth of IP enforcement.* Does your country enforce its IP regulations? If so, are the resources your country dedicates to IP enforcement more numerous and effective than those in countries with which your country competes for venture capital?
- *Court system efficiency.* Does your country's court system prosecute IP violations more efficiently than countries with which your country competes for venture capital?
- *Ability to monitor IP enforcement.* Is your country more transparent in reporting on IP enforcement than countries with which your country competes for venture capital?

If a policymaker answers yes to most of these questions, it is likely that the country already attracts significant global capital flows. By contrast, if a policymaker answers no to these questions, then it is likely that his or her country attracts limited global capital and is not receptive to the change required to attract it. Thus this framework is likely to be most useful to those policymakers who answer the questions roughly half yes and half no. These are countries that are stuck in the middle with regard to their EE and they must decide whether they are willing to make the changes needed to increase the flow of global capital to their country.

Policymaker Framework for Shaping the Entrepreneurial Ecosystem

The GRI should help policymakers identify where the biggest gaps exist between their country's current receptiveness and where it needs to be in order to attract global capital flows. Having uncovered these gaps, policymakers can develop a clear set of potential changes that they would need to make in order to close the gap. Based on these changes, they could then set about the task of trying to assess whether the benefits of these change initiatives would outweigh their costs. And if the benefits outweigh the costs, then the policymaker should make the changes to upgrade the country's EE. Here's a way to approach this process:

- *Form an EE team.* The policymaker should assemble a team of people within the country who can represent the key stakeholders likely to be affected by any change in the EE. This team might include key business regulators, leading financial markets officials, leaders in education, and experts on intellectual property regulations. Outside the government, the EE team should include leaders of public companies, key financial institutions, executives of major financial exchanges, and representatives of potential foreign capital providers.
- *Identify key EE improvement opportunities.* The EE team should conduct an assessment of the country's EE along the lines outlined in the previous section. This analysis will highlight the biggest gaps between their current EE

and the one that they need to attract big flows of global capital. For example, if a country offers little IP protection and it wants to attract foreign venture capital, upgrading the country's IP protection may be among the high priority EE improvement opportunities.

- *Rank the EE improvement opportunities.* The EE team should brainstorm and generate a list of EE improvement opportunities. The team should then decide on criteria for ranking these priorities—for example, how much the opportunity will increase the chances of attracting global capital flows or the political costs of changing the EE to effect the change. The team should then rank the EE improvement opportunities.
- *Analyze the costs and benefits of implementing the high priority EE improvement opportunities.* Next the team should pick three–five top-ranked improvement opportunities and analyze their costs and benefits in great detail to provide policymakers with information to decide which to implement and which to defer. Factors to consider might be the initiative's impact on tax revenues, employment by domestic firms, potential to create new companies—leading to new sources of tax revenue, political opposition and/or support for the change, and the budget requirements for implementing the change.
- *Implement those EE improvement opportunities with the highest net benefits.* Finally the EE team should pick the EE improvement opportunities that are likely to have the greatest net benefit and develop a plan to implement the change. One thing that might help the team in forming an implementation plan would be to study other countries that had made similar changes and figure out which approaches worked; which ran into problems; and what key lessons they might learn from other countries' experience.

Ultimately policymakers whose countries are stuck in the middle must make a strategic decision about whether they perceive that the benefits of encouraging global capital flows will exceed the costs. It will not be possible for policymakers to anticipate all the potential benefits and costs ahead of time—although they should try to estimate them. Policymakers would do well to study and learn from the experience of other countries. But in the end, it will take a certain amount of courage for policymakers to make the changes needed to spur the flow of capital into their countries.

Conclusion

Policymakers have the potential to shape their country's EE to encourage the flow of foreign capital into their countries. The case studies reviewed here suggest that foreign capital will flow into countries and stay there if the long-term returns of that investment are likely to be high. If a country encourages quick entry of capital without a solid basis for a long-term return on capital, then investors will exit quickly at the first sign of trouble. And after that, it will be difficult to persuade other foreign capital providers to invest in the future. However, each country has a different level of receptiveness to foreign capital flows and we have provided a framework for helping policymakers decide whether the benefits of the changes needed to attract that capital exceed the costs of making those changes.

7

Implications for Capital Providers

Capital providers face a dazzling array of choices about where to invest their capital. Choices of the country and industry in which to place their capital and people are among the most crucial in determining whether capital providers can satisfy their limited partners. If they pick rapidly growing industries and partner with companies with the right strategy and management team, capital providers can earn returns that will be the envy of their peers. If they make the wrong choice on these dimensions, they can lose their entire investment.

In order to make winning choices, capital providers must answer the following questions:

- How should they choose the countries/industries/companies in which they invest?
- How should they build networks that will give them the best deals?
- How can they work with the companies in which they invest to enhance their value?
- How should they exit?

These questions pervade the world of venture capital, private equity, and bank lending. And in this chapter we'll explore 10 cases that scrutinize these questions through a variety of lenses.

In so doing, we'll explore the following answers to these questions:

Capital providers should invest in countries, industries, and companies where they can add value with capital and capabilities. We'll explore cases that suggest that no country had an ideal EE for a capital provider. Capital providers can succeed by using their unique insights and skills to overcome the flaws in a country's EE while investing in industries and companies that embody that country's strengths. In most cases, capital providers can succeed by supplying capabilities—such as access to customers, suppliers, and/or expertise—in addition to capital.

Capital providers can source the best deals by finding deal networks that fit with their selection criteria. Capital providers need to have a clear idea of how companies that might receive their capital perceive the value they can provide. This outside-in perspective is essential for capital providers as they decide on the criteria they'll use to pick deals in which to invest and others that they'll eschew. Once they know their deal selection criteria, they need to build deal flow networks that understand these criteria and will provide investment opportunities that satisfy them.

Capital providers can add value to their portfolio companies in a structured manner, while respecting the strengths of their existing management. Successful capital providers seek companies with good management that is willing to adapt to the corporate governance standards of the countries in which they hope to sell shares. Successful capital providers are good at setting goals, in partnership with management, that link new investment with achieving milestones that will add value to the company. Such capital providers also institute stricter corporate governance standards—including rigorous audit committees and separation of the Chairman and CEO roles. The result is that they can add value to the company and the company's original management can learn new skills.

Capital providers seek to exit through the door with the highest after-tax value. In considering exit strategies, capital providers generally may deem a variety of options—including IPOs, corporate acquisition, sale to a group of private investors, or even sales to the original investors or managers. Capital providers evaluate such options based on the after-tax proceeds they are likely to harvest over the medium term. In making comparative estimates, they consider tax rates, valuations, regulations regarding the timing of equity sales, and the volatility and depth of the market.

Capital Provider Case Studies

To explore these themes, this chapter presents case studies by country, for example, China, India, Vietnam, and France, and capital source—specifically bank capital, private equity, and venture capital—as follows:

- *Warren Buffett Buys 10% of a Chinese Electric Car Maker,* which illustrates the benefits and risks of betting on a successful Chinese entrepreneur focusing a new technology on a big market;
- *Western Banks Losing on Chinese Real Estate,* which shows the risk of pushing surplus capital on a business that can't use it profitably;
- *Sequoia Ventures to China,* which demonstrates the wisdom of investing in a country's real consumer needs and betting on an entrepreneur with a great track record;
- *Global Venture Network Invests in China,* which highlights the great investment returns that flow from screening investments and placing capital in fast-growing Chinese companies that comply with strict governance standards;

- *Kleiner Perkins Considers Its Exit Door,* which tracks a capital providers' weighing of the tradeoffs between short-term high IPO valuations and longer-term risks of a shallow market and weak governance;
- *Indian Private Equity Refocuses in Economic Downturn,* which offers a picture of how PE executives consider whether to leave when times get tough or to invest at the lower prices available when most players flee;
- *Warburg Pincus Profits in India,* which provides a look at the high profits that can come from investing when things look too risky to most players and selling when peers pile in to replicate your high returns;
- *Kleiner Perkins Hits It Big in India,* which offers a look at a successful investment strategy that flows from betting on a leader who can span the boundaries between the cultures of the capital sources and its recipients;
- *IDG Ventures Expands to Vietnam and China,* which shows the profits that can flow from adapting to an EE that does not respect IP by investing in service businesses that meet growing consumer needs while pressing to change that EE; and
- *French Private Equity Is Better Than Its Start-Up Culture,* which illustrates the benefits of digging beneath the surface to find opportunities in a superficially unattractive market.

Warren Buffett Buys 10% of a Chinese Electric Car Maker

Investment legend Warren Buffett decided to invest $230 million for 10% of BYD, a Chinese battery, mobile phone, and electric car maker. Did this investment signal that the 78-year-old Buffett has finally lost his mind? After all, the electric car business does not have a profitable track record and Buffett's decision to shun investment in technology stocks suggests that he has little appetite for technology companies. Nevertheless, Buffett concluded that BYD has the potential to become the world's largest electric car maker and a huge player in the solar energy business. And a big part of this conclusion is based on BYD's CEO—Wang Chuan-Fu—whom Buffett's partner, Charlie Munger, touts as a cross between Thomas Edison (for his inventiveness and persistence) and Jack Welch (for his ability to get people to achieve great results).[1]

While Buffett has a tremendous long-term investing track record, he has also made mistakes—which resulted in a 44% loss in Berkshire Hathaway's stock price during 2008. So it is not a given that his investment in BYD will generate a positive investment return for Buffett. Nevertheless, his rationale for making the investment reveals some insights into what he perceives as the sources of value that spring from the Chinese EE in which BYD operates. Of the four EE elements, Buffett is betting most heavily on China's human capital—Wang Chuan-Fu's entrepreneurial ability and his skill at using low-paid but highly skilled Chinese workers to engineer a lower cost way of building BYD products. What remains to be seen is whether the other elements of China's EE—its corporate governance, financial markets, and IP regime— will enhance or hinder the value of Buffett's investment.

How did BYD come into being? It started with former Chinese premier Deng Xiaoping who designated Shenzhen as China's first "special economic zone" in

1980, inviting capitalism to take root, it was a fishing village; today, it has a population estimated between 12 million and 14 million. Wang Chuan-Fu left his home in a poor rural village and came to Shenzen—which has since grown to 40 million people—raised $300,000 from family and friends to start BYD in 1995. By 2000, BYD had become one of the world's largest makers of mobile phone batteries—selling to Motorola, Nokia, Sony Ericsson, and Samsung.[2]

In 2003, BYD bought its way into the Chinese car business—turning its F3 sedan into China's best selling sedan—ahead of Volkswagen's Jetta and Toyota's Corolla. BYD has also begun selling a plug-in electric car with a backup gasoline engine—its F3DM (for "dual mode") goes farther on a single charge—62 miles—than other electric vehicles and sells for about $22,000, less than its competitors such as Toyota's plug-in Prius. By April 2009, BYD had 130,000 people in 11 factories, 8 in China and 1 each in India, Hungary, and Romania.[3]

But all this is in the past, so what business opportunity could appeal to Warren Buffett's desire to boost the value of his holdings? The answer is a large potential market for batteries that run electric cars. David Sokol, an energy executive who runs Buffett's Mid-American Energy, argued that energy companies will need to produce more energy while emitting less carbon dioxide.

Electric cars—which generate fewer greenhouse gas emissions than cars that burn gasoline and have lower fuel costs—could meet this need. The reason is that electric engines are more efficient than internal-combustion engines, and because generating energy on a large scale (in coal or nuclear plants) is less wasteful than doing it on a small scale (by burning gasoline in an internal-combustion engine).[4]

Electric cars could save a significant amount of energy and money. Here are some estimates—for a car owner who drives 12,000 miles a year, gas costs $2 a gallon, and electricity is priced at 12¢ per kilowatt. A gasoline-powered car that gets 20 miles to the gallon will have annual fuel costs of $1,200 and generate about 6.6 tons of carbon dioxide. If these cars had electric motors, fuel costs would drop 67% to $400 a year and emissions would tumble 82% to 1.5 tons.[5]

The business opportunity for BYD is to make batteries that power cost-efficient electric cars. That's because currently electric cars that produce these levels of fuel efficiency are expensive to make—due largely to the high cost of the battery. Manufacturing a safe, reliable, long-lasting, and fast-charging battery for a car is complex and costly. But BYD claims that its lithium ion ferrous phosphate technology will do this cheaply. And since Warren Buffett does not have the technology background needed to assess this claim, he is betting on Wang and his people to fulfill it.[6]

So what is it about BYD's human capital that Buffett finds so inspiring? The answer is what Wang calls a human resource advantage—substituting inexpensive and talented Chinese workers for expensive Japanese robots. BYD first followed this strategy when Wang decided to enter the battery business that Japan then dominated. Wang observed that import duties and long delivery times made it expensive to import Japanese batteries to China. So Wang studied Sony and Sanyo patents and unpacked their batteries to understand how they were made.[7]

Wang realized that he could make the batteries less expensively in China by replacing Japan's robots with cheap Chinese migrant workers. While Japanese battery-making assembly lines used robotic arms that cost $100,000 each, BYD could cut costs by hiring hundreds, then thousands, of people. To control quality, BYD broke every job down into basic tasks and applied strict testing methods. By 2002, BYD had become one of the top four manufacturers in the world and China's largest in each of the three rechargeable battery technologies. Moreover, BYD's quality is higher than Sony and Sanyo—unlike these Japanese rivals, BYD never faced a battery recall.[8]

Wang now employs 10,000 engineers to help invent new products or improvements to existing ones. He claims that he trains the top students from China's best schools and that he can afford to hire so many because they are willing to accept low salaries ranging from $600 to $700 a month. Moreover, he grants these hires subsidized housing in company-owned apartment complexes and low-cost meals in BYD cafeterias so that they can spend all their time working. And these engineers investigate technologies, from automobile air conditioning systems that can run on batteries to the design of solar-powered streetlights. And thanks to its lower costs, BYD claims that it can make nearly the entire car itself—including the engines, body, air conditioning, lamps, seatbelts, airbags, and electronics—which BYD's Japanese and U.S. competitors try to outsource to lower their costs.[9]

As of April 2009, Buffett's investment in BYD was still awaiting Chinese government approval. Yet there were other risks that remained for Buffett's investment. For example,

- Would the battery technology that Wang touted actually deliver on its promise?
- Would BYD's disclosure of its financial condition and prospects be sufficient to warn Buffett of problems?
- Was there sufficient management strength at BYD to protect Buffett in the event that Wang left the company?
- Was there a risk that China could decide to unilaterally expropriate Buffett's stake in BYD?
- Was there any IP protection to keep a BYD competitor from copying its technologies?

Western Banks Losing on Chinese Real Estate

Some of the West's largest banks lent an estimated $10 billion to Chinese real estate developers. One such developer, a 48-year-old property tycoon, cost a handful of Western banks an estimated $400 million in sour loans after the tycoon's plans to sell stock to the public evaporated as the price of Chinese real estate plunged. The Western banks structured deals in offshore money havens that offered tax breaks and freed them from Chinese restrictions on foreign capital flows. The success of these deals hinged on converting bank debt into cash by issuing pre-IPO shares at a discount and then swapping the debt for pricey common shares after the property developer went public.

At fault were a combination of factors—Western bankers were too clever by half with their complex financial structures, Chinese property developers were overly optimistic in their estimate of demand's ability to keep up with the supply of property they were scrambling to add to the market, and all involved were speculating on a continued rise in the Chinese currency relative to the dollar. Will this convergence of bad bets leave an indelible mark in the minds of Western capital providers that keeps them from considering Chinese investment? Or will Western investors return to the Chinese market after a few years with more conservative financial structures to hedge themselves against a recurrence of such losses?

Not unlike Warren Buffett and BYD, the Western bankers were building their hopes for an investment killing on the belief that they were hitching their wagons to a Chinese entrepreneurial star. More specifically, in early 2007, bankers from Merrill Lynch and Deutsche Bank lent $400 million to a 48-year-old property developer named Xu Jiayin, who was expected to become China's next billionaire, and pushed him to use the funds to acquire land with the idea that his company, Evergrande Real Estate Group, would sell $2.1 billion in stock on the Hong Kong exchange and use the proceeds to pay back the loans. But things did not work out as planned—China's housing market collapsed, Evergrande is crippled with its debt, and the Western banks face huge losses because the IPO never happened.[10]

The Evergrande collapse is just one example of how $10 billion in foreign capital from banks and private equity firms flowed into China looking for a way to make a quick killing. In so doing, the money burning a hole in Western investors' pockets pushed itself onto Chinese entrepreneurs and in return those investors demanded a more aggressive expansion strategy than would have been justified by a rational analysis of the cash flows from such projects. For example, a Morgan Stanley real estate fund bought a tower in Shanghai for $240 million; Carlyle Group acquired luxury villas; and in 2008 JP Morgan Asset Management bought 12% of R&F Properties, a big Chinese developer. When the downturn hit, property prices plunged as much as 50%.[11]

The key to drawing in all the foreign capital to China was a clever tax and capital control dodge put in place by Western investors. To earn big returns, the investors in these real estate deals created complex offshore investment vehicles, such as convertible bonds and preferred equity, which gave them tax advantages and allowed them to bypass Beijing's strict controls on investing in Chinese companies listed overseas. Often the investments took a detour through the Cayman Islands or the British Virgin Islands, which permitted these dealings.[12]

With the huge quantities of Western money looking for a home, one of the most popular ways to get the funds to China was to invest it in a preinitial public offering deal. The Western investors issued convertible bonds through an offshore entity and then funneled that capital to a Chinese property developer. When the developer was ready to sell stock in Hong Kong, it would pay back the initial investment or bond by giving the foreign investor pre-IPO shares at a discount.[13]

The biggest preoffering investment deal was for Evergrande, based in Guangdong province and controlled by Xu, a respected entrepreneur. Evergrande, which was building large developments such as the Royal Scenic complex in Guangzhou, raised hundreds of millions of dollars from foreign investors and then started buying large tracts of land all over China. When Evergrande marketed its public stock offering in 2008, promoters bragged that Evergrande's offering would be larger than Google's $1.7 billion offering in 2004 and that its founder, Xu, would become China's richest man, with a net worth approaching $7 billion.[14]

Despite their efforts to bypass Chinese efforts to control capital flows into their country, Western investors were ultimately held hostage by the power of the Chinese government to control the housing bubble. Those efforts helped to slow down housing sales thereby crimping developer profits. Moreover, Hong Kong's booming stock market lost altitude after a multiyear rise. By withdrawing its IPO there, Evergrande was forced to go back to many of those same foreign investors who had hoped to cash out in the IPO and ask them for more cash to pay down the debt it incurred to buy the land. By April 2009, it had borrowed $1.8 billion, mostly from Merrill Lynch, Deutsche Bank, and Credit Suisse. At that time, it was unclear whether Evergrande would ever be able to get out from under that debt and whether those Western capital providers would end up getting repaid or take big losses.[15]

There are important lessons from Western banks' money losing bet on Chinese real estate:

Trouble follows when too much money is in search of too few good deals. In retrospect, the global availability of capital in search of a place to invest was bound to create trouble for capital providers and recipients. The capital providers would push themselves into deals that could not make profitable use of additional capital and the recipients would have spent the money too quickly at the urging of the capital providers. As economic conditions changed, the bubble burst and both parties lost.

Capital's efforts to bypass a country's capital controls can often backfire. Western capital providers thought that they could bypass Chinese capital controls and Western taxing authorities by issuing capital through complex structures in Caribbean tax havens. Ultimately, those capital providers proved unable to escape China's sovereignty over its housing industry. When China slowed down housing's growth, the Western capital that had been invested there plunged in value.

Capital should be a means of enabling a business strategy not a driver of strategy. One of the most powerful factors in expanding a credit bubble is that capital's role changes from one of supporting a business strategy to driving that strategy. In the case of Evergrande, bank loans forced a change in its business strategy. Xu followed the request of bankers to use the money to buy land, even though it had not been part of his development strategy. In a unique application of Say's Law, the capital's excess supply created its own demand—and in so doing ruined what had been a respected company.

Capital providers should base their investment decisions on a project's cash flows, rather than trying to arbitrage global capital markets. Had Merrill and Deutsche Bank based their decision to provide capital based solely on the cash flow projections of Evergrandes' properties, they may never have made the loans. However, it appears that their true motivation was to take advantage of the relatively low cost of debt capital in the West compared to the high value of Chinese property developer IPO shares on the Hong Kong exchange. When the cost of Western debt suddenly spiked as the credit crunch accelerated even as the Hong Kong IPO market lost value—the arbitrage opportunity evaporated.

Sequoia Ventures to China

Sequoia, a hugely successful Silicon Valley IT venture capitalist, has also succeeded in China. However, Sequoia's Chinese success springs from very different roots. It partnered with a successful Chinese entrepreneur, Neil Shen, to jumpstart its entry into China. Shen made a killing when he founded and sold Ctrip to public investors. And he does not focus on IT; instead he invests in the basics—food, clothes, housing, and travel. Moreover, he looks for entrepreneurs who have specific traits—brains, persistence, enthusiasm, and salesmanship. His portfolio of successes is focused and it appears that if Shen sticks to his principles, Sequoia will continue to profit by venture investing in China.[16]

By 2006, Shen had achieved great status among China's wealthiest citizens in the wake of his entrepreneurial success. Forbes rated him number 252 on its list of China's 400 richest. Shen cofounded Ctrip, a Nasdaq-listed travel booking company with a 2006 market capitalization of $1.5 billion. In September 2005, Shen left Ctrip to cofound Sequoia China in a joint venture with Silicon Valley's Sequoia Capital.[17]

Then in November 2006, Shen again hit it big when Home Inns, an economy hotel chain with 85 lodges that he and his Ctrip partners cofounded with their own money, had a successful Nasdaq IPO. Shen owns a piece of Nasdaq-traded Focus Media, an outdoor advertising company.[18]

Shen's investment strategy at Sequoia China differs from that of his U.S.-based VC partner. Shen prefers to put capital in things Chinese people need that he dubs the "four necessities" that include "food, clothes, housing, and travel." Shen himself has a background that helps him appreciate both the needs of China's consumers and the wants of the U.S. capital markets. He grew up in Shanghai, and earned a Yale MBA. He next jumped to Wall Street where he sold emerging market bonds in the 1990s when China was less of an investment fad. He later worked for investment banks in Hong Kong.[19]

By November 2006, Shen had invested Sequoia in nine companies including the following three:

- *China Linong*, a supplier of upscale, freshly packaged vegetables, which Shen chose because he believes that China has a hugely fragmented vegetable market, and that its middle class will demand premium products. A similar company, Chaoda Modern Agriculture, was founded by Guo Hao, who Forbes ranked thirty-seventh among China's 400 richest in 2006.

- *Palm Commerce*, Palm sells software to lottery operators and is a Chinese version of Nasdaq-listed Scientific Games—Shen considers the business to be poised for profitable growth because it is "extremely scalable once you set up the platform and system."
- *Great Dreams*, an animation company that he calls, "The Disney of China."[20]

How does Shen decide where to invest? Much of it has to do with human capital. Specifically, he looks to invest in entrepreneurs with three traits: brains and persistence, consumer focus, and salesmanship.

- *Brains and persistence.* As Shen said, "I think, 'Who is the smartest person in a business?'" Citing Robin Li—China's twenty-sixth richest person—who founded Chinese search engine Baidu; Shen considers him "smart, did a good job and has been very focused. In the early days, his revenue didn't take off, but he stayed with it."
- *Strong consumer focus.* Ma Huateng—CEO of China Internet service portal, Tencent, who ranked thirty-fourth on Forbes' 2006 Chinese rich list—is an example of this trait. As Shen said, Ma has a "good feel" for his products, "which is especially noteworthy because he doesn't come from a sales or marketing background."
- *Salesmanship.* Focus Media's success springs from its CEO's enthusiasm. As Shen said, "It's such a young company, and you have to ask yourself, 'How can this company do so well?'" Shen explains its success by describing its CEI Jason Jiang, then fortieth on Forbes China rich list. According to Shen, "Even now, after his success, he still loves to sell. The customers feel a lot of attachment to him. There was a board meeting recently, and he was late because he was still out with a client."[21]

Sequoia China's success suggests these important lessons for capital providers:

Partner with a local expert who has a great investment track record and can understand both capital source and recipient markets. Shen was the ideal candidate for such a role because he had achieved success founding and selling a company based in China in a U.S. IPO. And his academic and work experience prepared him well to understand how Chinese consumers and entrepreneurs operate and what Western capital providers seek in a start-up investment.

Tailor the investment strategy to the market. Sequoia China was wise to focus its attention on consumer needs rather than on technology. While this approach differed radically from that of its U.S. partner, which has a track record of success investing in enterprise technology companies, it made sense for the opportunities Shen saw in China. By tailoring its approach to China, Sequoia was able to achieve its overarching goal—high investment returns—through a different means.

Invest in people who model the best entrepreneurial behavior. In addition to picking companies poised to take advantage of attractive market opportunities, Sequoia recognized the importance of investing in the right people. Specifically, Shen tried to pick entrepreneurs who exhibited traits he believes are correlated with new venture success in China—brains and persistence; consumer focus; and salesmanship. While such traits would not make sense for all new ventures, they seemed to be important in China. The implication is that venture investors should know the traits of successful CEOs for their particular companies, and make people who exhibit these traits the stewards of their capital.

Global Venture Network Invests in China

Global Venture Network, a private equity investor, has earned high returns by taking big equity stakes in small, fast-growing Chinese companies. GVN's returns averaged 100% between 2002 and 2006. GVN's focus for these extraordinary returns has been on companies in rapidly growing industries like healthcare, media, and education. But GVN selects companies from those industries that pass three tests: they are well managed, they comply with strict U.S. accounting standards—such as Sarbanes-Oxley (SOX), and their businesses have the potential to expand into new markets. Will GVN be able to sustain this performance?[22]

Economic conditions for PE investors were very attractive in early 2006. For example, in April 2006, GVN CEO James Hahn was convinced that one of the biggest risks to those high returns was the potential for too much foreign capital—but he did not see that problem emerging until after the 2008 Olympics or the Shanghai World Expo in 2010. In Hahn's view, the growth in China was so attractive that it would be difficult not to profit from PE investing there. From his perspective, Chinese companies with good management were growing "at a rate of 30% internally and 30% globally."[23]

However, that rate of growth did not guarantee high PE returns. To achieve the kinds of triple digit returns about which Hahn bragged, it was important to filter from the millions of the privately held companies in China a far smaller subset that could satisfy tough U.S. corporate governance standards. His review of the numbers suggests that even the tiny percentage of companies that comply with U.S. governance standards makes a tempting target for PE investors. According to Hahn, in 2006 there were at least 3 million privately owned companies in China. Of those, GVN believes 300,000 would qualify to list on Nasdaq or NYSE today. Of these, 1% or 3,000 companies are what GVN believes are "jewels" that have sound management, that is, comply with Sarbanes-Oxley, and could be scaled up.[24]

GVN invests only in Chinese companies run by CEOs who are willing to operate under U.S. rule of law and accounting standards. As Hahn said, "We will spend time with any Chinese CEO who has made the first step by showing his or her commitment to the process by having the company audited under U.S. GAAP rules. We are betting on the current quarterback."[25]

GVN made it sound as if achieving triple digit returns investing in China in 2006 would be like shooting fish in a barrel. According to Hahn, "In China, today, the average investment is $5 million for a 30% stake in a Chinese growth company grossing $10 million with net income of $3 million and a pre-money valuation of $15 million, or 5 times net income. Comparable U.S. public companies in the same high-growth sectors such as healthcare, media, and education are trading at price-to-earnings ratios of 25 times. Buying low and selling high has delivered a minimum return of 100% a year for a five-year, $100 million size fund in China."[26]

The profits that PE firms like GVN earned in China seem to defy economic reality. The rapid growth, high investment returns, lofty exit valuations, and lack of competition all appear inherently unsustainable. As we saw in the Evergrande case, the high returns and large pools of capital seeking such returns generally lead investors to pile into "good" investment opportunities quickly. This leaves less good opportunities to soak up the excess capital. Ultimately, the lower quality costs investors money. And word of their losses spreads quickly to other market participants who withdraw their funds. The result is a burst investment bubble that enriches only the investors who got in early and got out by selling as their slower peers piled in.

Kleiner Perkins Considers Its Exit Door

How should a capital provider decide where to take public a portfolio company? Kleiner Perkins Caufield and Byers partner Ted Schlein's struggle with this question illustrates how one such capital provider made this choice when he was trying to decide whether to seek access to Chinese markets for initial public offerings of its portfolio companies. Schlein weighed the advantages and disadvantages of using financial markets in Shanghai, Shenzhen, London's Alternative Investment Market (AIM), and exchanges in Japan, Hong Kong, and India.

Specifically, Schlein made his decision by weighing the potential benefits of much higher IPO valuations—for example, in Shanghai, Schlein learned that companies going public could expect earnings multiples of 30–40 times—compared with 13–15 times in Hong Kong or 20 times on the Nasdaq, against the potential costs and risks including the costs of learning new laws and regulations, the risk that trading interest and volumes in these foreign markets will be too low to yield a meaningful return and the risk that less regulatory oversight could lead to scandals or collapse.[27]

Schlein's analysis began with a November 2006 meeting in Shanghai with local investment bankers promoting the original idea that a VC like KPCB should take companies public on China's stock exchanges. Why would a Western VC take such a proposition seriously? One reason might be frustration with the difficulty and expense of taking start-ups public in the United States. While Schlein saw Chinese exchanges, like those in Shanghai and Shenzhen, as more exotic choices for an exit, he was giving serious consideration to the London Stock Exchange's AIM, and to exchanges in Japan, Hong Kong, and India.[28]

As Schlein considered these other options, he knew that the United States had become a far less satisfying place in which to launch a VC-backed IPO. A December 2006 National Venture Capital Association (NVCA) study had found that 57 percent of 200 investors surveyed say there would be a growing industry push to take American companies public in overseas markets. How? The number of VC-backed IPOs had plummeted. In 2005, 56 venture-backed companies went public in the United States, nearly half of the 93 in 2004 and a less than a quarter of the 273 in 1996. And while VCs blamed the Sarbanes-Oxley Act, the 2002 corporate accountability law, they also admitted that the collapse of the dot-com bubble in 2000 had taken away the U.S. public's appetite for equity in VC-backed technology companies.[29]

As Schlein considered these options, he was quite cognizant of the challenges facing investors seeking to take their companies public in overseas markets. Among those hurdles were the following:

- The need for investors to learn new laws and regulations;
- The risk that trading interest and volumes in those foreign markets will be too low to yield a meaningful return; and
- The concern that less regulatory oversight in overseas exchanges would result in scandals or collapse.[30]

It seemed to many VCs in the United States that London's AIM had the greatest potential since England's legal system most closely resembled that of the United States. But at the time there was significant uncertainty about whether AIM would yield sufficient value and trading volume to enable VCs to sell their interests there. Investors were concerned that AIM would basically be like the so-called pink sheets in the United States—an illiquid exchange for tiny companies with limited potential. And one investment banker, Charles Cameron, managing director of Jeffries International, suggested that VCs were not sure what would be the appropriate size and shape of a VC-backed company targeting an AIM listing.[31]

One U.S. VC firm with success at international listings is DCM Doll Capital Management. By December 2006 its founding general partner, Dixon Doll, had taken five Japanese companies public in Japan since 1996. More recently he had made an investment in a mobile phone software company in Scotland that partnered with a Japanese handset manufacturer. Doll anticipated listing the company dually on British and Japanese exchanges. But even Doll questioned whether a U.S.-backed venture could use this formula to take itself public on an overseas exchange.[32]

The 30–40 times earnings valuations that Shanghai investment bankers had pitched to Schlein suggested to him that the Chinese government might have been helping to prop up start-ups and valuations to establish the exchanges' credibility. He remained skeptical and said, "I don't have answers yet, but I'm trying to figure it out."[33]

Schlein's dilemma about which exit door to pick suggests a need for a framework that such investors can use to analyze the decision. Capital providers comparing different countries' capital markets may wish to consider the following factors:

Breadth and depth of market participants. Capital providers are likely to achieve the greatest returns if they list on exchanges that feature a wide variety of investors, many of whom have significant amounts of capital. Ideally, these investors would include pension funds, foundations, endowments, mutual funds, and individual investors. Conversely, exchanges that feature few classes of investors—such as the government and individual investors—would likely be less attractive because of the high volatility and inability to predict outcomes.

Market transaction volume. Capital providers would similarly be better off selling shares in markets with high transaction volumes. Such volumes would provide sufficient market depth to keep the sale of a large portion of a VC's interests from collapsing the price of a venture's shares. In thinly traded markets, capital providers would likely suffer big drops in the value of their holdings if they sought to sell their interests.

Relative valuations of issued companies. A capital provider would ideally want to list a company on the exchange that put the highest value on the earnings prospects of their companies. To assess these relative valuations, a capital provider might consider the longer-term evidence, say, 5 or 10 years worth of valuations of IPOs of companies in the same industry. Such track records would help capital providers consider the reliability and sustainability of the valuations for their ventures on those exchanges.

Relative capital provider returns. Furthermore, capital providers would seek to sell shares into markets that had offered other capital providers the highest long-term investment returns. While high past returns would not guarantee a bright future, they would provide a basis for evaluating the exchange's experience in working with capital providers and offering them real value. By contrast, capital providers might seek to avoid exchanges with no track record of previous returns—unless they had solid evidence on which to believe that the risk of pioneering on such exchanges would be rewarded.

Rigor of financial reporting and other regulatory requirements. While rigorous financial reporting, disclosure, and other regulatory requirements may accord an additional burden on capital providers, they also protect them by blocking scam artists from gaining access to exchanges. If a capital provider lists a company on an exchange that permits fraudulent activity, then that capital provider's reputation is likely to be damaged—however inadvertently. Therefore, strict reporting and other regulatory requirements for listing shares on an exchange protect capital providers—even though such requirements add to their costs.

Track record of legal problems among investors and issuers. An obvious corollary to the previous consideration is that capital providers should avoid listing shares on exchanges that have hosted legal and regulatory violations—particularly violations that have garnered significant publicity, fines, and other punishment. Although exchanges may take abrupt action to stop such violations in the short term, these moves might last only until the next investment boom. Capital providers should shun the reputational damage of listing their companies on exchanges with potential legal and regulatory problems.

Were Schlein to have considered these factors, he probably would have decided to pass on using the Shanghai market as a place to sell shares to the public. Due to the lack of depth and breadth of market participants, the absence of a well-established track record of successful IPOs there and the relatively limited requirements for listing, Schlein may well have used this framework to conclude that KPCB would not achieve sufficiently high returns to warrant the risks of a Shanghai listing.

Indian Private Equity Refocuses in Economic Downturn

Western private equity (PE) firms entered the Indian market with the hope that they could make big bucks quick in an emerging market only to be brought up short. They discovered that Indian executives lacked enthusiasm for Westerners to come into their companies with wads of capital, give up control, grow the business, and sell it at a huge gain. To succeed in India, PE firms found that they needed to adopt different approaches—taking smaller stakes, finding management teams that were mutually acceptable, adding value by introducing a company's products to other portfolio companies, and having a much more patient attitude toward exits.

And by 2009, that patience was being tested even more—as huge drops in India's Sensex led those PE firms to try to limit their risk of loss by sharing their deals with other firms. Would India ultimately prove to be a cash sink for PE investors or would their patience ultimately be rewarded?

Before examining prospects for PE investors in India, it is worth considering in greater depth the specific requirements of India's PE capital *recipients* and how PE *providers* have adapted their strategies to satisfy those recipients. What do India's PE recipient company executives want? It is simpler to start off with what they don't want—which is for Western PE executives to use their capital to take over their company, cut costs, and quickly sell the company for a big gain. Indian company executives are looking for the opposite of this—a PE firm that offers patient capital willing to take a minority stake and to provide the company access to a wide network of potential customers, talent, and suppliers who can help the company grow without unduly upsetting the company's management team.[34]

Perhaps surprisingly, some PE firms have found it worthwhile to adapt their traditional methods to meet these requirements. Western PE firms have employed the following tactics to achieve their aims—high investment returns—while simultaneously playing a more supportive role with their Indian portfolio companies by filling important unmet needs for the Indian companies. These unmet needs include the following:

A global growth strategy. PE firms that have worked in different industries around the world can help Indian executives hoping to grow their companies. For example, in mid-2006, managers at Claris Lifesciences, an Ahmedabad-based pharmaceutical manufacturer took a $20 million investment from U.S.-based Carlyle Group. Claris wanted to penetrate key export markets by tapping a variety of Carlyle capabilities. Claris used Carlyle's technical experts to help it devise strategies to satisfy U.S. FDA standards and worked with a Carlyle unit in Japan to source reliable, yet cheap raw material suppliers.

Access to new customers and suppliers. Many Indian firms lack the access to global customers and suppliers that might help them achieve their growth goals. For example, Nimbus Communications, a Mumbai media company used 3i, a London-based PE firm, to help it grow. Nimbus' CEO Harish Thawani sold 3i 33% of Nimbus for $45.5 million in August 2005. Moreover, Thawani wanted 3i to boost the value of Nimbus by providing introductions to potential partners from 3i's 1,500 companies. Furthermore, Nimbus wanted 3i's 300 investment professionals to help it acquire broadcast rights, fund TV and feature-film production, and develop digital content for wireless distribution.

Strengthened corporate governance. Since many traditional Indian companies operate through close personal ties, they are not always comfortable with Western standards of talent, transparency, and independent oversight. Some Indian companies have recognized that Western PE firms can infuse these corporate governance standards into their companies; thereby making them more attractive to potential Western investors. For example, Sunil Mittal, the founder of Bharti, was drawn to an investment offer by Warburg Pincus managing director Pulak Prasad as a way to obtain access to these corporate governance skills. In 1999, as members of Bharti's board, Prasad (who left Warburg in late 2006) and Dalip Pathak, the head of Warburg Pincus' Indian funds, helped Bharti formulate an expansion strategy, bring aboard experienced senior managers and guide it through an initial public stock offering in early 2002 that raised $172 million.[35]

While such insights proved valuable to PE firms during the India boom years, by 2009, the downside of Indian PE was in full swing and PE firms were rapidly responding by taking steps to limit their risk. While an extraordinary five-year run-up in India's stock market attracted private equity, an even more abrupt collapse in 2008 triggered an equally large drop in PE investment there. More specifically, India's Sensex stock index fell 52.4% in 2008, its worst year ever, ending a five-year upward march during which it rose sixfold. And through February

2009, the Sensex had fallen an additional 6.3%. Indian PE investments fell in sympathy—down 38.1% to $10.7 billion in 2008. And the pain was expected to continue into 2009—PE allocation to India was expected to fall 33% to between $5 billion and $7 billion.[36]

What was driving the drop in PE investment in India? The evidence suggests that PE firms had overallocated their capital to the equity of public companies traded on India's Sensex. And as PE firms saw the value of those equity investments plunge, so did their ability to make new PE investments. Specifically, 66% of Indian PE between 2007 and 2009 was invested in Sensex-traded equity and its drop inhibited "PE firms' ability to invest," according to Nitin Deshmukh, CEO of private equity at Kotak Investment Advisors. Moreover, PE firms were expected to shun cyclical industries such as real estate due to the sliding prices of what had previously been a popular investment choice. As Ashish Dhawan, senior managing director at ChrysCapital, which manages $2.5 billion of assets, said, "It is a cycle. In good times you raise and invest oodles of money; in bad times you try and stay away."[37]

While different PE firms pursued varying investment strategies during the downturn in the Indian stock market, the downturn seems to have inspired them to pursue a common means of sharing PE investment risk—so-called club deals. More specifically, by February 2009, foreign and India-based PE firms were spreading the risk of investing in assets by banding together—forming a syndicate to acquire stakes in companies in order to limit the amount of capital each PE firm commits and, therefore, each PE firm's risk.[38]

From the capital recipient's standpoint, such club deals made sense because the absolute level of capital required for a company to reach maturity was increasing. At the same time, PE firms' appetite for risk was tumbling. Firms were resorting to clubbing together to form a syndicate when acquiring stakes to limit both funding requirements and risk. Evidence of the growing popularity of such club deals was compelling. Between January and July 2008, about 18% of all private equity transactions were syndicated. However, that proportion spiked to 29% between August 2008 and February 2009. Moreover, 60% of PE managers polled expected deal syndication to rise in 2009, while most expected the number and size of investments to drop because of investors becoming more risk averse.[39]

Wisely, PE club deals were being forged while bearing in mind the specific requirements of the company receiving the capital as well as the investment preferences of fellow club members. According to Rahul Chandra, director at Helion Ventures, "What you need in a syndicate partner is complementary values in business building and a similar kind of time frame (for growth and exit). The patience factor has to be similar." And the entrepreneur receiving the club's capital must be in synch with the syndicate members. According to Sandeep Singhal, Director, Nexus India Capital, "The entrepreneur should be the one driving the syndication and should come to the lead investor asking for another fund with certain preferred characteristics. We then connect the two together."[40]

Western PE firms' efforts to adapt to the unique conditions in the Indian market reveal several important principles for capital providers:

Capital providers must not apply a one-size-fits-all approach to investing in different market. Rather capital providers are more likely to succeed if they bring the strengths that matter most to the capital recipients in the countries where they seek to invest. The most effective PE investors in India shunned their traditional approach of taking a control position, replacing management, making rapid cost cuts, and quickly selling the restructured company. Instead, Western firms investing in Indian companies tended to work more closely with existing management after taking a minority stake—and in exchange for letting the PE firms into the company, its executives expected the PE firm to provide access to customers, talent, and suppliers who could boost the company's revenues.

Capital providers should seek out companies that value their corporate governance and financial markets skills. A corollary to the first principle is that capital providers are more likely to succeed if they partner with Indian companies that recognize their weaknesses and are eager to bolster themselves by partnering with a PE firm with relevant strengths. Bharti's decision to partner with Warburg Pincus reflects its realization that it could obtain access to deeper pools of capital if it could strengthen its corporate governance. When both partners are mutually dependent for different reasons—and the partners reinforce each other through their unique strengths—then both parties are likely to end up better off.

Capital providers should consider increasing their investment in down markets and lessening it in up markets. As we explored above, capital providers tend to follow just the opposite of this advice. When times are flush, PE firms tend to raise huge amounts of money from limited partners and invest as much of it as they can. And when stock market values drop, they suddenly become very reluctant to commit capital and seek to invest as little as they can themselves—instead opting to share the risk with other PE firms. But this approach may be unprofitable since it will tend to encourage the maximum amount of risk when company values are high and the minimum risk when values are low. This approach has the advantage for PE managers of putting them in a position to tell disappointed limited partners that they were in good company. However, those limited partners would likely be happier if the PE firms bought low and sold high.

Warburg Pincus Profits in India

All this Western PE interest in India likely sprang from envious peers seeking to replicate the early success of Warburg Pincus (WP). WP was earlier than most and it invested in well-established companies to which it added capital and made well-timed bets on big changes in India's attitude toward foreign capital. Specifically WP profited from changes in Indian government policy that were more open to foreign capital flows and permitted those investors to take their profits and gradually walk them back to their limited partners.

Moreover, Indian government efforts to reduce inflation helped boost the bottom line of companies in which WP invested. In addition, WP tried to invest in companies Indian policymakers wanted to boost—those involved with upgrading its creaky infrastructure. WP's success has invited competition. Can WP continue to profit as it faces more rivalry for deals and the challenges of a shrinking global economy?

The proverbial shot heard round the world for Indian PE investors was WP's March 2005 sale of a $560 million stake in Bharti Tele-Ventures, India's largest publicly traded mobile telephony company. At the time, that transaction was the Bombay Stock Exchange's largest block trade and it took only 28 minutes to complete—surprising analysts with the unexpected depth and maturity of India's equity markets. After a series of trades, WP reduced its 18.5% stake in Bharti to about 6%.[41]

The sale let WP walk away with an $800 million profit after selling two-thirds of the stock it took following its $300 million investment in Bharti between 1999 and 2001. And by November 2005, WP's remaining 6% Bharti stake was worth $700 million, or more than twice what it originally invested. Since that initial 1999 WP investment, Bharti's market capitalization and subscriber count grew from a mere $100 million and 104,000 to $15 billion and 14 million respectively.[42]

WP has generated high returns from this and other Indian PE investments. According to WP's copresident, Charles R. Kaye, WP has earned returns in "the mid-30s over 10 years." How did WP accomplish this feat? Simply put, it saw opportunity where others saw problems. More specifically, other investment gurus, such as commodities investor, Jim Rogers, perceived India as having a very weak infrastructure—meaning roads, bridges, and telephone lines—and a government that appeared to deter foreign investment. But WP saw that very lack of infrastructure as an opportunity to invest in firms, like Bharti, that could profit from growing demand for services—such as cellular communications— that would enable India's population to communicate without a radical upgrade to India's infrastructure.[43]

And WP saw before other PR firms that India's government was committed to changing its stance toward Western capital flows. Specifically, in 1991, India's policymakers began to open India to foreign capital and to create a more stable economic environment—accelerating growth—achieving GDP growth in the 6.5%–8% range, while stabilizing the Rupee and tamping down inflation.[44]

Moreover, India's IT sector gained great self-confidence after helping to save the West from the potential ravages of the Y2K problem. These moves attracted significant amounts of foreign capital—more than $12 billion between 2003 and 2005. And pleasantly, for WP and other PE firms, India permitted Western PE firms to repatriate their Indian profits quickly—in 48 hours, according to Dalip Pathak, WP's managing director in charge of its Indian strategy.[45]

By late 2005, WP was beginning to see that it might make more sense to sell its stakes rather than invest further. Nonetheless, its diverse holdings suggested that WP saw the best investments in consumer and infrastructure companies including the following:

- Rediff Communication, the country's largest consumer web portal;
- Gujarat Ambuja Cement;
- Sintex Industries, an industrial plastic-goods manufacturer with a 60% share of the market for water-storage tanks;
- Kotak Mahindra, a financial services conglomerate;
- Nicholas Piramal India, a major pharmaceutical company; and
- WNS Global Services, a business process outsourcing company.[46]

These investments suggest that WP was attracted to companies with the greatest assurance of meeting a real market need which were subject to the stricter corporate governance standards which India imposed on its larger public companies. According to Pathak, "Larger companies are less risky; listed companies are less risky," due to the transparency of India's capital markets. Moreover, with bigger Indian companies seeking capital and acquisitions outside the country, Pathak believes that they won't risk running afoul of WP because if they did, "they know they will never get investment abroad."[47]

WP's success brought competition from the United States to India. These competitors included Intel Capital, Oak Hill Capital Management, the Carlyle Group, Citigroup Venture Capital International, General Atlantic Partners, CSFB Private Equity, and the California Public Employees Retirement System (CalPERS)—most of which had invested only in the tens of millions. But WP realized that it needed to respond to these competitors and concluded that investing in companies that could capture a share of India's expected $20 billion to $25 billion in infrastructure investment—for greater power generation, better highways and more efficient ports—would be a good place for WP to focus. Kaye concluded that WP would be best off following India's policymakers who were trying to lift 200 million people out of abject poverty. In his view, infrastructure projects, far more than IT, had the potential to generate the large numbers of jobs needed to accomplish that task.[48]

WP's success in India suggests two important lessons for capital providers:

- *While demanding more courage, investors willing to go their own way outperform their meeker peers.* A significant reason for WP's success was its willingness to invest when its peers were afraid of India's problems and to exit when its peers were piling in. Forming an independent perspective on investment opportunities based on objective, fact-based analysis often yields high investment returns. India rewarded WP for its prescient investment picks and its timing.
- *Capital providers should invest in companies that satisfy the growing needs of a country's government and its populace.* Ahead of its peers, WP saw both a growing need for Indians to communicate and the limitations of its telephone

infrastructure. Rather than viewing this as an obstacle to profitable investing, WP recognized cellular as a quicker solution and profited from that insight by placing a bet on Bharti. Moreover, WP recognized that India had decided to change its posture toward global capital flows and invested at a low price before that transformation had fully flowered. India rewarded WP for betting correctly on what proved to be an inexorable trend

Kleiner Perkins Hits it Big in India

Silicon Valley venture capital legend, KPCB has similarly achieved success with venture investing in India by partnering with the right executive there, Ajit Nazre who worked out of KPCB's Silicon Valley office to find, capitalize, and IPO Info Edge (India)—which had a spectacular 2006 offering. Nazre's approach to VC investing in India reveals some important principles—find successful entrepreneurs who need your contacts, not your capital; be patient because the time from investment to exit is longer in India; and focus on businesses, such as real estate development and infrastructure, which are likely to grow.[49]

Nazre's pre-KPCB pedigree was impressive and boundary-spanning in the sense that it gave him insights into Indian companies and Western capital providers. Nazre earned an undergraduate degree in mechanical engineering from the College of Engineering Poona in India; holds a master's degree in mechanical engineering from Michigan Tech; a Ph.D. in biomechanics from the Technical University of Hanover, Germany, and an MBA from Harvard Business School. At SAP, Nazre claims that he helped to formulate and execute its Internet strategy (mySAP.com) and cofounded and led SAPMarkets. And in addition to Info Edge, by 2007 KPCB had invested in Indian industries such as enterprise software and services, material science pertinent to energy, environment and life sciences through stakes in Cleartrip, Kovio, Spatial Photonics, SpikeSource, Virsa, Visible Path, and Zettacore.[50]

KPCB first began investing in India in 2004 however it had been exploring India for decades before investing. According to Nazre, in the mid 1980s and early 1990s, KPCB "got familiar with Indian entrepreneurs in [Silicon] Valley." And many of KPCBs' U.S. ventures established operations in India during the 2000s. Indian entrepreneurs who had succeeded in the United States went back to India to start companies—yielding investment opportunities for KPCB.[51]

KPCB's first big investment success in India was with Info Edge, which operates job website Naukri.com. Together with another Indian entrepreneur, Ram Shriram, Nazre spoke with the founder and CEO of Info Edge, Sanjeev Bikhchandani, in July 2004. In 2005 KPCB had more concrete discussions—ultimately investing in the latter part of that year. Nazre's reasoning for the investment was that Info Edge was "cash-flow positive and generating revenues. Sanjeev is just a great entrepreneur and we were fascinated by him. He did not need capital. He was looking for people that can help him."[52]

Naturally, the success of Info Edge's 2006 IPO brought in many new entrants eager to make a killing in less time. In contrast to these recent imitators, Nazre believed that Info Edge spent a long time building up its business and thus had truly earned its financial success. According to Nazre, "For a lot of the folks who have just started in the last two years or so to compare themselves to Sanjeev is a little premature. He's been at it a long time. This guy started the business as printed job listings in 1987. At that time he wasn't doing it on the Internet, but he had a list of employers and he used to sell his listing sheet on campus. Then in the mid-1990s, he made a database and he went online in 1996. He's been online since then. He's overcome all the hurdles. The growth numbers are staggering. It's a huge success story—every aspect of it."[53]

Despite this success, many challenges remain for VCs seeking to profit from investing in India-based consumer Internet companies. As Nazre suggested, despite the Indian returnees, there were not as many talented employees in India as in Silicon Valley. Moreover, the level of Internet penetration in India did not compare favorably to that of China or the United States. In 2007, Nazre estimated that there were between 20 million to 25 million Internet users [out of a population of 900 million] and broadband there was a slow 256 Kpbs—far below the six to 10 Mbps broadband rates prevalent in the United States.[54]

Moreover, although India presented unique challenges related to IP protection and financial markets, Nazre believed these challenges were not difficult to surmount. In Nazre's view, IP theft in India was "a moot point" because investors had access to a legal system—albeit one that was slow to respond. He cited as support for the strength of India's legal system a January 2007 victory by Pfizer against an Indian generics manufacturer. He also suggested that without IP protection, GE and others would not have been establishing R&D centers in India.[55]

Finally, he argued that India's requirements for listing companies on its exchange were different in minor ways from those in the United States. For example, Securities and Exchange Board of India (SEBI) rules required entrepreneurs to hold their IPO shares for a year—much longer than the 180 days typical for Nasdaq. Nevertheless, Nazre believed that India's markets had liquidity and since its rules were based largely on those in the UK, U.S. investors needed only make minor adjustments to their normal procedures.[56]

KPCB's success in India suggests two important lessons for capital providers:

Partner with boundary spanners. A significant reason for KPCB's success in India was its ability to partner with Nazre and Nazre's relationship with Shriram. Nazre's deep technical expertise, experience working with Western companies, and his Indian roots helped him to operate as an effective ambassador between the worlds of Western VC and Indian entrepreneurs. Moreover, Nazre's insights into the challenges of Indian VC investing and means of overcoming those challenges proved critical to KPCB's success there.

High returns flow from investing in entrepreneurs with the talent to use available technology to meet the needs of local consumers. In retrospect, it's clear that KPCB benefited from investing in the right entrepreneur who was able to create a popular job search site in India which would work effectively with India's slower broadband speeds. KPCB was also able to overcome the natural resistance of Info Edge's founder to cede control in exchange for capital—particularly when the company was growing, cash flow positive and not in desperate need of KPCB's capital.

IDG Ventures Expands to Vietnam and China

How do different countries' intellectual property (IP) regimes influence where capital providers invest? We explored this question in chapter 1 when we first met Michael Greeley. Greeley's views on investing outside the United States come from an unusual set of life experiences. He spent considerable time in Hong Kong during his childhood before entering business school and then heading into the world of venture capital. He has worked with a number of leading VC firms including Polaris Venture Partners, Boston-based IDG Ventures Atlantic, and Flybridge Capital Partners.[57]

Greeley founded Boston-based IDG Ventures Atlantic in 2001 and served on the board of International Data Group, the flagship Limited Partner for the IDG Ventures global network of funds including funds in China, Korea, India, and Vietnam. Greeley's firm, IDG Ventures Atlantic, changed its name to Flybridge Capital Partners in 2008. While the firm is no longer part of the IDG Ventures network, Greeley retains close relations with the IDG Ventures international funds.[58]

Greeley is convinced that it is impossible to invest outside the United States without a local manager who has deep roots in that country. As Greeley said, "My big insight is that venture capital is hyper-local. If I were to go back to Hong Kong, I would be ineffective for years—since it would take me so long to get up to speed with what is happening there now. IDG Ventures does a great job at this. All of their regional firms are run by nationals from each country with a local orientation seeing local entrepreneurs."[59]

While Greeley believes a track record of prior investment success in the United States makes it easier to raise capital for a fund seeking to invest outside the United States, this track record may not help much when it comes to investing that fund. As Greeley explained, "In the mid-2000s, some VC firms who had been successful in the United States moved to Asia to start up VC funds there. They were able to raise capital because they had a good reputation from their successes in the United States. But they thought they could export the U.S. VC model to Asia. Although they were successful at raising money, they were not successful at investing because they did not recognize the importance of hyper-locality."[60]

Greeley believes seeking out countries with a large, fast-growing consumer market that is eager for technology is key as well. As he said, "How should firms choose which countries in which to invest? They should look for hyper-growth—which means an emerging consumer middle class which is a big consumer of technology."[61]

Greeley offered an interesting perspective on the various regions in which to invest venture capital. According to Greeley, "There are two countries that have local technology talent which they export to the U.S. and around the world—India and Israel. Clint Harris at Grove Street Investors has said that the Silicon Valley model only works in two other places in the world—Boston and Israel. These regions have talent in abundance, but small local markets, so they need to sell their products globally."[62]

Greeley continued, "The venture capital community in Israel is really hurting in the economic downturn so it is relying more on U.S. VCs. Unlike India, China has a language barrier because there English is a very distant second language. In India, English is spoken widely which is why outsourcing is such a strong business there."[63] And he reiterated his concerns about how a lack of Asian IP protection makes it unattractive to invest in IP-based businesses there. Greeley explained, "In Asia, IP issues will make it difficult to obtain venture money for medical and technically-based businesses. I don't think Asia will ever change enough to protect IP. It takes a cultural position that IP is owned by the people. It would take a generational change to make it safe for a venture capitalist to invest in IP-based companies in Asia."[64]

Greeley took the position that the best way to exit an Asian service company investment would be to sell it to a U.S. company seeking to expand into that country. According to Greeley, "As far as exiting, it's likely that Google or Yahoo would find it to be cheaper to buy a local company than to build one."[65]

Greeley also described how Flybridge uses board meetings in which directors compare expected outcomes to actual ones to manage the companies in which they invest. As he explained, "We're on the board of all our companies and we have monthly (if not more frequent) board meetings where we review performance versus plan and set priorities for the year. These meetings are absolutely metric-driven. We focus on factors like hiring, staffing and monthly burn rates. We have rules of thumb like no more than $15,000 for employees per month. We assess whether the business is scaling."[66]

Much of the value that Flybridge adds to its portfolio companies is the result of introducing them to potential partners and to helping recruit managers. According to Greeley, "We make CEO to CEO introductions for prospective partners, customers, or acquirers. We co-exist in an ecosystem of partnerships—helping our companies think through deals and approaches to partners."[67] Greeley also takes an active role in recruiting. As he said, "I am heavily involved in recruiting—I try to meet two new companies and one new relevant person a day. 90 percent of venture capital goes to salaries. We are investing to staff up businesses."[68]

Greeley finds it difficult to explain how he picks great CEOs. As he said, "It is hard to answer the question about how to pick great vs. good CEOs. It has to do with pattern recognition. We talk to customers and ask whether a company is good to do business with. We talk to a company's employees and ask how moral it is. Ultimately it has to do with whether the company is hitting plan."[69]

Moreover, Greeley finds it difficult to fire CEOs who are not meeting goals. As he described, "If the company is not hitting plan, changing out leadership is hard. We are reluctant to do it and tend to stay with a CEO longer than some other firms. On the other hand, there is a big morale boost if you change out a weak CEO."[70]

Flybridge relies on networks of people to generate investment opportunities. As Greeley explained, "We get deals from what I call micro-clusters. They are thought leaders and entrepreneurs. I have one CEO who I have backed four times in a row at different companies. It's not easy because for every 150 companies we see, we only invest in one. We've found that a CEO who has been successful in the past is likely to remain so in future start-ups and a failed CEO is likely to fail in the future. This has been confirmed by research at Harvard."[71] And Greeley prefers entrepreneurs to thought leaders—who have great ideas but often lack the ability to carry them out—when it comes to investing. As he explained, "Entrepreneurs are more focused than thought leaders. The most successful ones have a sense of the voice of the customer and they are obsessively focused on solving big problems. Weaker entrepreneurs tend not to understand customer needs and they keep changing their minds about what to do. Bob Langer and Michael Cima are great examples. They are two of the most successful entrepreneurs who we've backed in the biomedical and drug delivery device markets. Both are driven about how to make a device more perfect."[72]

IDG's approach to investing globally offers useful lessons for capital providers:

Adapt to a country's EE rather than trying to change it. IDG's decision to invest in service businesses with good management teams represents a pragmatic way to deal with a weakness in China's EE. Rather than waiting for some far off day in the future when China would willingly change its IP regime, IDG chose to accept the particular strengths and weaknesses of its EE and to structure its investments in Vietnam to take advantage of the strengths and protect against the weaknesses.

Invest in local managing partners. Greeley's personal observation on the hyper-locality of venture investing means that capital providers should make a significant effort to find the best possible local partners to manage their investments. Such partners must have deep networks of relationships with government officials, entrepreneurs, suppliers, and others who can help find and manage the best investment opportunities.

Think carefully about an exit strategy when initiating an investment. IDG's idea of offering its portfolio companies as a quick way for an established U.S. firm to expand into Asia appeared sound. However, after investing, IDG discovered that its Vietnamese ventures targeted a market opportunity that the potential acquirers thought was too small to be worthy of their attention. To solve this problem, IDG came up with the idea of expanding its Asian ventures into a broader regional market that might be large enough to appeal to these acquirers.

French Private Equity Is better Than Its Start-Up Culture

On the surface, France would appear to be a poor market in which to profit from private equity or venture capital investing. After all, it is known for having a strong anticapitalist bias, strong labor unions that strike frequently, and workers who take long vacations. In the case of venture capital and start-ups, the perception is right. But in the case of private equity, there may be opportunities. As we'll see, France discourages entrepreneurs—sending them to Silicon Valley.

But things are slightly different for private equity investors. The antiprivate equity perception acts as an intangible barrier to entry that leaves the French private equity market to investors who understand the unique nature of the opportunity to invest in mid-sized French companies. Astorg Partners is one such firm that has succeeded by helping family businesses achieve some liquidity should they have trouble finding family successors when the founders are ready to retire. Is Astorg Partners' success in France a fluke or does it reveal important insights about European private equity investing?

First, let's explore how France treats citizens who aspire to start new companies. Even though the word entrepreneur is of French origin, France's culture seems to expel entrepreneurs—or more precisely they migrate to Silicon Valley. How many French entrepreneurs have migrated there? According to French trade groups, there are between 400 and 500 French companies operating in Silicon Valley including the following:

Talend—a data integration company founded in France in 2006 that now has offices in Los Altos, CA (and the UK, Germany, Belgium) and serves clients such as Yahoo!, Virgin Mobile, Honda, Sony, and the United Nations;

VirtualLogix—a French virtualization software start-up based in Silicon Valley, which got financing from Cisco Systems, Intel, and Motorola; and

Qualys—another privately held company offering network security software as a service eBay, Cisco, and Hewlett Packard; it was started by a French entrepreneur and is now based in Redwood Shores, CA.[73]

France's culture deters entrepreneurs. It places emphasis on attending the most prestigious schools and employing these graduates in the biggest companies and government organizations. Moreover, France punishes failure in a way that would make it way too risky to start a company and expose its founders to the normal challenges that a small company must overcome.

According to Isabelle Lescent-Giles, an associate professor of international business at San Jose State University, "Overall France has been much more friendly to big firms than it has been to start-ups. Launching a start-up in France is like playing Russian roulette in some ways. Failure is not tolerated in French business culture as it is in the United States and both the legal and social consequences of bankruptcy are much direr in France. The government dominates the economy, and the business elite is almost exclusively recruited from the elite schools, the Grandes écoles."[74]

This culture has convinced some of France's best known native entrepreneurs to flee into the arms of Silicon Valley. Two of the best known in the United States are Eric Benhamou, a serial entrepreneur who founded 3Com and was formerly CEO of Palm, and Jean-Louis Gassée, a one-time president of computer products at Apple and the founder of Be Inc., the creator of the Be operating system.[75]

It's France's loss that these entrepreneurs leave the country. That's because France traditionally produces engineers who excel in mathematics and graphics, two academic disciplines that matter to two very popular technology areas at the moment—gaming and algorithm-driven programming that Google and other search engines use. And thanks to the years of French entrepreneurs coming to Silicon Valley, the pioneers have the capital to invest in more recent French start-ups. One beneficiary is Talend that, in January 2009, secured $12 million in its third round of investment during a time when the economy was in dire straits. A leading investor was Balderton Capital, one of whose general partners is Frenchman Bernard Liautaud, who joined Talend's board.[76]

Although France appears quite hostile to entrepreneurs, it displays a similarly prickly hide to PE investors. However, at least one PE investor views that crusty exterior as a useful barrier to competitors. As we discussed above, Astorg Partners has found a way to profit from the barriers that France puts in the way of PE investors. According to Thierry Timsit, its managing partner and cofounder, France is often depicted as one of the most difficult European markets to address for foreigners. "We don't speak English. We hate capitalism and globalization. We love smelly cheeses and our president [is married to] a top Italian model. This is not easy to address for Anglo-Saxon investors."[77]

Astorg sees opportunity helping the founders of family businesses to cash out when their children are not interested or not able to succeed them. According to Timsit, France has a large number of family businesses spawned by post–World War II entrepreneurs who have trouble with succession plans and would like to find a way to liquidate at least some of their equity; 50% of Astorg's business is with family-owned firms, with owners reinvesting between 25% and 49% of the firm's value.[78]

But helping founders cash out is not the only area where PE investors can make money in France. Despite some difficulties, Astorg has also profited from investing in the market for spin-offs from large corporations that were created by the government from the 1950s through the 1990s and that are now being turned over to private investment. According to Timsit, "That has created bread and butter for private equity players stripping out these large corporates." He pointed out that it is more difficult to take public companies private in France than in the United States because of tax rules and other regulations. For example, to deduct interest on loans, private equity sponsors must control 95% of the target firm. In addition, conditional offers are not permitted.[79]

Other difficulties face PE investors placing capital in France. For example, worker benefits are much higher. According to Timsit, French companies must offer rich benefits and protections to labor, but at least those costs are clear to acquirers before the deal closes—which enables PE investors to factor these costs into their pricing. As Timsit said, "When you know that in advance, it's not going to get any worse. The only way it will move is to get better."[80]

Astorg has come to accept that it will face competition for deals. However, he seeks out complex transactions whose very complexity will tend to repel other PE firms. If it can focus on these more proprietary deals, then it is in a better position to control the negotiating process and end up with a more attractive price and structure. As Timsit said, "First of all, no deal is proprietary. I mean the only proprietary deal is the vendor. Anyone can claim they own the deal, but the real owner is the owner of the company."[81]

Astorg shuns such shopped deals and focuses on those with complications that he hopes will repel other PE firms. According to Timsit, Astorg concentrates on "complex situations where we have conflicting shareholders or regulatory hurdles which are very French-specific, or virtually no free cash flow or very poor bankability of the deal. In these situations, you sometimes find a proprietary deal or deals where the owner is ready to talk to you without an investment bank." Even with proprietary deals, he said, "the owner is going to talk to someone else to see whether he's getting a fair price. In that case, he normally continues with you if you've been fair."[82]

The response to France's EE of Astorg and France's entrepreneurs suggests two important lessons for capital providers:

Dig beneath the surface of a country's EE. PE investors are better off if they can limit competition for deals. In France, the apparent hostility to foreign capital and entrepreneurship seems to be somewhat of a deterrent to potential entrants. But PE investors willing to dig beneath the surface can find profitable niches—as Astorg did among company founders trying to get liquidity in retirement and large companies spinning off divisions. Ultimately, the only way for a PE firm to keep finding such niches is to embrace complexity where peers will not.

Adapt to a country's EE, don't wait for it to change. A corollary for digging beneath the surface is that capital providers must accept the reality of a country's EE. For example, France's entrepreneurs bolt for Silicon Valley because the career-killing costs of a failed start-up deter not only company founders but also venture capital investors. Capital providers should not wait for a country to alter its EE for their benefit. Instead they should place capital in countries that value the benefits they can provide.

Implications for Capital Providers

What should capital providers do to profit from the lessons of these cases? They should use a formal methodology to manage the investment lifecycle—the process that begins with deciding to invest and ends with harvesting the fruits of that investment. An awareness of the differences between the EE from which capital originates and the EE in which the capital is invested forms the basis for the methodology that follows. Simply put, this methodology is intended to break capital providers out of a possible comfort zone that might lure them into thinking that the EE they know (the one in which they gather capital) is the same as the one in which they aspire to invest and profit.

What follows is a six-step methodology we believe will help capital providers to sniff out the best opportunities while sidestepping the pitfalls of global private capital investing. We illustrate each step in the methodology with examples from an Indian PE firm that has followed many of these steps.

1. *Assess the opportunities and risks in the country's EE*

Capital providers seeking to invest outside their countries of origin must develop a clear rationale for their choice. Should they invest in China, India, Russia, France, or some other country? What factors should they consider in that decision? As we suggested in chapter 3—and as illustrated in figure 7.1—capital providers can compare each country on the basis of the drivers of its EE's capital receptiveness.

The factors in this model can provide the foundation for enabling capital providers to construct a capital receptivity index (CRI).[83] But one of the most useful insights revealed by our case studies is that no country's EE scores a perfect 100% on the CRI—in order to profit, capital providers must decide

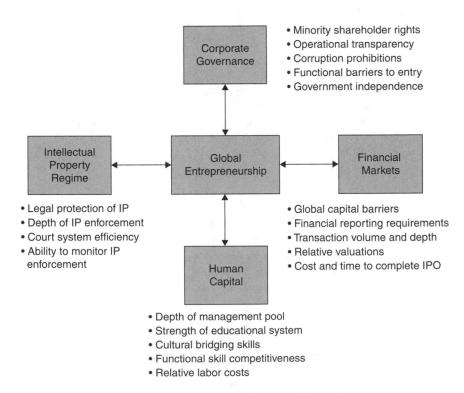

Figure 7.1   Drivers of Entrepreneurial Ecosystem Capital Receptiveness

whether the strengths of a country's EE make it worth devising a strategy to work around its weaknesses. Earlier in this chapter we saw examples of how capital providers at IDG Ventures and Astorg did this in Vietnam and France, respectively.

Now let's examine how Motilal Oswal Venture Capital Advisors Private Limited (MOVCAPL), a subsidiary of Mumbai-based Motilal Oswal Financial Services, thought about why investing in India made sense. In 2007, MOVCAPL raised $42 million of a proposed $100 million to invest in promising Small and Medium Sized Enterprises (SMEs) in India.[84]

MOVCAPL was clearly familiar with the strengths and weaknesses of India's EE since it had operated there for years. However, according to its CEO, Vishal Tulsyan, there were specific factors that encouraged MOVCAPL to focus on Indian SMEs. As Tulsyan explained, "We strongly believe that, in an economy that has grown at an average of more than 7.5% for the last four years, the biggest beneficiaries have to be small to midsize enterprises. If the economy were to grow at that rate going forward, these SMEs would continue to be its nerve centers."[85]

In his view, the growth of SMEs flowed from the way India approaches what we think of as human capital. According to Tulsyan, "[India] has always had a strong culture of entrepreneurship cutting across all regions. It's just that capital was a bottleneck, but now capital is easily available to many corporations."[86]

Clearly MOVCAPL saw that India's EE offered significant human capital benefits in lights of MOVCAPL's knowledge of the country based on its experience. MOVCAPL lacked sufficient capital to raise its $100 million fund without partnering with Stone & Youngberg (S&Y) of San Francisco—suggesting a possible limitation in India's financial markets. MOVCAPL concluded it could not raise sufficient capital on its own; however, it clearly believed that its insights into India's EE would enable it to persuade S&Y clients to provide the balance of the capital and to generate high returns for these investors.[87]

Why did S&Y decide to invest in India and why did it pick MOVCAPL? S&Y had spent years considering investing a portion of its investors' money in PE and had already put some capital into China, so it considered India as a good possibility due to its economic growth and its ambitious and more highly paid work force. According to an investment banker familiar with S&Y's thinking, "By 2003/2004 we decided to start PE funds in China and India. But being a PE investor from a long distance was not adding value. We needed to understand how commercial markets think. We already had China exposure and my parents knew people at Motilal Oswal Venture Capital Advisors Private Limited (MOVCAPL) so we started talking with them in 2005 and signed a contract in 2007."[88]

S&Y needed to focus on specific segments of the Indian market. According to the investment banker, "We started to think about where we could add value. Our conclusion was in a private Small or Medium Sized Enterprise (SME) with five to 10 years of operating history, seeking growth domestically [only in India], and not in the technology sector."[89]

S&Y had clear reasons for believing that it could succeed in this segment. As the investment banker said, "We focused here because we saw that the growth in India was coming 50% from people under the age of 25. And their annual income was growing from between $800 to $900 to between $5,000 and $10,000. Therefore we believe that local consumption will grow. Debt markets are not easy to access and money lenders only lend to those at the bottom or the very top—such as TATA."[90]

But this is not to say that everything in India is perfect for PE. In fact, S&Y perceives significant risks there. According to the investment banker, "The risk in India is fraud. But we invest in companies that are small enough and we have board seats, accountants and lawyers; and a quarterly review process. There is also the risk that the company we invest in won't grow so we have to pick the right sector. And there's the exit risk—'when will we be able to exit and how much will we get?' Finally, there's a technical risk—'what will the exchange rate be between rupees and the dollar?'"[91]

S&Y also sees PE competition in India from large U.S.-based PE players; however, it does not believe that this competition has sufficient knowledge of local conditions to be effective. The investment banker argues, "Equity is a natural outgrowth and is sold to a founder. There are two to three PE funds catering to India. India has become hot. Large PE funds like Carlyle and Blackstone are raising massive funds with capital from the U.S. and going after the market without knowing what they are doing—their funds are between $400 million and $600 million or more."[92]

2. *Identify the industries in those countries most likely to benefit from foreign capital*

Having decided on the country in which to invest, capital providers must focus their attention on industries likely to offer them the highest returns with the least amount of risk. To draw conclusions about the most appropriate industries, capital providers should conduct industry analysis—focusing on the size, growth rate, and profitability for the average participant of a variety of industries in the country. Moreover, capital providers should think about how the determinants of industry profitability are likely to evolve in the future. Finally, capital providers should assess whether they have specific capabilities—such as a network of potential customers, suppliers, or management talent—that might enable them to compete effectively in the most attractive industries.

Not surprisingly S&Y saw itself as taking a better approach to India than Carlyle Group. As the investment banker suggested, "We are doing things differently. We are looking to invest in SMEs with revenues in the range of $5 million to $15 million who can double or triple sales to between $50 million and $60 million and we are looking to buy these companies in a price range between $5 million and $9 million. More than between 10 and 12 companies will be more than I can control with a fund between $100 million and $150 million."[93]

S&Y tried to create an investment opportunity for its limited partners that would satisfy their specific PE investment criteria. As the investment banker explained, "Large pension funds have a limited amount of resources that they can invest in PE—perhaps $50 million to $100 million at a time. They don't have time to monitor. Their PE investments are checking a box [they are making their minimum required allocation to PE]."[94]

Bearing in mind the objectives of its limited partners, S&Y embarked on fund raising. According to the investment banker, "We raised money in India, the Middle East, and Europe. And we launched in April 2007 and have invested about 50% in 8 to 10 companies. It will be another year to completely invest the rest of the money and another five to seven years to exit. As we see it, the exit options are equity IPO, a private buyback of shares, or other funds that take it over."[95]

S&Y believed that MOVCAPL would be the right partner to help achieve these goals. As the investment banker noted, "With MOVCAPL we get deal flow, managers, and local knowledge. Philosophically, we like them—there is no arrogance; they are research oriented. They ask 'Does this sector make sense?' They have access to managers and experts in the field. For example, they have chemical engineers and petroleum engineers who have been useful for getting advice on our 'Indian Rubbermaid' investment."[96]

How did MOVCAPL help S&Y carry out its goals? It used some of the analytical techniques mentioned above to conclude that the most attractive Indian industries to invest in might be vehicle manufacturing and parts supply and consumer retailing. As Tulsyan explained, "Let's take an example. If the four-wheeler industry expects to grow at 15% annually, some [suppliers] serving Maruti [India's biggest car maker] would grow at probably 30%." And as MOVCAPL director, Anantkumar Kulkarni, amplified, "The second scenario is the rising purchasing power of many Indians and the opportunities thrown up by the changing demographics. A case in point is the retail boom triggered by increased consumerism."[97]

MOVCAPL further elaborated on the industries in which it would invest and the specific kinds of investments it hoped to make in them. According to Tulsyan, "We will make 15 to 20 investments, averaging $5 million to $6 million each. We'll wait three to five years for each company to attain a particular size and then take them to the IPO market."[98]

He further elaborated on the attractions of specific Indian industries in which he hoped to invest and the forces driving their attractiveness. As Tulsyan said, "Broadly, one can see growth from two aspects. One is businesses that leverage India's key competitive strengths—its highly skilled English-speaking manpower and the opportunities for cost arbitrage. In the first phase of [economic] liberalization, we saw more of outsourcing low-end jobs. Now that Indians have established their track record, Western companies are more comfortable outsourcing high-end work."[99]

This broad trend led MOVCAPL to identify engineering services as an industry of interest. According to Tulsyan, "One of the companies we are talking to provides high-level engineering design services. In a tie-up with a fairly good-sized U.S. company, it has designed an unmanned kiosk for immigration [checkpoints]."[100]

And Kulkarni pointed out another group of industries that would likely attract MOVCAPL's investment. He explained: "The second part [of our strategy] is to build upon the appeal of India itself. Today everyone wants to have a share of Indian consumer spending. With India's rising income levels and demographics—60% of its population is below the age of 30—a lot of opportunities are thrown up. These could be leisure and lifestyle, media and entertainment, or retail and infrastructure."[101]

3. *Build deal source network within those industries*

Having chosen which country and industries in which to invest, capital providers need good deal flow. Such deal flow will consist of a series of candidate companies—ideally whose managers are skilled enough to take their capital and use it to enhance the value of the company. If a capital provider is investing in a country its peers have already discovered, it will be essential for each capital provider to attempt to generate deal flow that is somewhat proprietary.

To create such deal flow, capital providers must build a network that can provide candidate companies for their review, and ideally such candidates will fit with each capital provider's source of expertise. Some capital providers may already have a network of contacts within the target country/industry and others may need to forge partnerships in order to jump start such a network.

As we saw in the cases we explored above, it is difficult to sustain a proprietary deal network for any period of time. That's because companies seeking to raise capital recognize that they are likely to obtain better terms if they can create a bidding war among capital providers. Therefore, capital providers seeking to avoid such bidding wars must create countervailing capabilities—such as a deeper level of industry expertise and contacts—that raise the costs to a company of shopping a deal to other capital providers well above the benefits of such shopping.

MOVCAPL devised such a strategy for obtaining proprietary deal flow—first, it believed that its PE peers were seeking larger transactions than those on which MOVCAPL focused. According to Tulsyan, "The sector we are targeting—SMEs—was the target for many private equity funds of Indian origin between 2001 and 2005. Most of these funds seem to have raised large amounts of capital over the past two years, and many of them are managing anywhere between half a billion dollars and $2 billion. They are no longer interested in, say, a $6 million transaction. That puts us in a unique position."[102]

Tulsyan also believes that the distribution network of MOVCAPL's parent gives it proprietary deal flow. As he explained, "To be successful in India, it is very important to have a deep penetration into the market. We [through parent company Motilal Oswal] have a thousand outlets all over India. We service more than 200,000 retail customers, many of whom are high net worth individuals and owners of SMEs. Our own distribution network will be an excellent base for sourcing investment opportunities."[103]

MOVCAPL's deal flow network is based on the respect in which its name is held in India. As Tulsyan explained, "Our name is one of the most respected in the equities market in India. Many of the franchisees in our vast distribution network are boutique accounting and advisory firms that service a lot of the small to midsize firms in their respective regions. That is one of our sourcing pools."[104]

Yet Tulsyan was keenly aware of competition and seemed to hope that MOVCAPL's deal flow would be so voluminous that there would be enough to satisfy its competitors without impinging on MOVCAPL's. According to Tulsyan, "I am not saying that all the transactions will come to us and that the Kotaks and Reliances—[Kotak Mahindra Financial and Reliance Capital are active private equity investors]—will not be able to get them. But the opportunities are so many that there is probably a place for everyone. And I don't know how keen a Reliance or Kotak will be on the space we are targeting."[105]

4. *Based on your firm's strengths, find the best companies within those industries in which to invest*

How should capital providers choose among the various investment possibilities that their deal flow network generates? They need investment ranking criteria. Such criteria are likely to include specific factors that are correlated with investment success. The case studies we explored suggest that success flows from investing in a company that passes the following tests:

- It's growing and generating cash;
- It targets a large and growing base of customers;
- It can benefit from the capital provider's strengths;
- Its CEO is skilled at identifying new opportunities and exploiting them well; and
- It's willing to adapt its corporate governance practices to suit the requirements of the country in which the capital provider hopes to exit.

By May 2007, MOVCAPL had made a single investment that appeared to satisfy many of these criteria. While Kulkarni was not willing to name the company, he did make it clear that it had a significant market share in a growing market segment and was generating significant cash flow. Specifically, he described the investment as a company in "the polymer-based bulk-packaging business. It makes 100- to 200-liter drums that are used to store specialty chemicals or other liquids that could be very reactive if they were stored in metal containers. It is a licensee of a $1.3 billion German company with patented packaging-products technology. The company we have invested in has a market share of more than 75% in India, revenues of about $100 million and after-tax profits of $10 million. It has diversified into businesses related to polymers and plastics."[106]

Moreover, its investment criteria reveal the importance to MOVCAPL of the industry, the company's strategy, and its management team. Why did Kulkarni pick the company? As he said, "Three things. The business itself. It is near monopolistic. It is a high technology-based business started by first-generation entrepreneurs. That fits with our investment philosophy. And the management has very high integrity and execution capability. We have known these managers over the past 10 years since they started this business."[107]

5. *Work with the entrepreneur to set goals and obtain the capital and other capabilities needed to achieve the goals*

Once a capital provider has picked a company in which to invest, how does it structure its investment and manage its relationship with the company in order to realize an attractive return? First, unless it is a majority investor—a position that is frequently difficult to take—it must work well with the other investors with larger stakes in the company. Nevertheless, it is important for the capital provider to obtain a board seat and to work well with other directors and top management. Second, the capital providers must structure their investments so they are linked to the company's achievement of specific milestones that will raise the value of the company. And finally, capital providers must have the power to work with company executives to monitor their progress in achieving these milestones—and to take necessary action if the executives are not meeting objectives. Ultimately, it is clear that a big part of making an investment pay off is betting on an entrepreneur with whom the capital provider is comfortable.

How do companies accomplish this in practice? In the case of MOVCAPL, a big part of the ability to manage the company comes from linking capital to meeting key milestones along the road to building the value of the company. According to Kulkarni, "We will do thorough due diligence. We will structure each investment in such a way that the valuation is linked to milestones to be met by the company in terms of revenue, profits and other things. In addition to that, we would like to play an active role at the strategic level by getting onto the board and also having a very well defined shareholders' agreement that gives us specific rights to protect our investment."[108]

And S&Y brings some ideas to the table about how to work with portfolio companies. For example, it focuses on helping with corporate governance and product development. According to the investment banker, "One thing we bring the companies we invest in is corporate governance. They are usually family companies with three to four brothers and their father. As you start accessing public capital markets, you have to formalize corporate governance. This means structuring the board in a certain way, separating the roles of Chairman and CEO, creating an audit committee."[109]

While upgrading corporate governance is always important, S&Y also brings value to portfolio companies depending on each company's specific needs. For companies that depend on product innovation for growth, S&Y offers management ideas that make product development more effective. As the investment banker explained, "And as far as product development, we often find that there is a bright pool of ideas in R&D that are never drawn out—[they are never turned into revenue-generating products]. To cure that problem we put the CTO and CIO in a role on the management committee."[110]

S&Y also helps portfolio companies form global partnerships. As the investment banker said, "We help form global partnerships to expand a company. For example, our 'Rubbermaid of India' investment partnered with a European firm that developed a protocol for using a chemical that could make a low weight battery. And we partnered with a Swedish firm to get advice on how to run a dairy farm. We were able to get graduate students from a non-profit who were willing to work with local villagers to implement some improvements."[111]

S&Y believes that portfolio companies are better off with the structure it provides them as they seek to capitalize on growth opportunities. The investment banker suggested, "We do set targets for sales and/or introduction of new products with our companies and review the results quarterly. If the company misses the target, we try to understand why and to get a plan for fixing the problems. And every year our CEOs join us for a formal review with our investors."[112]

Interestingly, S&Y has found that its portfolio companies are open to accepting its input—possibly due to the international experience of the children whose parents have brought them home to manage the family business. According to the investment banker, "The companies are willing to accept Western-style corporate governance because the younger generation is very international. It has been exposed to both Indian business culture during childhood and to Western business—often after being sent away to school in the U.S. or Europe and working in senior jobs for big companies. When the younger generation returns to run the family business it understands how global capital markets work and knows the benefit of getting equity investment. So the parents are willing to accept the change—although it is a gradual process."[113]

Moreover, the nature of shareholder agreements reveals some important insights about how a country's EE shapes how capital providers can exert influence over the companies in which they invest. MOVCAPL strives to negotiate shareholder agreements that give it the chance to decide who gets to exit and when, to have consent over a change in business strategy, and to review budgets before the company finalizes them. According to Kulkarni, a shareholder agreement could "include clauses such as who gets the first opportunity to exit if, at any point, the company's promoters want to divest their equity for non-business purposes. [The companies] will also not be able to unduly expand or diversify without our consent. Other minor aspects are, they should take us into confidence when they finalize their budgets, their accounts and so forth."[114]

As minority shareholders, a capital provider's rights might be limited. MOVCAPL expected to be a minority shareholder and, therefore, it ran the risk of not controlling enough of the company to block a big change in strategy with which it disagreed. As Tulsyan explained, "Given the fact that we will have a shareholders' agreement backing the investments, whether we own 10% or 15% won't really make a difference in terms of voting rights."[115]

Moreover, if he did not like a company's business plans, such a stake might not be sufficient to block the plans. According to Kulkarni, "Under India's Companies Act, you need a minimum of 26% equity to block such proposals. But here, even if we do not own 26%, our contract will give us the right to do so." Tulsyan continued, "Such rights or covenants are available as long as the company remains private."[116]

6. *Pick the best means of exiting the investment*

If a capital provider has the skill and good fortune to invest in a company that meets or exceeds the milestones referred to above, which exit option yields the greatest benefits? There is no clear answer that works in all situations. If the company founder wishes to continue to lead the company after capital providers have liquidated their interests, then that desire could be an important factor in the choice of exit option. That's because a company founder who lacks the skills to manage a publicly traded firm might naturally resist the IPO—particularly if a corporate acquirer might be willing to guarantee the company founder a leading role after the deal closed.

However, if the company founder is willing to step aside, then the capital provider may seek the exit option that yields the highest after-tax return. How can a capital provider evaluate the exit options—which might include an IPO, a merger with a corporation, or a sale to another group of private equity or venture capital firms? As we saw above, the answer depends on several factors. Perhaps the ideal option would be for the capital provider to conduct an IPO in a market that will place high valuation on the shares in a country that permits the capital provider to sell with favorable tax treatment without collapsing the share price (due to lack of liquidity). Absent that, a stock swap with a corporate acquirer could generate a high return—only if the acquirer has a long track record of integrating acquisitions effectively—leading to a rising stock price.

MOVCAPL was clearly thinking about these considerations back in May 2007. For example, if by 2010 or 2012, equity markets would not support an IPO, Tulsyan was considering other options. As he said, "There will definitely be an opportunity for us to sell our investments to other private equity funds. There are a lot of funds eying the Indian market right now and looking for opportunities in the $25 million to $30 million range. We have seen some transactions where one private equity fund has sold off its investments to other funds. As the market matures, there will be more transactions. That is the first option."[117]

But MOCVAPL also had a second option shy of an IPO—a buyback by the original company promoters. Tulsyan explained: "Second, many of the shareholders' agreements will also have a clause for buyback by the promoters of the company. And there will always be consolidation plays. Say a company reaches a certain size. There would be other larger companies willing to buy it."[118]

Conclusion

Capital providers have a wide array of options for generating high returns as they survey the global markets. In order to increase the odds of generating high yields and minimizing the chances of getting wiped out, capital providers must conduct independent, fact-based research into a country's EE to identify opportunities and risks. Within the most attractive countries, capital providers must pick the industries most likely to prosper and build a deal flow network that will surface investment opportunities that best fit with their strengths. Capital providers should screen the deals rigorously—investing only in companies that enjoy a competitive advantage in an attractive market whose CEOs have entrepreneurial ability and a willingness to commit to and achieve value-creating milestones. Ultimately, capital providers must select an exit strategy that yields the highest returns for their investors and the best opportunities for the company founder.

Implications for Managers in Existing Industries

Should managers in existing industries do anything differently following the globalization of entrepreneurship? Perhaps not—if one defines entrepreneurship as the creation of new firms. But as we discussed earlier, we believe entrepreneurship is all about Schumpeterian creative destruction. As a result, managers of existing industries face difficult questions:

- Should they preserve the corporate strategies that got their companies to their current position?
- Do those strategies represent a core rigidity that makes their companies unable to adapt to change and thus vulnerable to up-start competitors?
- If so, do acquisitions represent a profitable means of reviving a moribund company's growth?

Chapter 8 addresses these questions by exploring seven case studies of managers in existing industries who have decided to make acquisitions—and in so doing these managers have flowed with the globalization of entrepreneurship. As we explore each of these cases, we examine specific lessons that we believe managers can use to help them as they consider whether to pursue global acquisitions. And we conclude with a methodology that we believe can help managers apply these lessons to their own businesses. In so doing, we'll explore the following answers to the questions we just mentioned.

In some cases, global acquisitions can represent a logical way to extend a firm's corporate strategy. Deals that make the most strategic sense target large, rapidly growing markets and assemble a set of capabilities that enables the combined company to take significant share in those growing markets. Such deals are likely to pay off for managers by reviving a stagnant company.

In other cases, acquisitions are a mistake because the availability of private equity and bank debt enables deals that would otherwise not make strategic sense. Deals that are driven primarily by the availability of capital to finance them, rather than a sound strategic logic, tend to fall apart rather quickly once the appetite for such financing switches off. Such failed deals should be a cautionary tale for managers in existing industries. Their key lesson is that managers must separate the investment and the financing decisions. If the availability of financing causes managers to seek investments that make little economic sense, the managers will later regret their inability to resist the deal.

In general, managers make their companies vulnerable if they do not remain keenly attuned to changes in their competitive environment. A manager's willingness to break out of the bubble separates her from those who would rather bask in the glory of their past successes than continue to push forward. The globalization of entrepreneurship represents a threat to companies that refuse to pay attention to how this force can upend their business. Yet for managers willing to tap its power, the globalization of entrepreneurship can revive a moribund company in a mature industry.

Existing Industry Managers Case Studies

To explore these themes, we present seven case studies that examine how existing industries grapple with the opportunities and challenges of using acquisitions to grow globally:

- *Mittal Acquires Sicartsa* illustrates the profits that flow to a skilled acquirer of undermanaged assets in a country with untapped profit potential;
- *Japan Tobacco Buys Gallaher* demonstrates how a global acquisition can provide a company in a declining industry with new life by opening access to a rapidly growing new market;
- *Tata/Corus* provides an example of how a rapidly growing leader in developing country can overtake a more staid peer in a relatively static market. While pride may have played a part in driving the initial bargain—cost cutting at the target took on an important role as demand slumped;
- *Lottomatica Buys Gtech* shows how a smaller Italian company took over a larger U.S.-based one to create a more vertically integrated competitor for global lottery market opportunities. But in a surprising twist, the management of the Italian company concluded that its U.S. executive team should stay to run the show;
- *Riverdeep Buys Houghton Mifflin* exemplifies the danger of too much money chasing after too few good deals. That's because private equity investors including Thomas Lee, Bain Capital, and Blackstone Group clubbed up to help Riverdeep, an Irish software company, close a successful bid for the staid, but money-losing Boston publisher, Houghton Mifflin. Riverdeep's auditor then resigned and Moody's downgraded its debt—leaving a messy situation for investors;
- *Sabic Acquires GE Plastics* illustrates the payoff to a Saudi petrochemical company of its $20 million in Washington lobbying expenses—granting it access to a leading U.S. plastics company that provided entrée into the more

lucrative market for consumer products without producing a peep of objection from the American public; and

- *Vodafone Acquires Hutchison Essar* looks at how a British firm navigated around foreign ownership limits to take a commanding stake in a leading Indian cell phone service provider—boosting its profits and accelerating its corporate growth.

Mittal Acquires Sicartsa

Global capital flows make it possible to revive a previously moribund industry if the CEO of an existing business has the right mindset. Combining the factors of an industry that has long been declining; a recent boost in demand from emerging markets for its product; and access to copious equity capital from Western markets, you may have a recipe for entrepreneurial action by a CEO in that industry.

That was the result when Mittal Steel's CEO decided to acquire Mexican steel mill Sicartsa in 1992. In that case, he used Mittal's superior corporate governance—specifically its highly sophisticated pre- and postacquisition process—to transform Mexico's struggling Sicartsa steel plant.

In 2004, Sicartsa had revenue of $956 million, but its sales were hindered by a 46-day strike that stalled production in 2005 and for four months in 2006—but Mittal was able to transform it into a rapidly growing and much more efficient operation that it ultimately bid to acquire for $1.4 billion in December 2006. Having listed its shares on the New York Stock Exchange (NYSE), Mittal enjoys access to massive pools of capital that it uses to finance such deals as part of its global acquisition strategy.[1]

How exactly would the merger create a more muscular steel industry competitor? The deal added to Mittal's steel making capacity. And at the time, Mittal was in the process of combining with Arcelor—yet it was still able to execute this capacity-adding transaction. Specifically, the combination would create Mexico's largest steel producer with an annual capacity of 6.7 million tons by combining Vinton, TX-based mini mill Border Steel Inc., and an integrated steel making plant, a mini mill and two rolling mills in Mexico.[2]

It appears that the rationale for Mittal was to give it entrée into the rapidly growing Mexican steel market and to capture cost savings. Arcelor Mittal CFO Aditya Mittal argued that "With the Mexican market expected to grow by up to 6 percent per year over the next 10 years; this is the ideal time to expand our presence in this country. We see significant potential for improving the profitability of Sicartsa." In addition to gaining access to Mexico's growth, Mittal anticipated to achieve $130 million in cost savings from the combination.[3]

And one unusual aspect of the Sicartsa merger was that it was taking place in the context of an even bigger merger—between Arcelor and Mittal. Specifically, in December 2006, when it announced the Sicartsa merger, Mittal Steel Co. NV was completing its $33.4 billion acquisition of Arcelor SA—a combination that was due to be completed in May 2007 creating a new company with about 10% of global steel production.[4]

Moreover, Mittal's Mexican acquisition spree was not limited to steel making capacity—it also entered into a distribution joint venture for the Mexican and Southwestern U.S. markets. Specifically, Arcelor Mittal also entered a 50–50 joint venture with Grupo Villacero to distribute and trade its long steel products in Mexico and the southwest of the United States.[5] Mittal's acquisition of Sicartsa reveals some important insights about how a CEO can tap global capital flows to reshape the business ecosystem:

- Mittal's NYSE listing gave it access to capital and the credibility of Wall Street advisors who could analyze its expansion plans and support its stock as a currency for consolidation;
- Mittal recognized that Mexican management techniques were inferior to its own. It could tap global capital markets to transfer its superior management skills to an undervalued asset; and
- Mittal believed that the Mexican market would grow relatively quickly and that it could cut costs to help it earn back the price premium it paid to get control of the Mexican production capacity.

Japan Tobacco Buys Gallaher

The limits to growth can be painful for a large existing company if it is in an industry that—due to the fatally addictive nature of its product—government after government around the world appears to be trying to destroy. But thanks to access to global capital markets and the differences in attitudes toward that toxic product between developed and emerging markets, a CEO of such a company can acquire rivals to boost growth—by tapping into growing demand in those emerging markets—while lowering its unit costs.

These were the forces at play when Japan Tobacco made its December 2006 bid to buy the UK's Gallaher for $14.7 billion. Japan Tobacco, the former state tobacco monopoly, which had $18.75 billion sales in 2005, was privatized in 1985, but the Japanese government still holds a 50% stake. In 1999, Japan Tobacco bought the non-U.S. rights to the Camel, Winston, and Salem brands from RJR Nabisco for $7.8 billion. Though Japan Tobacco has 66% of the Japanese cigarette market—Japanese are still heavy smokers, and its Mild Seven brand is most popular there—its domestic sales were slowing and it made most of its profit outside Japan.[6]

Why was Japan Tobacco interested in Gallaher? Although Gallaher marketed Benson & Hedges and Silk Cut cigarettes in Europe, Japan Tobacco was really paying up to gain access to its robust position in the growing market for Russian cigarettes. How big were the stakes for Japan Tobacco? At the time, it represented the largest acquisition in the tobacco industry, the third-largest M&A deal in Europe in 2006, and also the largest foreign takeover by a Japanese company, much larger than NTT DoCoMo's 2000 acquisition of AT&T Wireless for $9.8 billion.[7]

While there may have been fear in Europe of a resurgent Japan seeking to control the world, Japan Tobacco's goal was to gain access to Europe's largest tobacco market, Russia, which was growing, unlike the market in Western Europe, which was a declining one due to smoking bans and tobacco taxes. Why were these markets declining? The UK had long banned smoking in pubs, and the French stopped allowing smoking in cafes. This caused tobacco consumption in Western Europe to fall by about 2% a year between 1996 and 2006—a decline that pushed tobacco makers selling there to look elsewhere, including emerging economies in Eastern Europe, for growth.[8] These emerging markets were enormous, accounting for 75% of world volumes. Moreover, emerging markets consumers, who were accustomed to state-owned products, tended to switch to fashionable Western brands to confirm their new middle-class status.[9]

To tap into such opportunities, Gallaher acquired Russian cigarette maker Liggett-Ducat in 2000. As a result of Japan Tobacco's already strong position in Russia, the deal with Gallaher propelled Japan Tobacco into the top spot in Russia—surpassing Philip Morris's Russian market share and leaving Japan Tobacco with a 34% market share. Moreover, the Russian tobacco market was enormous compared to those in the more developed world—66% of Russian men were smokers—twice the ratio in the United States and United Kingdom—consuming a total of 370 billion cigarettes a year.[10]

But Japan Tobacco now could satisfy only about 19% of that demand—operating a plant at St. Petersburg with the capacity to make 70 billion cigarettes a year. And the acquisition added an additional 15% market share from Gallaher's LD brand, one of the biggest tobacco labels in Russia, and its Sovereign cigarettes, which were widely smoked in Ukraine and Kazakhstan. Moreover, Gallaher also owned tobacco business in Sweden and Austria, which Japan Tobacco believed would help it to enter the still smoking markets of Eastern Europe via the Western flank.[11]

With help from Merrill Lynch, in the form of a loan, Japan Tobacco hoped to complete the deal within months of the December 2006 announcement.[12] According to Japan Tobacco president and chief executive Hiroshi Kimura, "The integration of our business operations and our portfolios will position our international tobacco business for continued growth." By April 18, 2007, Japan Tobacco had successfully closed its $15 billion deal for Gallaher—thus realizing Kimura's ambition.[13]

Japan Tobacco's acquisition of Gallaher demonstrates how the market for global mergers enables a declining company to revive itself by applying the strengths it developed from competing in a mature market to new markets with more vigorous growth. Japan Tobacco's acquisition of Gallaher also reveals some helpful tests that CEOs in mature industries can apply as they consider acquisition candidates:

Does the target have a strong position in attractive market segments? Gallaher clearly passed this test—insofar as it had a strong position in the large and rapidly growing market for Russian cigarettes.

Does the target benefit from the acquirer's capabilities? Gallaher clearly benefited in Russia from combining with Japan Tobacco's presence—the combination led to a company with a dominant 34% share of the market.

Does the purchase price capitalize future profits? This question is difficult to answer in the case of the $15 billion acquisition of Gallaher—however, the price paid was consistent with those paid for similar companies at the time. Although it is difficult to answer this last test definitively before a deal has been completed, Japan Tobacco clearly perceived significant growth from a dominant share of Russia's tobacco market as being worth the price it paid to attain that dominance.

Tata/Corus

Existing businesses in countries on the rise may have the competitive edge when it comes to reviving peers in more staid countries. When those advancing businesses enjoy higher stock market valuations due to their more rapid growth, they can use the more highly valued currency to acquire at a lower price the stock of more moribund peers. However, if such moves are made out of national pride—rather than a quest for efficiency—they may ultimately prove costly to the acquirers.

It appeared that this might be the way Tata Steel's $12 billion acquisition of Anglo-Dutch steelmaker Corus—a 47,000-worker company with plants in Belgium, Britain, France, Germany, and the Netherlands which was created in 1999 through the combination of Royal Hoogovens of the Netherlands and British Steel—might turn out.[14] After the deal closed in January 2007, Tata was determined to avoid labor and political troubles by keeping Corus's workers in place. However, a 48% plunge in profits in 2008 led Tata to reconsider the wisdom of its hands-off policy.[15] As Tata faced the profit implications of a slowdown in global demand, its skills at cost reduction would be tested as it sought to fulfill the initial promise of the Corus acquisition.

Before delving into the details of the Tata/Corus merger, it is worth taking some time to explore the evolution of Tata Steel's parent company—Tata Group. The reason for exploring this evolution is that Tata Group—with its broad array of business interests—represents the growing industrial muscularity of Indian industry. Moreover, the Corus acquisition was a signal event in tipping Tata from a group that stayed within India to one that set its sites onto a broader, global stage.

Tata Group is among India's oldest and most widely diversified industrial conglomerates. It exports software via Tata Consultancy Services; makes steel through Tata Steel; runs hotels via its Indian Hotels Co.; and makes mini cars— such as its three-meter-long, four-seater Nano with a top speed of 65 miles per hour and a price of about $2,500—through Tata Motors. And by March 2008, Tata had announced a deal to acquire Ford Motor Co.'s luxury Jaguar and Land Rover brands for $2.3 billion.[16]

The deal represented another in a string of global acquisitions—intended to take Tata beyond its Indian strategy. According to Ajit Surana, managing director at brokerage Dimensional Securities in Mumbai, "They [the Tatas] have become far more outgoing and aggressive in their approach. Ten years ago, they were seen as a staid, conservative group. That perception has changed completely... If there is a (merger-and-acquisition) deal out there, and if it makes sense, they'll go for it, even pay a premium."[17]

The result? Tata Group controlled almost 100 companies with $28.8 billion in 2008 in 27 listed companies with a market value exceeding $65 billion. Some of Tata Group's global acquisitions have been bigger than Tata in terms of revenue. For example, Tata Tea acquired UK beverage company Tetley in 2000 for $540 million. And as we'll explore below, Tata Steel's $11.3 billion takeover of Anglo-Dutch steelmaker Corus Group in 2007 was also a shocker for investors.

The Tetley acquisition was the largest-ever cross-border takeover by any Indian company in 2000, while the Corus buy was the largest-ever overseas acquisition by an Indian company as of March 2008.[18]

Not all of Tata's global deals were big. Since 2002, Tata completed other smaller global acquisitions such as Tata Steel's 2004 purchase of Singaporean firm Natsteel for $486 million; Videsh Sanchar Nigam Limited's 2005 acquisition of U.S. firm Teleglobe, a provider of voice, data, and mobile signalling services, for $239 million; Tata Tea's 2006 buy of a $677 million stake in the U.S. water manufacturer Glacea; and Tata Coffee's 2006 deal to buy United States's Eight O'Clock Coffee for $220 million.[19]

Tata shocked the investment world with the boldness of its Corus deal because it boosted Tata Steel's global market rank and because it stirred up pride among Indians. Since Corus was several times bigger than Tata Steel, the acquisition boosted its market position from the fifty-sixth to sixth in the world steel making ranks. As Rahul Bajaj, chairman of India's second-largest motorcycle and scooter maker, Bajaj Auto (BJJAF), said, "Their acquisition of Corus made every Indian proud and that, in my view, is a very significant milestone in the march of the Indian industry from a closed economy." By "closed economy," Bajaj was referring to the Indian economy prior to 1991, when India ended state controls over industry and opened the doors to foreign direct investment.[20]

Was there a danger that Tata's global acquisitions were the triumph of management ambition coupled with access to capital over the interests of shareholder's in building long-term value? Given the large amount of debt that Tata undertook to finance its acquisitions, its global acquisition strategy increased Tata Group's short-term financial risk and placed significant short-term management hurdles in the path of its executives—such as integrating operations in different countries and cultures and managing the high amounts of debt Tata Group firms typically raise to fund these deals.[21]

At least one observer found these short-term risks somewhat daunting. According to I.V. Subramaniam, chief investment officer at Quantum Advisors in Mumbai, "As long as the group's acquisitions are made at a reasonable price and there are new markets which get added, I think it is a positive sign. My worry is less on the financial part and more on the people-management aspect."[22]

Tata and Corus clearly did not share Subramaniam's doubts when they announced the merger in December 2006. For example, Ratan N. Tata, Chairman, Tata Sons, was thrilled with the deal that in his view was consistent with Tata's strategy of growth through international expansion. As Tata proclaimed, "It is a very exciting moment for both companies because the deal pulls together two companies which have a similar global vision." Moreover, he stressed that Corus would retain its identity in the "foreseeable future" and remain an Anglo-Dutch company with the existing management structure. Tata defended the deal being "not an opportunistic, agenda-driven" one but that built on a shared vision of a "global strategy."[23]

Furthermore Tata did not perceive any integration risk from the merger. As he said, "Corus and Tata Steel are companies with long, proud histories. We have compatible cultures of commitment to stakeholders and complementary strengths in technology, efficiency, product mix and geographical spread. Together we will be even better equipped to remain at the leading edge of the fast changing steel industry."[24] He also emphasized that Tata Steel wouldn't impose its leadership on Corus. "Our intention is that Corus will retain its identity for the foreseeable future, will remain an Anglo-Dutch company. The management will be substantially the same."[25]

Tata also tamped down fears that the takeover would mean loss of jobs at Corus. According to B. Muthuraman, managing director of Tata Steel, the deal represented an uninterrupted century of Tata Steel's leadership in the steel industry—reflecting its commitment to remaining at the cutting edge of the new global market. Muthuraman sought to allay fears of job losses at Corus as a result of the takeover and planned cost cutting. He said the threat to jobs would have been greater had the deal not taken place. Although he did not exclude the possibility of future job cuts, Muthuraman noted that "The deal makes it more competitive and that means more job security."[26]

Corus former Chairman, Jim Leng, joined the happy chorus. Leng described Tata Steel, which it chose over companies from Brazil and Russia, as the "right partner at the right time and on the right terms. This creates a well-balanced company, strategically well-placed to compete in an increasingly competitive global environment." The deal, he explained, was prompted by his company's decision to seek access to low-cost production and high-growth markets.[27] And there was no doubt a huge production cost difference Tata produces steel at one of the lowest costs in the world—$160 a ton, far lower than $540 a ton cost, mainly attributable to its high raw material costs.[28]

In order to close that cost gap, Tata eventually needed to take steps to create a more efficient organization. To that end, it formed a new organization structure that went into effect in January 2008, which combined the corporate functions of Tata and Corus while leaving the latter to operate independently in its direct activities. This new structure took the form of what Tata called a "common strategy and integration committee" for all its operations, while Corus remained a separate corporate identity. The committee included top management of both companies—with Ratan Tata heading the committee as the Tata Sons chairman. It also comprised Corus' Leng and Philippe Varin and Tata Steel managing director Muthuraman.[29]

Efforts to achieve efficiencies on joint overhead activities took the form of a "group center" that would span the business operations across Tata Steel (which include Thailand and Singapore plants) and Corus. The overhead functions participating in the group center included technology and integration, finance, strategy, corporate relations and communications and global minerals, a raw materials purchasing activity. Moreover, Tata Steel and Corus operated executive committees chaired by Muthuraman and Varin. And a joint Tata/ Corus executive committee for Tata Steel Group would meet every quarter to review overall performance and would be cochaired by the Tata Steel managing director and the Corus CEO. While the Corus deal brought Tata Steel enough capacity to make 21.4 million tons of steel per year, these management commit- tees were charged with a bigger goal. Tata hoped to control more than twice that level of production—operating 50 million tons of annual steel making capacity by 2015.[30]

Unfortunately, for all its positive rhetoric, Tata was unable to keep the global recession that began in 2008 from putting some of its glossy promises to the test. A drop in steel demand led Tata to conclude that it would no longer be able to let Corus operate independently—instead it would merge Corus into Tata to cut costs by firing thousands of Corus workers. Although Tata clearly did not rel- ish contradicting itself, it had already taken steps to adapt to declining demand including cutting production by 30% and asking workers to take a 10% pay cut—a request to which the unions had not agreed.[31]

Tata's stated policy of going easy on labor unions had helped it close the Corus deal and the Jaguar-Land Rover one as well. One analyst suggested that Corus accepted Tata's bid in part because it had agreed with its labor unions not to engage in massive layoffs for a few years after the acquisition. This agreement made Ford's labor unions comfortable with Tata in the Jaguar-Land Rover deal. But the plunge in capacity utilization and steel prices put tremendous pressure on Tata to cut costs. And while it could count on the Netherlands government to cover lost wages if it laid off the Corus workers there, it could not obtain the same benefit from the UK—where most of Corus's steelworkers were employed. Thus Tata would likely be stuck with high wages in a declining market.[32]

Declining demand, high costs, and plunging steel prices combined to put continued pressure on Tata management. By May 2009, these pressures forced it to take even harsher measures as it struggled to come up with the cash flow it needed to meet repayment demands of the bankers from whom it had bor- rowed billions to pay for the Corus acquisition. At that point Tata Steel carried $9 billion, $4 billion of which it used to finance the Corus deal. Tata hoped to restructure its loan—extending the loan repayment period for three years to help Corus weather the economic slump. While Tata Steel's repayment schedule did not require it to pay back any of the loan in 2009, its subsequent cash calls rose steeply—to $795 million in 2009–2010 and $1.3 billion in 2010–2011.[33]

Not surprisingly, the debt service demands constrained Tata's expansion plans. According to a Mumbai-based analyst, "The Company may use part [of] its $1.9 billion reserves for the loan repayment, but that will adversely affect its expan- sion plans in India. The company requires $1.2 billion for its capital expenditure during this fiscal [year]." The analyst also pointed out that Corus had already cut 40% of its production after the demand slump, so cash flows from Europe also will be lower. As he said, "The restricted cash flow will affect Corus' plans to acquire iron ore and coking coal mines for raw material security."[34]

While Tata tried to take a variety of steps—including selling plants, closing service centers, and restructuring management—it remained unclear whether it was doing enough to satisfy the demands of its creditors. Here are four tactics it tried:

Divest steel plants. In May 2009, Tata was considering the fate of plants in Spain, France, and the Netherlands, which it could sell to raise capital. Unfortunately, the financial crisis made it difficult to close such sales—for instance, early that month an Italian buyer, Marcegaglia, backed out from a deal to buy Corus's Teesside plant in northern England, because the proposed $480 million deal would put too much of a financial strain on Marcegaglia.

Sell downstream businesses. Moreover, Corus had already decided to divest downstream businesses—arranging a deal for Briand Investments, an affiliate of UK-based investment group Klesch, to acquire Corus' aluminium smelters at Voerde in Germany and Delfzijl in the Netherlands.

Close steel service centers. Corus closed its three UK-based steel service centers. As part of restructuring its building systems division, it had closed units in South Wales and relocated the facilities to Shotton in northeast England.

Change management. The Tata Steel and Corus managements changed after Philippe Varin resigned as chief executive to head French car maker PSA Peugeot Citroen. Kirby Adams, former chief executive of BlueScope Steel in Australia, succeeded Varin.[35]

As of this writing, it appears that Tata Steel's acquisition of Corus could ultimately be judged a blunder—in which management overpaid to achieve ambitions that exceeded its grasp. Although unresolved, Tata Steel's acquisition of Corus raises some important questions about whether management ego can overwhelm sound business judgment when it comes to tapping global capital flows to energize a mature company. Such questions represent warning signs, which can keep managers from crossing the line that separates confidence from arrogance, and include the following:

Was Tata Steel too optimistic about future steel demand and prices? Tata management clearly made the Corus deal at a time when demand and prices were peaking. At the time, Tata concluded that the market would continue to boom and discounted evidence that there might be global financial problems that could send the industry into a tailspin. In retrospect, it appears as though it should have given more consideration to more pessimistic industry scenarios.

Was Tata Steel overly generous in its union agreements in order to win the bid? Tata management clearly recognized that its Indian plants had much lower steel production costs than Corus'. Nevertheless, Tata was so eager to win the Corus deal that it gave assurances to Corus' union workers that it would not conduct mass layoffs for years after the deal closed. It appears that Tata had concluded that such layoffs would not be needed and that the benefits of adding the new production capacity would more than offset the resulting higher steel production costs. This assumption proved invalid when demand plunged in 2008.

Was Tata Steel realistic about how much it could lower Corus's production costs? It appears that Tata may have been overly optimistic about how much it could lower Corus' production costs. Initially, its hands-off approach clearly kept Corus's costs at about the same level as they had been prior to the deal. But as demand declined through 2008 and 2009, Tata took increasingly aggressive steps to lower those costs. Unfortunately, as it shed production capacity, it lost some of the economies of scale that might have helped it get lower costs absent wage cuts.

Did Tata Steel take on more debt than it could afford to repay? As of this writing, it appeared that Tata's ability to repay its debt depended in part on bankers' willingness to extend its repayment schedule. But given weak economic prospects and the dire straits within which many banks found themselves, it appeared more likely that banks would look for a reason to demand immediate repayment of the entire loan rather than satisfying Tata's request for a delay in the repayment schedule.

Lottomatica Buys Gtech

Thanks to the alchemy of global capital markets, in 2006 a slightly smaller operator of the Italian lottery was able to acquire a larger U.S.-based maker of gaming technology. But in a very unusual move, the acquiring company was convinced that the management of the U.S. target was better suited to run the merged company. The acquiring firm reasoned that its investment would be better off with the target's management since it envisioned greater opportunity emerging from a team that had expanded into 50 countries and was considered a technological innovator. Thus the merged company would be in a position to bid for global lottery contracts in many countries besides Italy—and the combined company's capabilities in lottery technology and operations would present unrivalled value to potential customers.

The details of the deal were complex. In January 2006, $707 million in sales and 1,000 employee, Lottomatica, which operated the world's largest single lottery, in Italy, agreed to buy the larger ($1.26 billion in revenues and 5,300 workers) Gtech Holdings, the world's largest operator of computerized lotteries, with contracts in a majority of U.S. states and many foreign countries. The combined company was expected to operate in more than 50 countries, with revenues of $1.9 billion and more than 6,300 employees.[36] The $4.8 billion Lottomatica bid was backed by a private company, De Agostini S.p.A., which was the majority owner of Lottomatica. And the financing for the deal was particularly complex—coming from $0.48 billion of available cash, a $1.7 billion rights issue, and $0.9 billion of nonconvertible subordinated securities both expected in May 2006, and a $2.3 billion senior loan to be extended to a special purpose vehicle to merge into Gtech at the close of the transaction.[37]

Without the involvement of leading Wall Street banks to provide debt capital, this deal would not have been feasible. In this case Credit Suisse First Boston and Goldman Sachs have agreed to underwrite Lottomatica's rights issue and subordinated securities and committed to provide the senior loan financing. However, in order for Credit Suisse and Goldman Sachs to follow through on their commitments, Lottomatica needed to maintain a proforma investment grade credit rating. The subordinated securities, due 2066, were to be listed on a European stock exchange and offered to institutional investors.[38]

In an unusual move, Lottomatica management decided to step aside and let Gtech's team take over—while preserving Lottomatica's representation on the company's board. For example, Gtech's president and CEO, Bruce Turner, was expected to become CEO of Lottomatica, while maintaining his position at Gtech and joining Lottomatica's board. By contrast, Rosario Bifulco, then chairman and CEO of Lottomatica, was expected to give up his executive roles. Moreover, Jaymin Patel, Gtech's CFO, was expected to take on the CFO role at Lottomatica after the deal closed.[39]

In addition to the financing risks that made the deal possible, the two companies faced numerous regulatory bodies that needed to approve the deal. That's because each state lottery Gtech helped operate needed to approve the deal. As Tom Burnett, director of research at Wall Street Access, a New York–based brokerage firm, said, "This is not as clean as Gtech holders might have hoped for. It involves a number of risks. It could take some time." Burnett continued, "They [Lottomatica] get a very good cash price. But they're also getting it from somebody who makes the whole transaction kind of suspect because so many moving pieces are involved," referring to the financing and regulatory issues the deal faces.[40]

Nevertheless, a leading ratings agency appeared to bless the deal. Specifically, Standard & Poor's credit analyst Guy Deslondes saw the main benefits of the deal as deriving from "product and geographic diversification, technology synergies covering the gaming sector's entire value chain, as well as certain commercial advantages."[41] Despite this optimism, S&P put Lottomatica's BBB/A-2 rating on credit watch with negative implications, saying it expected to lower the company's rating to BBB-/A-3 once the deal closed.[42]

Despite these risks, there were some obvious benefits to the deal—mostly resulting from the combination of the two firms' strengths that gave the new company access to new revenue opportunities. According to Turner, "Lottomatica is a lottery operating company, while Gtech is a lottery technology and services company. So it's a vertical integration."[43]

And at least one analyst agreed with Turner. ABN Amro analyst Michael Pacitti said, "Strategically it makes a great deal of sense." By "strategically," Pacitti meant that the deal combines Lottomatica's skills in running lottery, gaming, and other services via its network, with Gtech's strong technology and extensive lottery concessions. Moreover, Pacitti anticipated that the combined operation would be able to bid for the UK's lottery since Gtech was the technology supplier to the operator of that lottery, known as Camelot. In addition, the combined company would be able to sell to the growing market for video lottery games, which are located in bars and other outlets, but run from a central database. According to Pacitti, "That is a growth market, mainly in Europe."[44]

As of the first quarter of 2009, it appeared that Lottomatica's gamble on Gtech had paid off. Its revenues for the quarter rose 20% over the same quarter in 2008 and its net income rocketed up 69%.[45] The success of this deal suggests important lessons for managers in existing businesses seeking to tap global capital markets to revive a slow-growing business:

Analyze potential markets to identify the most attractive growth opportunities. Lottomatica was relatively objective in its evaluation of the potential markets that it could tap outside of Italy since the combination would take advantage of Gtech's far broader geographic scope. While Lottomatica did identify many growth opportunities, it was wise not to stop its analysis with a consideration of these markets' size and growth.

Determine the skills needed to gain a meaningful share of these attractive segments. Lottomatica clearly realized that it lacked the technological skills and geographic access that would enable it to win new business opportunities—such as managing the UK's lottery. However, both parties recognized that their combined skills in technology and lottery management services would create a formidable global competitor.

Keep in place the people who can manage those capabilities to win new business. Lottomatica shrewdly recognized that it could not simply take over Gtech and fire its executives without losing the skills it would need to make the deal pay off. So it kept on key people in Gtech's management team. However, by the end of 2007, Gtech's CEO, Bruce Turner, departed and the CEO of Gtech replaced Turner.[46] Despite Turner's departure, it appears that his predeal CFO was a worthy successor. Moreover, Lottomatica's postdeal financial results suggest that its approach to global mergers is worth following.

Riverdeep Buys Houghton Mifflin

What happens when excess private equity and debt supply meet a dodgy Irish software company with ambitions to gain respectability in the United States by acquiring a money-losing educational book publisher with a storied heritage? In the $5 billion merger between Ireland's Rivergroup and Boston's Houghton Mifflin, financial troubles were the result. While the deal no doubt enriched the club of private equity investors who helped finance it, Rivergroup's auditor resigned when it refused to certify the financial statements that put rating agencies, such as Moody's, in a skeptical mindset toward the deal.

Before delving into these complications, let's examine the basic details of the transaction. HM Rivergroup, a holding company, acquired Riverdeep Holdings Limited, an Ireland-based producer of web- and CD-ROM-based education and personal productivity products targeting the consumer and school markets with 2005 sales of $141 million and pretax profit of $17 million, and Houghton Mifflin, a $1 billion (2006 sales) Boston-based educational publisher in a $5 billion deal.[47] Just as with Lottomatica and Gtech, the smaller company Riverdeep—with 300 workers—was acquiring the larger one, Houghton Mifflin, with 3,500 employees.[48]

And that $5 billion deal size reveals the important role that global capital flows played in making the merger possible. That's because the $3.4 billion purchase included $1.75 billion in cash plus the assumption of approximately $1.61 billion in net debt. In addition, as part of the transaction, certain Houghton Mifflin management and employees converted $40 million of their equity into equity of HM Rivergroup. And no doubt, private equity firms that owned Houghton Mifflin—Thomas H. Lee Partners, Bain Capital Partners, and the Blackstone Group—made an attractive return on their investment.[49]

But that was not all; even as a new holding company, HM Rivergroup was acquiring Houghton Mifflin; it also bought Riverdeep Holdings Limited, the educational and personal publishing products controlled by Barry O'Callaghan, executive chairman of HM Rivergroup and former Credit Suisse investment banker, in a stock swap valuing Riverdeep at $1.2 billion, including the assumption of net debt. The combination of Houghton Mifflin and Riverdeep was thought to create a sizeable company with reasonable cash flow—specifically, $1.425 billion in revenues and adjusted earnings before interest, taxes, depreciation, and amortization (EBITDA) of $392 million for the year ending September 30, 2006.[50]

Executives at both companies waxed enthusiastically about the benefits that would come from combining Riverdeep's technology with Houghton Mifflin's access to the U.S. educational market. As O'Callaghan put it, "We are excited about the future of HM Rivergroup and the ability to capitalize on the convergence of print and digital education platforms. The combined business will leverage Houghton Mifflin's brand names, established relationships and large sales force to provide customers with an unrivalled product offering."[51]

While it was difficult to decipher the strategic intent of the deal, it appears that the biggest part of it was to use Houghton Mifflin's much larger sales force to push Riverdeep's products into new accounts. Evidently, the move from print to electronic delivery was seen as an inexorable growth trend. As Collin Earnst, a Houghton Mifflin spokesman, said, "By putting these two companies together, we've created the competitive advantage beyond all standard competitors who are trying to grow these things organically, as was Houghton Mifflin before."[52]

Earnst seemed to believe that print was passe and the future was in electronic learning. In his view, "Where the market's heading is actually moving toward an electronic format, so that loop between instruction, assessment, and remediation is closing tightly around technology." The company's executives seemed to believe that having acquired the textbook assets of Houghton Mifflin, Riverdeep would be able to offer more integrated learning materials to schools. And since Mifflin's sales force was four times larger than Riverdeep's, the executives concluded that a combination with Houghton Mifflin would extend Riverdeep's reach.[53]

Finally, the deal would involve a series of complex debt refinancings with help from two leading investment banks—Credit Suisse and Citigroup Global Markets Limited. The new company would buy back all sorts of debt issues such as its 9.25% senior notes due 2011, 8.25% senior notes due 2011, and 9.875% senior subordinated notes due 2013—to name a few. This refinancing would put 50% of the new company in the hands of O'Callaghan and the management group, 15% under the control of former Riverdeep shareholders, and 35% to be owned by new shareholders.[54]

All the excitement around the deal could not fully mask two nagging problems—first Riverdeep's auditor resigned within months of the deal and then Moody's downgraded those bonds used to finance it. After raising $660 million in new equity for the deal that was completed on December 22, 2006, Riverdeep auditors, Ernst & Young, resigned the account a bit over a month later—on January 31, 2007.[55]

Why? Ernst & Young claimed that Riverdeep misrepresented some information that evidently resulted in a $1.5 million accounting restatement. In its resignation letter, Ernst & Young wrote, "as a result of incorrect representations made to us by the company's parent in respect of a material contract, the professional relationship between us and the company has irretrievably broken down, and we have concluded that we cannot continue to act as the company's auditors." O'Callaghan dismissed the importance of Ernst & Young's resignation saying the matter that led to his auditor's resignation resulted in only an "immaterial" adjustment to Riverdeep's accounts.[56]

But Warren Buffett's ratings agency, Moody's, used Ernst & Young's resignation to spark a possible credit rating downgrade, and given all the debt that Riverdeep took on as part of the deal, such a downgrade could raise its costs of funds. How? In February 2007, Moody's put Riverdeep's ratings under review for a possible downgrade "following the announcement that the auditors of its parent have resigned." Moody's also indicated that the review would only conclude "on receipt of audited financial statements, currently expected by the company to occur on or before March 31, 2007."[57] Needless to say, this put sharp pressure on Riverdeep to come up with a top accounting firm to bless its financial statements.

Two years later, the combined company was poised to collapse. That collapse was near in May 2009 when Moody's withdrew its ratings on the company— expressing its view that there was a high probability of the company defaulting on its debts. At the time it owed $6.7 billion and Moody's withdrawal of its ratings covered $6.4 billion worth of that total—including senior secured debt. In withdrawing the rating, Moody's stated that it took into account "the business risk and competitive position of the company versus others within its industry; the capital structure and financial risk of the company; the projected financial and operating performance of the company over the near-to-intermediate term, and management's track record and tolerance for risk."[58]

The failure of Riverdeep's acquisition of Houghton Mifflin highlights an important reality. During a period of credit expansion, a financial wizard can persuade investors and lenders to part with their money to finance deals that make little economic sense. This is clearly what happened with Riverdeep. As such, the case offers managers in existing industries some important lessons:

Make sure to sell all your holdings at the close of such a deal and don't lend to it. The private equity firms who sold Houghton Mifflin to Riverdeep were no doubt thrilled to get out of the deal with their original investment intact. Although it is not clear, those PE firms probably extracted dividends and fees early in their ownership of Houghton Mifflin and likely sold all their holdings at the close. The managers of Riverdeep and Houghton Mifflin who ended up owning 50% of the new company got totally wiped out. And most likely, so will the bondholders and other lenders.

Avoid investing in a declining market unless enormous cost cutting can ensue. While Riverdeep and Houghton Mifflin probably realized that the U.S. textbook market was very mature and unprofitable, they probably had convinced themselves that combining the two companies could magically transform that frog of an industry into a prince. Unfortunately for all associated with the deal, that magic was unhooked from any rational analysis of the industry structure.

Run away from deals that promise vague statements of synergy. Riverdeep clearly did not grasp how difficult it is to sell textbooks to schools and probably overestimated how much those schools would be willing to spend on its CD-ROMs and Web-based educational tools. Simply put, the competitive advantages about which Riverdeep and Houghton Mifflin crowed were a mirage.

Sabic Acquires GE Plastics

What do you do if you're sitting on the world's biggest oil and gas reservoir and the price of that black gold is going through the roof? What if you believe that you're leaving money on the table because you're good at extracting the raw materials and converting them into petrochemicals but don't have the capabilities needed to turn those raw materials into consumer products that will yield a much higher price? What if the key to achieving those higher profits is to acquire the plastics business of an American corporate icon? How do you overcome the potential political obstacle to such a deal when it turns out that only 6 years before 12 of your citizens had joined 7 citizens of other countries to hijack a few airplanes and fly them into that country's tallest buildings—killing 3,000 of their citizens?

When Saudi Basic Industries (Sabic)—one of the world's 10 largest petrochemicals manufacturers with an $80 billion market capitalization that is 70% owned by the Saudi government and 30% controlled by private Middle East investors[59]—acquired GE's Plastics division for $11.6 billion in 2007, it needed to solve all those problems. It also tapped into the global appetite for selling bonds to finance that deal—in so doing it deviated from its traditional Islamic approach to finance—presumably in order to widen the base of investors who would help finance the deal. Moreover, it overcame political opposition that might have arisen by spending $20 million annually on Washington lobbying and talking up the value of GE Plastic's management team.

The details of the deal were fairly straightforward. In May 2007, GE announced it would sell its plastics division for $11.6 billion to Sabic, which was the largest public company in Saudi Arabia. Sabic beat out other bidders—including Basell, the Dutch plastics maker, and Apollo Management, the American private equity firm—to win control of the GE division that employed 11,000 people in 20 countries.[60]

For Sabic, the deal represented a way to forward integrate—getting closer to its customers and charging a higher price in exchange for producing products that more uniquely meet consumer needs. Mohamed al-Mady, the vice chairman and chief executive of Sabic, said: "This business is complementary to our existing business without any overlaps. Sabic's intention is to grow the business globally." Meanwhile GE's CEO Jeff Immelt took care to praise Sabic for its intent to invest in GE's people, saying, "Sabic is the right owner for our customers and our employees. This transaction will transform the plastics industry by combining Sabic's low-cost materials position and global reach with GE Plastics' strong marketing and technology capabilities. Sabic also has a record of investing in acquired businesses and their people."[61]

Why did GE chose to sell the plastics division to a company instead of a private equity firm? It decided that it would be better for its people if it could sell to a company that would use the division and its products, rather than cut costs or otherwise conduct financial engineering in preparation for an eventual public offering or resale. To that end, Sabic's access to Saudi Arabia's vast petroleum supplies made it a logical partner. After all, it was the ever-rising cost of benzene, a petroleum derivative and a key raw material for GE's plastics products that had cut into the unit's profitability. Since Sabic had access to an inexpensive and virtually unlimited supply of benzene, it would have an easier time profiting from the division.[62]

And Sabic's top management broadcast its view that GE plastics' human capital was a valuable asset that would help it capture more downstream value in the plastics business. As Al-Mady said, "Our plans are to keep the business running under the leadership" of incoming CEO Brian T. Gladden, a GE Plastics executive. "We have no other plans at this time. This is the corporate part of our operations, and we leave the company here in good hands. [GE Plastics] is one of the best companies in the world. And I'm sure they know how to run the business in the best way."[63]

How did Sabic intend to use these people to earn a return on its investment? According to Al-Mady, "The strategy is for our company to be a global leader and to add specialty businesses to our portfolio. So the acquisition of GE Plastics is going to play very well with our ambitious plans. We'll integrate some of our operations in the Kingdom (of Saudi Arabia) into supply chains and utilize technologies of GE Plastics into other areas that we have there. And GE Plastics can rely on the financial position of Sabic to grow the business in the future."[64] Despite the potential for the deal to fuel public opposition—due to the role of Saudi Arabian citizens in the 9/11 attacks—Sabic was able to close the deal without a whimper. This despite the fact that Saudi Arabia's political system was far more totalitarian than that of the United States'—thus requiring it to decide whether to impose Saudi governance on GE Plastics or let it run in accordance with U.S. law.

To that end, it was interesting that there was no effort to extend the review of the deal by the Committee on Foreign Investments in the United States (CFIUS)—a process that helped to derail other deals proposed in the preceding years. Examples of other deals derailed by protectionist sentiment included the proposal by the People's Republic of China's state-owned CNOOC in the summer of 2005 to acquire UNOCAL of California, the ninth largest oil company in the United States and Dubai Ports World, of Dubai Holding, a United Arab Emirates (UAE) government-owned corporation, and its buyout of the United Kingdom corporation, Peninsular and Oriental Steam Navigation Co. (P&O), for its port operations of six major U.S. East Coast ports in early 2006.[65]

The Sabic deal sailed through without opposition despite the potential for discomfort in light of GE Plastics' government contracts[66] even as the United States was embroiled in two wars in the Middle East. The key to Sabic's success in closing this deal was a long track record of lobbying Congress. The Saudi Arabian government spends $20 million annually to lobbying organizations and law firms representing them in order to gain exclusive access to lawmakers in advancing such financial interests or specific foreign trade policy agendas.[67]

For example, former secretary of state James Baker, a senior partner in the law firm, Baker Botts, LLC, of Houston, TX is a legal representative to Saudi Prince Sultan bin Abdul Aziz, one of several Saudi persons, entities, Islamic foundations, and financial institutions named as defendants in a pending lawsuit brought by the 9/11 Families to Bankrupt Terrorism.[68]

Thanks to all its political firepower, Sabic was able to get the deal past any potential political opposition. And the only major hurdle thereafter was getting the $9 billion in debt it needed to finance the transaction. Fortunately, Sabic had little difficulty tapping the global financial markets—gaining access to the European and U.S. debt markets via bankers Citigroup, ABN AMRO, HSBC, and JPMorgan. In July 2007 it issued two "tranches" of debt—a euro tranche totalling EUR590 million and a dollar tranche worth $1.95 billion. Both matured in eight years and were noncallable for four years. Overall, Sabic hoped to raise a total of $9 billion worth of debt by the end of the third quarter of 2007.[69]

It certainly appeared that Sabic had done everything right in its deal with GE Plastics. However, it could not escape the negative impact of the global economy—moreover, it may have overpaid for GE Plastics. By the first quarter of 2009, Sabic reported a net loss for the quarter ended March 31, 2009 of SR0.974bn—including a SR1.181bn charge for impairment of goodwill resulting from a decline in the value of assets it acquired—compared to net income of SR6.924bn in the same period of 2008.[70]

The very benefit that Sabic hoped to get from its investment in GE Plastics turned out to be a negative for its financial results when the economy went into reverse. As Al-Mady said, "The financial and economic crisis that hit the world's major economies, and the credit crunch have led to difficulties for customers accessing credit facilities from banks and financial institutions. This has contributed to the decline in demand for petrochemical products and metals, in particular engineering plastics, which have been impacted by the recession in the automotive, construction and electronic industries."[71]

In retrospect, the logic of the deal between Sabic and GE Plastics may have been sound. However, it appears that the deal was based on a set of assumptions that may have proven overly optimistic. Specifically, it appears that Sabic over-paid for GE Plastics based on a belief that its lower benzene costs would yield far higher profitability whereas the deal closed at a time when the global economy was on the verge of a credit-led implosion that drastically cut demand for plastics. As a result, Sabic's acquisition of GE Plastics reveals some important lessons for managers of existing industries:

Lay the political groundwork for a potentially sensitive deal years before the deal is announced. Saudi Arabia's decades of lobbying in Washington clearly paid off in the form of a quiet acceptance of its deal to acquire a huge division of an American icon, GE. Sabic's timing was perfect given the close relationship between then president Bush and the Saudi government.

Be wary of a hands-off management approach to an acquisition. While it is politi-cally popular to close a deal while offering assurances that existing managers will stay in place, the reality is that this policy generally works best during a time of economic expansion. However, often the management that weakened the company enough to get it into a position where its parent wanted to sell might not be the best managers to boost its future value. Although GE Plastics' human capital may have been a reasonable basis for Sabic's deal, it may turn out that this assumption was overly optimistic.

In considering how much to pay for a global acquisition, consider worst case sce-narios. In 2007, with oil prices rising, it appeared unlikely that Saudi Arabia would ever need to be concerned about overpaying. However, given the cyclical nature of the energy industry it may not have been too difficult to imagine that prices could decline along with credit quality. Had Sabic considered a more pes-simistic scenario, it may have structured its deal for GE Plastics more conserva-tively and have avoided overpaying.

Vodafone Acquires Hutchison Essar

Imagine you're CEO of one of the leading cell phone providers in Europe and you'd like to tap into the faster growth opportunities in an emerging market. Even though it might be possible to acquire a market leader in that country, it has laws that limit how much of that company you're allowed to own. However, it turns out that these obstacles are not insurmountable. When the UK's Vodafone closed its $11.1 billion cash acquisition of a 67% stake in India's Hutchison Essar, it was able to satisfy its 20% ROE benchmark for investment returns while tap-ping into a market with 40% growth even as it met India's limits for foreign investment control.

Vodafone's deal for Essar was complicated by the latter's ownership by a Chinese company, Hutchison Telecom. In February 2007, Vodafone paid $11.1

billion in cash for Hong Kong–based Hutchison's 67% stake in India's fourth-largest mobile operator, Hutchison Essar. Vodafone's goal was to launch its wireless service into what it perceived as the world's second biggest mobile market in terms of potential subscribers and the fastest growing major market.

Vodafone's deal gave Hutchison Essar an enterprise value of $18.8 billion—since the group assumed a net debt of around $2 billion as part of the acquisition.[72] At the same time Vodafone sold off a stake in an Essar competitor. More specifically, Vodafone closed a parallel deal to sell its 5.6% share of India's top mobile operator Bharti Airtel for $1.6 billion back to Bharti group, and announced an agreement with Bharti to share network infrastructure in India to cut costs. Vodafone, which acquired 10% of Bharti for $1.5 billion in 2005, retained its 4.4% interest in Bharti—leaving Vodafone competing with a piece of itself in the Indian market.[73]

And that Indian market represented a big opportunity. The deal would give Vodafone a presence throughout India, including 24 million customers and a 16% market share. Moreover, the business was growing fast and generating cash flow—with revenue growth of 51% and an Earnings before Interest Taxes Depreciation and Amortization (EBITDA) margin of 33 percent in the six months ending June 30, 2006. Not only did the deal help it increase its exposure to emerging markets—increasing its EBITDA from emerging market businesses from 20% in 2007 to an expected 33% by 2012—but also exceeded Vodafone's investment hurdle rate—yielding a 14% 2012 internal rate of return.[74]

Vodafone also needed to comply with Indian law limiting its control of an Indian telecommunications company. Vodafone anticipated that it would offer to buy Indian conglomerate Essar group's 33% holding in Hutchison Essar at the same price it agreed to pay Hutchison Telecommunications. However, since Indian law prohibited Vodafone from holding more than 74% of an Indian telecommunications company, if Essar decided to accept Vodafone's offer Indian law would have required Essar to arrange for Indian companies to buy minority stakes—so the Indian companies would own as much as 26% of Hutchison Essar.[75]

Gaining control of Essar while satisfying Indian law proved to be a bit tricky—however, Vodafone succeeded within about two months of announcing the deal. The deal needed approval by India's Foreign Investment Promotion Board (FIPB)—which cleared the case in April 2007 and sent it on to India's finance minister for formal approval. That's because Vodafone figured out a way to assure FIPB that it would comply with India's restriction of no more than 74%. In February 2007, Vodafone had acquired a 52% majority stake in Hutchison Essar from Hutchison for $9.8 billion. Another 15% stake was being held by local Indian businessmen Asim Ghosh and Analjit Singh—Vodafone valued the entire 67% stake at $11.1 billion. As noted above, Essar Group held the remaining 33% stake in Hutchison Essar—22% of which was already foreign owned through Essar's overseas unit. Although Vodafone sought FIPB clearance in March, it delayed the decision three times because it was concerned that Ghosh and Singh—who held 15% of Hutchison Essar—were fronts for Hong Kong's Hutchison Telecommunications.

If that had been true, then Vodafone's deal would have given it 89% of Hutchison Essar—15% more than it is allowed.

Since Singh agreed not to sell his stake to a foreign investor, FIPB approved Vodafone's deal.[76] Having obtained approval for the deal, Vodafone completed the transaction on May 8, 2007 at a slightly lower price. Ultimately, Vodafone paid a discounted price of $10.9 billion in cash for Hutchison Essar, $180 million from the originally agreed price of $11.08 billion, which reflected retention and closing adjustments as agreed with seller Hutchison Telecom to complete the deal. As Vodafone CEO Arun Sarin said, "I am delighted that, having secured all the necessary regulatory approvals, we are now able to complete this important transaction and move onto the process of integration. The transaction was completed on May 8."[77]

Ultimately, Sarin's delight turned to sadness as he left Vodafone in May 2008. He was able to fight off efforts by institutional investors who voted against his reelection to the board, accusing him of being too quick to spend millions of pounds on foreign acquisitions. But Sarin, who had previously worked at Pacific Telesis Group in San Francisco, after which he joined its subsidary AirTouch as chief operating officer, became CEO of Vodafone's U.S. and Asia-Pacific operations, also joining Vodafone's main board after Vodafone bought AirTouch. Sarin was appointed CEO of Vodafone at a time when the investment community wanted it to concentrate on managing its businesses efficiently and returning cash to shareholders, after its dramatic takeover-driven expansion between 1999 and 2002. But Sarin refused to comply with the investment community's wishes—leaving on his own terms in July 2008—to be replaced by Vittorio Colao, who ran Vodafone's European operations.[78]

But a year later, Vodafone executives credited Sarin's efforts to expand outside of Europe for helping to dampen the negative impact of a contracting European economy on Vodafone's 2008 results. Successor Vittorio Colao acknowledged the contribution made by operations outside Europe when he presented Vodafone's 2008 results to investors in London. Although revenue was up around the world—32% in Asia-Pacific and Middle East, 14% in Europe and 11% in Africa and central Europe—EBITDA was up in March 2009 from £13.2bn in 2008 to £14.5bn. As Colao said, "These results demonstrate the impact of the early actions we took to address the current economic conditions and highlight the benefits of our geographic diversity."[79]

Ultimately Sarin's efforts to use global M&A to accelerate Vodafone's growth led to a bittersweet result. Sarin's aggressiveness cost him his job but his deals appear to have helped dampen the negative economic impact of Europe's contraction in 2008 on Vodafone's results. In this context, Vodafone's acquisition of Hutchison Essar reveals some important lessons for managers of existing industries:

Analyze the growth opportunities. Vodafone conducted a well-considered analysis of the slow growth in Europe and the far more rapid growth available to the company were it to take a bigger share of the mobile phone market in India. Such analysis should be the first step a manager in an existing industry conducts prior to evaluating acquisition candidates in growing countries.

Follow the rules. While Vodafone ran into some speed bumps, it made the offer for Hutchison Telecommunications' and Essar Groups' stakes in Hutchison Essar with a clear understanding of India's rules limiting foreign ownership of its telecommunications companies. Ultimately, Vodafone was able to sell off enough of its stake in the company to satisfy India's regulatory requirements and win the deal.

Leap over your hurdle rate. Vodafone set a 14% internal rate of return hurdle rate for its Hutchison Essar acquisition. As of this writing it is too early to tell whether the deal will ever meet that standard. Perhaps more relevant to Vodafone's current financial position, Vodafone set specific goals for how much of its revenues and profits would come from emerging markets. And the Hutchison Essar deal helped Vodafone come closer to those goals. These examples of financial discipline in evaluating acquisitions should serve as a good case in point for managers of companies in existing industries.

Implications for Managers

What should managers in existing industries do to profit from the lessons of these cases? They should use a formal methodology to help them figure out how to use acquisitions in growth markets as a means of reviving an existing company. Such a methodology can help managers willing to follow the steps as a way to inject entrepreneurial energy in a corporate gas tank operating at too low an octane level.

This methodology begins by helping managers identify the most attractive countries in which to invest and ends with a reshaped company that grows faster than it did before. This methodology is built on the assumption that there may be meaningful differences between the EE in which the acquirer operates and that of its target. More specifically, this methodology is intended to help acquiring managers to think through whether the differences between their EE and that of their target company represent a threat or an opportunity. We seek to direct managers to capture the opportunities—in the target's financial markets, corporate governance, human capital, and IP regime—and protect themselves against the threats in the target's EE.

What follows is a six-step methodology we believe will help managers to exploit the opportunities of global M&A to revive a moribund company in an existing industry. Here they are:

1. *Pinpoint large countries growing fast with industries in which your company competes.* As illustrated in cases such as Vodafone/Essar, managers in existing industries have an opportunity to scan the world and look for other countries in which they might want to offer their products. For managers in existing industries, the most attractive countries are likely to be ones that

have a large number of potential customers with rapidly growing demand. The reason such countries are attractive is that an existing company that has reached significant scale can grow only in a way that is meaningful to investors if that growth springs from big, growing markets.

To find such markets, managers may seek to focus on developing countries with large populations where there is demonstrably rapid growth in demand for their products. It is worth noting that unless the manager's company can satisfy that demand better than competitors already do, then the investment it might make in trying to take a share of that market is likely to be wasted. To avoid that fate, managers ought to conduct research into the specific criteria that channels and end-users apply to competing suppliers to assess which one to pick. Such analysis can help managers to assess their odds of winning a share of that country's markets.

2. *Identify the risks and opportunities in the country's regulations regarding foreign ownership and other corporate governance matters, its capital markets, its human capital, and its IP regime.* However, if managers see an opportunity in meeting customer needs better than the competition, they should next consider whether the country's EE is at odds with their own. Such differences do not necessarily mean that the managers should not seek to enter that new market. However, managers will find themselves at a disadvantage if they do not explore those differences early in the process of considering a new country in which to expand.

To that end, managers should conduct research into the details of the EE of the country where they perceive growth opportunity. Such research should seek to answer questions such as the following:

- Are the country's financial markets deep enough to be a good source of capital for the business or will capital need to come from other countries?
- Does the country have a sufficiently rigorous set of corporate governance principles and enforcement mechanisms to protect their investment?
- Does the country have limits to how much of its companies can be in the hands of foreign investors?
- Can the country's human capital enable them to achieve their growth objectives? If so, what is the best way to manage that human capital?
- Does the country protect IP or would they be better off assuming that the country will permit its companies to steal their IP?
- Based on the responses to such questions, managers can decide whether a country's EE presents more opportunities than threats. And they can consider how they might protect themselves against those threats while taking advantage of its opportunities.

3. *Identify companies in those countries/industries that could be acquisition candidates.* Having settled on a particular country in which to invest, managers

may wish to consider whether they should seek to take market share through a de novo venture, partnership, or acquisition. The cases we've presented here suggest that acquisition is a common mode of entry—particularly for managers of companies in existing industries.

The primary reason for acquisition's popularity among managers is that the other options generally take more time to generate sufficient revenues and profits to get the attention of investors. To develop a list of potential acquisition candidates, managers should seek out lists of companies in their industry in those countries ranked by market share. Managers should further collect data on each of these companies on their management team, financial performance and prospects, current products, R&D projects, and key capabilities.

4. *Rank the companies based on their fit with your company's skills and the potential for an attractive investment return.* Such data can help managers as they decide which of those companies they should approach first, and which they should shun. Before making an approach to one or more of these companies, managers should consider these questions:

   - Will the target company combined with their company be better able to take market share in that new country?
   - Will the cash flows from the combined company exceed the target's purchase price?
   - Will they be able to integrate the target effectively after the deal closes?

   Managers should rank the potential candidates based on how they stack up on the answers to these questions.

5. *Complete the acquisition and integration of the company that best fits these criteria.* The next step is to execute. In general this involves a huge amount of management effort, in conjunction with advisors, capital providers, target company management, and regulators, to complete all the tasks from contacting the target company to completing the integration of the target into the acquiring company. As we've noted above, execution is fraught with landmines—including satisfying the needs of regulators and working effectively with the target company's managers so they'll be onboard with the idea of joining the acquiring company's management team.

6. *Set performance milestones and manage the company to achieve them.*
   Once the deal has been concluded, managers need to get down to the brass tacks of running the business. This means

   - Setting performance goals for the combined company;
   - Putting in place managers who will be held accountable for achieving these goals;

- Formulating the strategy that will enable the combined company to win in the marketplace;
- Getting the resources—in capital, technology, and people to implement the strategy; and
- Making adjustments based on whether the strategy works or falls short.

Conclusion

Managers in existing industries can revive their companies with carefully planned and executed acquisition strategies that open up their companies to growth opportunities in large untapped markets. In order to capture the opportunities and avoid the risks in these new countries, managers should research the differences between the EE of the country in which they operate and that of the country that they seek to enter. As we've seen from the case studies in this chapter, the best strategies result from careful consideration of how to avoid the pitfalls while finding the right acquisition targets, not overpaying, and integrating and managing those companies with care. By contrast, acquisitions built on the availability of too much capital seeking too few good deals can cost investors and managers dearly.

Implications for Entrepreneurial Managers in New Firms and Industries

Should entrepreneurial managers in new firms and industries do anything differently as a result of the globalization of entrepreneurship? Certainly such globalization makes it possible to consider far more options around the world for where to source capital and labor. The globalization of entrepreneurship also makes it possible to design, build, and sell products for potential customers in far-flung locations that could represent big new opportunities for entrepreneurs or capital traps.

But such opportunities are not without risks. For example, raising capital from a different country could expose a start-up to foreign control of its management, which might limit its decision-making speed as well as its strategic options. And hiring people in a different country might provide high skill at lower wages or could put the entire foreign venture at risk of appropriation by the country's leaders. And it may prove to be far more difficult to adapt a company's skills in its home country to the requirements of satisfying the needs of potential customers in more distant ones. Finally, entrepreneurs who invest in other countries may be putting their hard-won intellectual property positions at risk of theft.

How can entrepreneurs seize the opportunities of globalization while avoiding its pitfalls? There is no single easy answer to this question. However, the cases we'll explore in this chapter suggest that entrepreneurs can increase their odds of a net positive outcome by taking the time to explore—in a systematic and rigorous manner—a set of specific questions before deciding whether to ride the globalization wave. Often it is difficult for enthusiastic entrepreneurs who pride themselves on overcoming obstacles to conduct such analysis before committing to a goal. However, the cases we'll explore in this chapter suggest that rigorous analysis can lead to better outcomes.

So what are these questions? Here are some of the most important ones:

- Is it likely that there will be a big market in the country I seek to sell? If so, what trends will drive that market's growth?

- What capabilities are required to succeed in that market?
- Does my team have the skills needed to design and sell a competitively superior product in that market?
- If not, how can I close the capability gap? Can a foreign source of capital help bring the needed skills to the company?
- Will the benefits of bringing in such foreign capital outweigh its costs?
- Is there a reliable corporate governance process in the country to protect my investment in the country?
- Does the country respect intellectual property rights? If not, is there a way to build a viable business there?

This chapter illustrates the way entrepreneurs address these questions by exploring 10 case studies. As we explore each of these cases, we examine specific lessons that we believe entrepreneurs can use to help them as they expand their start-ups. And we conclude with a methodology that we believe can help entrepreneurs apply these lessons to their own businesses.

In so doing, we'll explore the following answers to the questions we just mentioned:

Effective analysis of a start-up's market opportunity depends on many factors which could vary by industry. Many of the cases we'll explore suggest that entrepreneurs should analyze many factors including changes in government policy, evolving industry structure, demographic changes, and the direction of competitors' product innovation.

Most entrepreneurs are better off acknowledging capability gaps from the start. We'll explore cases in which entrepreneurs succeed because they have an objective sense of the capabilities needed for their company to compete effectively. Entrepreneurs who can figure out which capabilities they lack and close the gaps through hiring and/or partnering with the right venture capital firms increase their odds of success. Moreover, entrepreneurs who know what they want from a VC tend to use that insight to the benefit of their start-up.

A country's corporate governance approach will generally not change to suit the entrepreneur. We'll explore cases in which entrepreneurs succeeded in part by positioning themselves to benefit from trends in a country's approach to corporate governance. And we'll also examine the disastrous consequences for a new venture of assuming that a *destination* country's approach to corporate governance is the same as that of the *home* country.

In countries with weak IP protection, service businesses that adapt the strategies of successful U.S. start-ups tend to do well. We explore several case studies that adapt a winning U.S. model to the Chinese market. These cases suggest that a direct copy of the U.S. business is not likely to succeed in China—the U.S. business strategy must be adapted to the differences in China's consumer expectations and competitive landscape. Nevertheless, as our cases illustrate, the adaptation of a successful U.S. business strategy to the Chinese market tends to lower a U.S.-based venture capitalist's perceived risk of investing in the Chinese start-up.

Entrepreneurial Manager Case Studies

To explore these themes, this chapter presents 10 case studies of entrepreneurs in new companies and industries as they attempt to take advantage of the opportunities and avoid the threats of the globalization of entrepreneurship:

Tutor Vista Bridges the India-U.S. Knowledge Gap illustrates how a successful Indian entrepreneur can use detailed market research coupled with carefully chosen U.S. capital providers to create a new industry.

Sonoa Systems Wins by Partnering with Venture Capital demonstrates how an entrepreneur with a successful track record can build a global company by coming up with the right idea, bringing in Venture Capitalists (VCs) who can add value through their industry contracts, and hiring an experienced CEO who can manage Indian engineers to build products that meet the needs of U.S. corporate customers.

Tejas Networks Focuses a Great Team on an Emerging Unmet Need provides an example of how a team of executives that built successful companies by crossing between India and the United States can create a start-up in Bangalore by building a product focused on an emerging unmet need. Despite the risks, this case shows that with the right team and product idea, such a start-up can persuade U.S. VCs to invest.

Sawyer Research Products Loses Its Investment to Russian Expropriation shows how risky it is to invest in Russia and also helps to illustrate the critical importance of addressing the questions we discussed above prior to investing. If Sawyer had done so, it would have realized that corporate governance practices in Russia virtually guaranteed that it would be lured into investing and making its quartz plant a success only to lose its investment to creeping expropriation managed through the political manipulation of its legal system.

Campus Media Helps Intel Capital Sell Chips to Chinese Students portrays how a carefully considered corporate venture capital strategy can provide access to new markets for its core product. For Intel Capital, Campus Media's strategy of advertising to Chinese students increased the market potential for Intel semiconductors, which it hoped those students would buy.

Changyou's Blockbuster IPO Is an Oasis in the Desert illustrates the power of a successful Chinese Internet company to generate significant investor interest in a fast-growing division to give its skilled game designers a chance to profit from the growth they generate from producing new hit games.

Focus Media Rewards Private Equity through Quick Thinking celebrates how a quick thinking entrepreneur can overcome the objections of a potential private equity investor—thus raising the capital needed to build a new company that captures a newly created market. The case also illustrates how the founding entrepreneur's quick thinking enables him to take the venture public and stay in control as its value exceeds $1 billion.

Dangdang Books Profit for Western VCs Makes clear the power of applying a business strategy that succeeded in the U.S. to the Chinese market. As a result of its superior ability to adapt Amazon.com's business strategy to the specific limitations of the Chinese market, Dangdang's founder succeeded in raising capital from several leading Silicon Valley VCs.

Bain Capital Blue-Printing Spurs Portfolio Company Growth provides an example of how a Western capital provider can transform a Chinese portfolio company. In Bain Capital's case, its blue-printing process provides a framework for sending signals to the market place. It tells entrepreneurs that it will not let their companies twist in the wind once Bain Capital invests. But it also signals that those entrepreneurs will only get that capital if they are willing to take a significant amount of direction from Bain Capital.

Worksoft's Sea Turtles Bring Home Venture Gold ends Chapter 9 with an example of a successful business built by Chinese entrepreneurs who spent time in the West only to return to China to build a venture that outsources work from American companies. Thanks to capital from another pioneering U.S. VC, Worksoft was able to grow rapidly to the point where it succeeded in listing its shares on the NYSE within a couple of years of receiving that capital.

Tutor Vista Bridges the India-U.S. Knowledge Gap

India has produced its share of highly skilled entrepreneurs. Such start-up gurus have the skill of knowing when and why to accept venture capital from overseas and when to self-finance. It turns out that one of the most important lessons for entrepreneurs is to view Venture Capital (VC) as a critical part of the bundle of capabilities needed for a venture to succeed. And in the case of Tutor Vista—a $300 a month online tutoring service for high school students delivered by Indian teachers—the VC brought capital, marketing credibility, and a useful knowledge of the industry which the company hoped to serve.

Krishnan Ganesh is the serial entrepreneur who founded Tutor Vista. As he explained, "Tutor Vista is my fourth venture. My previous ventures have focused on using Indian resources for addressing global markets."[1] An examination of Ganesh's previous ventures reveals just how much of a natural entrepreneur he is. Ganesh started in 1990, just as the Indian economy was being liberalized, by founding IT&T, a computer-maintenance business serving local firms.[2]

This decision required courage because capital was scarce and regulation discouraged entrepreneurship. To overcome the problems, Ganesh required clients to pay their maintenance premiums upfront. And it took 26 clearance permits and 9 months of battling to get IT&T up and running. Moreover, India had a strong cultural bias against entrepreneurship—his mother-in-law, who had blessed his marriage to her daughter because of his stable job in corporate planning, was unhappy with his decision to start a new company. But Ganesh was a success and by the time he stepped down from a hands-on role at the company in 1998, IT&T had 400 people, 16 offices, and a $4.8 million in sales.[3]

His next three ventures were also successful. He ran a telecommunications joint venture between Britain's BT and Bharti Enterprises for two years. Then, recognizing that the Internet would enable India to become a provider of out-sourced services to overseas firms, Ganesh and his wife founded CustomerAsset, a call-center business serving "old-economy" Western firms that ICICI, a business process outsourcing firm, bought in 2002 for $22 million. And then he started a venture focused on complex, knowledge-intensive services—joining Marketics, a data-analysis and modelling start-up, which asked Ganesh to invest in their business and to become their nonexecutive chairman. He sold Marketics for $65 million in March 2007.[4]

Ganesh turned next to Tutor Vista. As he explained, "I got the idea for Tutor Vista after visiting the U.S. and finding that two of the biggest areas of concern in magazines and newspapers were that health care and education in the U.S. were in crisis. I measured this in terms of the money flowing into these areas, the level of debate, and the degree of media buzz."[5]

Ganesh concluded that an opportunity might exist to capitalize on the buzz surrounding education. As he said, "It seemed to me that people in the U.S. perceive that the secondary school system is a major mess. However, U.S. colleges and universities—Stanford, Harvard, Berkeley, and Wharton—are the best in the world. And the U.S. is number one in the world in terms of Nobel laureates and patents. But in secondary education, the U.S. is 29th in Math and 27th in Science."[6]

He continued, "This gave me the idea to provide supplemental education in the U.S. at the secondary school level with tutors from India. It was a new field and had never been done before—personalized tutoring delivered online. I spoke to 100 parents, teachers and students in the U.S. asking them 'Will they accept the service? Will it work? Will parents pay? Will they accept teachers from India?' "[7]

Ganesh found that American students and parents reacted positively to his idea. As Ganesh explained, "The general reaction has been positive. Children were comfortable with having teachers from India. They thought it was cool. American parents had no reservations about Indian teachers. I was worried that they would have problems with the Indian accents and their knowledge of U.S. curriculum. But they said that they were comfortable with their children learning academic subjects such as Math and Science from Indian tutors. I find it funny that over the last three years, the second most popular area of demand after Math was English, with Science number three."[8]

Ganesh provided enough capital himself to get Tutor Vista off the ground and then sought venture capital. According to him, "I financed the company for the first six months to show that we could gain traction in order to raise venture capital. I said from the beginning that because this was a consumer Internet business it would require deep pockets. It was not a BTB like Wipro or an outsourcer who can get financing by signing contracts with U.S. companies.

Because we are a BTC, we are creating a brand directly to the consumer and asking him or her to pay $300 per month. I thought we needed a lot of money to do that."[9]

When he considered where to find VC funding, Ganesh concluded that the United States would be the best place to look since he thought it would understand his consumer-focused business. According to him, "I decided to go the U.S. for VC because the biggest online market was there—with Google, eBay and so on. I thought the U.S. investors would understand our model and that they would be more comfortable with the consumer Internet. For this business we thought it might be a problem for U.S. consumers to trust an Indian company offering personalized tutoring over the Internet—unlike buying a book from Amazon, how would American consumers know what they would be getting?"[10]

Ganesh chose his VC provider in part as a way to give confidence to potential customers. As Ganesh pointed out, "To overcome that trust barrier, we wanted to get a venture capital investor that was a marquis name and that would be patient and understanding of the ups and downs of a business in the Internet services space. We were willing to sacrifice on other financial terms in order to get these two."[11]

Ganesh chose the specific VC firms that he thought would understand Tutor Vista's industry and would be willing to tolerate the ups and downs of a start-up. According to Ganesh, "We chose a VC by first figuring out what kind of business we're running and its specific requirements. We want smart capital that can fill in the gaps in the requirements which we don't offer. There would be a different logic for the Indian infrastructure space."[12]

He continued, "We had offers from three firms and we picked Sequoia because it was a marquis name, it had invested in successful consumer internet companies such as Google, Apple, and Yahoo, and we knew the people from a previous relationship. They invested in us for two reasons: First, they liked the concept of investing in the consumer Internet a unique, value-creating business model and second due to our track record of three previously successful ventures."[13]

Ganesh was quite satisfied with the VC providers that Tutor Vista chose. He explained: "Our first round came from Sequoia and our second round from Light Speed Ventures and Silicon Valley Bank. The way they dealt with us was standard—nothing different. We got more freedom because they trusted us more than they would have if it had been a first-time start-up. They don't feel that they have to micromanage us."[14]

Ganesh has found that taking VC from the United States leads to specific expectations regarding corporate governance. As he explained, "Different decisions require different levels of approval. Sometimes it's the board that has to approve—other times it's the CEO who decides and then informs the board. When we decided to acquire a company in India we were getting into a new business and that required board approval."[15]

Ganesh offered an example of a decision that required board approval. He said: "We wanted to buy an Indian tutoring business that delivered classes through store fronts. We sold the board on the idea by pointing out that the student market in India was bigger than the Chinese market. And it's upscale. We got the investors and the board to agree. They asked 'Is this the best use of capital?' and we convinced them it was."[16]

Ganesh has learned some important lessons from working with VCs. He said: "When it comes to picking a VC, we learned that it is a mistake to pick one that has not been through a down-period and is not familiar with the Indian market. We got capital from such a VC in 2000 and when things got tough with the dot-com bust, they withdrew. Specifically, their house was on fire they closed down the fund and laid off people."[17]

This experience has changed how Ganesh looks at VCs: "So when we look for VCs we want ones that are grounded operators—e.g., they have six years experience in India and they have a strong track record. Such VCs will not be affected by the ups and downs of the industry."[18]

Ganesh has also changed his general working relationship with VCs as a result of his experience working with them. According to him, "I've learned some lessons since I first started working with VCs in 2000. Initially I was irritated by their questions and now I realize that it's important to bring them on the same page. I matured and learned that working with a VC is like running a business with a partner."[19]

Finally, Ganesh offered up some useful advice to entrepreneurs, specifically, "If I was to give advice to a first time entrepreneur in India I would tell the person to ensure that their VC will be around and will be their partner in India. You need to check the reputation of the person and make sure he is not an absentee person who will be harmful. You need to make sure the VC is committed to India based on the number of investors, the quality of its core team, and its partner."[20]

He offered a second important piece of advice: "Second, you need to find out how your company fits in with what they like to invest in. If they are used to investing in health care or biotechnology then you don't want to be their first consumer Internet company because they are going to measure your performance based on the trajectory of their earlier health care or biotechnology investments."[21]

Finally, Ganesh cautioned entrepreneurs to check out the people in the VC firm. Ganesh suggested: "Third is people from the VC firm. You need to be comfortable with the partner handling the investment. The partner with ownership in your company needs to be a person you can relate to. I have had that kind of person in six out of the seven firms that have invested in my companies. One out of the seven was a value detractor. You need to do due diligence to make sure there is a portfolio fit. In today's market, it is tough to raise money and you may not have too many choices."[22]

Ganesh provided some useful insights into how he gets information on VC people before taking their money: "During the dot-com boom you didn't have time to do due diligence. But I now know that the VC that invested in my company had never exited successful, had no track record, and had no reputation as a company builder. You should talk to other entrepreneurs and learn about their track records during tough times. We had been with Sequoia for a long time and we knew how they behaved when the chips were down. Entrepreneurs won't come right out and say something negative about a VC but they will give enough signals so that you get the message."[23]

Ganesh concluded with an important piece of advice about the risks of a start-up company and the means of overcoming them. He said: "Entrepreneurship is a lot about passion. It is extremely tough and only 5% succeed. 95% odds are against you. Picking the wrong VC can boost the risks. You could run out of capital if you pick the wrong VC. But if you pick the right VC, like Sequoia, you get other VCs wanting to come in on the second round because you had a quality VC in the first round."[24]

Although it's too early to know at this point whether Tutor Vista will reward its venture capital investors, Ganesh's progress so far suggests important lessons for entrepreneurs:

Bravado in assessing market opportunities is no substitute for market research. Ganesh clearly gained valuable insights into the willingness of American parents and their children to pay for tutoring offered by Indian teachers. Although such services had never before been offered, Ganesh's primary research revealed that his idea could work.

Partner to gain access to the complete bundle of capabilities required to succeed in the business. Ganesh realized that he could not succeed alone. Instead, it was clear that he would need to partner with others in order to make Tutor Vista a success. Interestingly, he viewed his Silicon Valley venture investors as a way to gain the credibility needed to persuade American consumers to pay a significant monthly fee for its service.

Working with VCs requires a commitment of time to keeping the key contact person up to speed with the venture's activities. Ganesh learned that he had to pick a VC carefully—investing time to make sure he was comfortable with the person from the firm who would be managing the investment. Ganesh also recognized that he needed to keep the person informed about the company's activities and seek advice on how to achieve their mutually agreed-upon goals.

Sonoa Systems Wins by Partnering with Venture Capital

Sonoa Systems similarly decided to partner with a VC that could help it grow. Its success was based on the track record of its founder that made it possible for him to attract investors in the industry around which he hoped to build the company. Sonoa's success is an example of how it often makes sense for entrepreneurs to start by assembling top people with similar interests—and then to pick the company's market and product based on the team's strengths.

Sonoa Systems provides so-called secure cloud gateways—a technology that enables computers to communicate with each other. In October 2008, Sonoa raised its third round of venture financing—closing a $10 million Series C round of funding led by Third Point Ventures, the venture capital arm of Third Point LLC. Previous investors included Norwest Venture Partners, Bay Partners and SAP Ventures, a division of SAP AG.[25]

Sonoa's CEO is Chet Kapoor who described the company's founding. As he said, "Sonoa was founded in 2005 and I was brought in as CEO in 2007. Raj Singh was the founder and he was a very successful serial entrepreneur from the Bay Area. He had created significant wealth and joined with a few others to incubate the idea for Sonoa."[26]

Singh developed the strategic vision for Sonoa. As Kapoor explained, "Raj saw an opportunity because he expected that computers would be using eXtensible Markup Language (XML) to communicate with each other. Singh saw that as XML was more widely adopted, there would be a need for a technology to operationalize XML. Raj was joined in founding Sonoa by several of the early folks from Cisco. Raj pitched to U.S.-based venture capitalists—such as Norwest. Ravi Krishnan headed up the engineering team in Bangalore. And before getting the funding from the VCs, Sonoa received Angel funding."[27]

Singh realized that in order to build up the technology he envisioned, he would need to raise far more capital than Angel investors could supply. As Kapoor said, "But Raj realized that the effort required to build Sonoa could not be accomplished on beans and rice—it would require VC. And since Raj had been successful before—founding companies that were sold to Cisco Systems and Redback Networks—he was able to raise capital from two Silicon Valley firms—Norwest and Bay Partners."[28]

Kapoor believes that Singh's process for choosing these firms made sense. According to Kapoor, "While I can't speak for Raj, I think there are two reasons he picked those two firms. First, both have a very successful track record investing in early stage start-ups. They know that at the early stage, an entrepreneur may have a nebulous idea that will morph over time. And both have experience working with start-ups over a longer period of time—they don't invest in companies that will build technology and then sell in two months. In order to design and test Sonoa's product—it needed patient capital. Promod Haque who had invested in Juniper Networks and Neal Dempsey who had invested in Brocade were early investors in Sonoa [which gave it a compelling pedigree.]"[29]

Sonoa was financed initially by a strong collection of Angel investors. According to Kapoor, "Raj's idea was very new but he had a good track record and a good idea. As a result, people who have done well in Silicon Valley were willing to write checks for $25,000 to $100,000—providing Angel money— after which they could raise money from VCs. And today, even VCs are providing incubation money—in the form of a $500,000 loan that converts into equity. And the Angel investors can bring in the VCs along with customer contacts."[30]

Bringing in a CEO to run Sonoa was typical of Singh's previous start-ups. As Kapoor explained, "Raj brought me in to run Sonoa in 2007. I had been running a business for BEA Systems. Then I had joined Gluecode, an open source application server company that IBM acquired, and I was on the board of Sonoa. I was at IBM running products for content management and search, while Raj and the board were interviewing CEO candidates. When I decided to leave IBM, the Sonoa board approached me. I ended up as CEO."[31]

VC funding should not affect the way a CEO runs a company. As Kapoor said, "If you have a good relationship with a VC firm, then running a company backed by a VC is no different than one that is self-funded. You are always working for the customer whether it is a company you started or one that is venture-backed. If you're doing a lifestyle business and you want four to eight people to operate a strategic consulting firm you can be self-funded. But if you're digging a hole for two years then you'll need to hire talent and pay salaries—this requires VC."[32]

Kapoor has learned some important lessons in working with VCs—the most important of which are that the CEO must be comfortable with the individual representing the VC firm. As Kapoor explained, "There are some important lessons I've learned from working with VCs. When you take VC, you are taking money from an individual—the partner who will be managing the VC firm's investment in your company. You have to make sure that you are creating a good relationship with that individual. You want to make sure that this person has experience with the ups and downs of a start-up. Second, you have to make sure that the individual who is working with your firm understands the industry and is not learning about it from you. Third, realize that VCs are a partnership and you want to be working with an individual who is high up in the partnership ranks. If you work with a junior guy then that junior guy might do things artificially that a more senior person will later reverse. A steady hand always helps."[33]

Kapoor believes that an effective start-up CEO will run the business well regardless of how it is funded. According to Kapoor, "You should run it like you own it—whether you take VC or it's self-funded. This means you monitor cash flow; focus on customers; hire the best people; and set clear, measurable, and quantifiable milestones with the board. If you have the right CEO and the right team then the board will not be setting the milestones, it will be offering advice to the CEO. But having an external board is helpful. That's because with self control comes blind spots. It helps to check with individuals to get a different perspective. If the board is running the company there's something wrong with the CEO."[34]

Kapoor also offered some useful advice to budding entrepreneurs. As he said, "Getting VC is not a milestone; getting the first customer or the first 100 customers is a milestone. As I said before, it is important to develop a relationship with a senior partner at the VC firm who has been through the ups and downs of a start-up and knows the industry. Also, make sure that you understand the problem you are trying to solve and that you are sure the problem is worth your time to solve."[35]

Kapoor advises entrepreneurs to figure out for themselves whether they're working on the right problem. Kapoor pointed out, "You won't necessarily get that answer from the VC because the VC might not be a deep a technologist.

In order to make sure you're working the right problem, you need to talk to customers to get validations. You have to convince yourself that it's worth your time. Start-ups are hard and you should be sure that you'll stick with it. You also need to hire the right people. And don't go it alone—have like-minded partners because doing it by yourself gets lonely. And ideas change—we started Sonoa with the idea of operationalizing XML but it morphed into how it applied to cloud computing."[36]

Finding the right people can be challenging. But Kapoor is confident in his ability to find such people. As he explained, "The table stakes are to look for somebody who is smart, hard-working, has high integrity, and a teamwork orientation. Skills are fifth or sixth on the list. The ones that get hired have a passion for the problem you are trying to solve. That pulsating passion about the problem becomes a magnet for customers."[37]

Passion is the critical element that separates those who Kapoor hires from those whom he rejects. He described how he finds passionate people as follows: "You talk about the problem and see the questions the person asks and how the person reacts. A passionate person has a can-do attitude. They convey excitement in trying to solve the problem versus just doing their job."[38]

And Kapoor is passionate about running Sonoa. As he said, "I love running the company. I work with the board and founders to get advice. On some decisions I talk with the team. I take some decisions to the board. So make sure you have both available."[39]

Kapoor's insights into working with VCs and hiring staff for his start-up appear particularly valuable. Among these, the following are most critical:

Pick a VC who is willing to put a powerful partner in charge of its investment in your company. Kapoor's experience working with VCs makes it clear that the CEO should feel comfortable with whoever is in charge of the VC's investment in the start-up. However, given a choice between a powerful partner and a weaker person, it is better to get venture capital that the powerful partner will oversee because a weak person will end up being overruled. And that lack of consistency will endanger the venture.

Solve the right problem. Entrepreneurs often decide they want to start a company without a fixed idea of what they want the company to do. Kapoor offered sound advice on how to conduct the research needed for entrepreneurs to convince themselves that the problem that they are trying to solve is worth spending time on. And if they can convince themselves, it will be easier for them to convince potential employees and investors.

Hire people with intellectual curiosity and passion for solving the problem. Kapoor's insights into how to hire the best people have general applicability. Any entrepreneur can benefit from his advice to take the time to assess a candidate's inherent intellectual curiosity and passion for the problem that the company is trying to solve. To some extent, Kapoor is looking for people like himself since he can't do everything himself.

Tejas Networks Focuses a Great Team on an Emerging Unmet Need

It would seem that the ideal entrepreneurial start-up would blend a team with a track record of significant start-up success with an emerging market growth opportunity. Combine these elements with a willingness to listen to these customers to understand their specific product requirements and the venture capital required to pay for the development of that product and you'd have an opportunity to build a company with prospects for an attractive return.

These are the elements that blended together to form Tejas Networks, a Bangalore-based start-up developing specialized computers for switching traffic for Indian telecommunications companies. Tejas started with a vague goal of building a company in India and proceeded to assemble a world-class team of top executives to conceptualize that opportunity. Tejas raised initial capital to talk with potential customers and develop a prototype. And, after bridging some of the gaps between the U.S. and Indian approaches to raising private capital, Tejas raised venture capital from U.S.-based firms to help build the company.

To gain insight into what a world-class start-up team looks like from the perspective of a VC, it is worth delving into the background of the key members of the Tejas team—many of whom had been born in India, gone to the United States for their education, and built successful companies there. In May 2000 four men founded Tejas in Bangalore, India: Sanjay Nayak, Dr. Kumar Sivarajan, Arnob Roy, and Guraj "Desh" Deshpande. Deshpande had founded and taken public or sold two companies in the U.S. telecommunications network equipment industry—Cascade Communications and Sycamore Networks. Deshpande had the capital and reputation to pull together the team based on a vague notion of wanting to build a company in India.[40]

Nayak had developed a reputation as a company builder in the semiconductor design software industry—twice running India-based engineering subsidiaries of U.S. software companies. He was born in 1964 in the state of Madhya Pradesh, and received his undergraduate degree in electrical engineering from a well-known engineering institute. After receiving his master's degree from North Carolina State University, Nayak joined a U.S. electronic design automation (EDA) company and returned to India to establish the company's engineering department. Cadence, a U.S.-EDA industry leader, acquired that company and Nayak stayed on to run Cadence India. He returned to California to join Viewlogic, another EDA company and then went back to India to set up its India-based engineering subsidiary. Synopsys acquired Viewlogic and Nayak stayed on to run Synopsys India.[41]

Nayak's experiences led him to realize that he was an entrepreneur. As he recounted, "I began to see myself as an entrepreneur at that time. I needed to do everything to start up Viewlogic's operations in India—recruit an excellent team, set up an office, get approvals, get legal advice on structuring the entity, establish and manage a budget, recruit for and oversee multiple functions, and so on. In 1999 Viewlogic was acquired by another EDA leader, Synopsys, and I was appointed managing director of the Indian subsidiary."[42]

Cofounder Roy had grown up in Calcutta and met Nayak at Cadence India. Roy was one of Synopsys India's first employees and in 1997 he left Synopsys to rejoin Nayak at the Indian subsidiary of Viewlogic. Synopsys acquired Viewlogic in 1999, merged their Indian operations, and chose Nayak to lead them.[43]

Kumar was a stellar academic engineer whose optical networking text-book was widely adopted. As a result, Kumar was a magnet for recruiting the most talented optical networking designers. Growing up in Bangalore, Kumar graduated from Indian Institute of Technology (IIT) and by 1990 had received M.S. and Ph.D. degrees in electrical engineering from California Institute of Technology (Caltech). After Caltech, Kumar joined IBM's Watson Research Center to work in optical networking and related fields. In 1994 he joined the faculty of the Indian Institute of Science (IISc) and he coauthored a text book on optical communications that became popular, giving Kumar great credibility in the field.[44]

Kumar met Deshpande at an optical communications conference in March 2000 just as interest in optical communications was starting to grow. Kumar wanted to be involved in a start-up but up until that point, no one had considered basing one in Bangalore. But when Deshpande said he wanted to start such a company, Kumar was interested. After meeting with Deshpande in Boston, Kumar decided he wanted to get involved but he ultimately could not do so while staying at IISc, which gave him two options: to resign from IISc to join the company full time or to consult to the venture. So Kumar quit IISc and joined the venture full time.[45]

Deshpande described his interest in the venture as a logical extension of his previous experience. As he recounted, "I had been in North America since 1973 and had founded several companies, most notably Cascade Communications and Sycamore Networks, both of which became leaders in their spaces. I had been itching for some time to do something in India because I sensed an opportunity there, and telecommunications was the natural area for me to look at. In addition, the telecommunications market in 2000 in India was beginning to take off."[46]

Deshpande recognized Kumar thanks to his textbook that was popular with Sycamore engineers. As Deshpande recounted, "[Kumar] told me that he wanted a shot at becoming an entrepreneur in India and I thought to myself, 'With this type of talent we ought to be able to start something exciting.' He would give the venture credibility and would be able to attract the best talents in the country."[47]

Deshpande set about hiring a CEO and quickly settled on Nayak. After Nayak met Kumar and other members of the team, Deshpande decided to hire him as CEO. Deshpande chose Nayak because he was "action oriented, had a good track record, was optimistic, and highly motivated to build something." He felt that Kumar more than compensated for Nayak's lack of experience in optical networking. Nayak immediately brought in Roy, who impressed Deshpande as also having excellent credentials and entrepreneurial potential, and the team was formed—without any clear idea of what exactly they would do. "That is how

I started all my companies," Deshpande noted, "with a very talented group of people and a large but ill-defined opportunity."[48]

Deshpande and his Sycamore Networks provided the seed financing for Tejas. In May 2000, the founders had agreed in principle to work together to start an Indian company that would be active in the optical telecommunications networking area. In return for their combined $5 million investment, Deshpande and Sycamore Networks together would own nearly 50% of Tejas's common stock. The remainder would be composed of shares distributed among the three fulltime founders (together about 40%) and a stock option reserve for future employees.[49]

At the time, Tejas had two options: it could become an independent company selling its own product or become the base for Sycamore India. Nayak's first hire was the financial controller, N. Ramanathan from Synopsys, and the team immediately began recruiting dozens of top engineers, which was relatively easy to accomplish because Nayak and Roy had excellent connections from their Cadence and Synopsys days in India.[50]

Since Sycamore was then recruiting 25 engineers per week, Tejas sent its own new recruits to Boston for several months of training at Sycamore. As Nayak explained, this gave Sycamore access to top engineering talent while providing excellent training to Tejas engineers in how to build optical networking equipment for the telecommunications industry—exposing them to key functions such as quality assurance, hardware design, software development, network design, responding to Requests for Proposal (RFPs), and customer support.[51]

Ultimately, Tejas settled on developing a less expensive version of the kind of optical networking equipment that was popular in the United States targeted at the specific needs of India's emerging telecommunications companies. Following the Indian government's 1992 decision to liberalize its telecommunications sector, various international and domestic vendors entered the market. And by 2000, Deshpande believed that the $6 billion equipment market was about to expand rapidly because the government had decided to leapfrog old technology and install the most technologically advanced systems on the market.[52]

Tejas was functioning as Sycamore's marketing, sales, and support arm in India and its top executives spent their time talking with potential customers in the telecommunications industry to understand their needs. As CTO, Kumar was also very involved in marketing, and he and Nayak met with many telecommunications carriers. They identified their product opportunity by talking with Tata Power, which owned a network of largely unused underground optical fiber and wanted to use the network to carry telecommunications in Mumbai. Tata had the architecture and equipment for a high-capacity backbone, but also needed equipment that would carry the smaller, slower streams of data into the fast backbone.[53]

Satisfying this unmet need became Tejas's strategic focus. It turned out that no company offered such low-capacity switches because all the equipment makers were focusing on adding more capacity to switches so they could sell them at higher prices. Tejas decided to satisfy Tata's need for the low-capacity switch and received its first order in January 2001. As Nayak explained, "We were honest with the customer and they appreciated it. By the end of 2000 most telecommunications carriers had tired of hearing all of the reasons they should make large capital expenditures to buy the 'latest and greatest' technology, and had become distrustful."[54]

Since Tejas engineers were located in India, they were much more responsive to the needs of its telecommunications companies. And Tejas found from listening to these potential clients that they had similar needs to those of Tata Power.

Nayak described the product requirements of Indian telecommunications providers such as Tata Power as follows: "We need a low-capacity, low-cost switch that has many of the features of the larger, higher-capacity switches that reside in the backbone. Getting the data and voice traffic from the customer to the backbone is our problem. And we cannot afford the prices the United States companies are charging, which are initially too high ex-factory, but become completely unaffordable as the various regional, country, and reseller or integrator margins are added on."[55]

Deshpande had a strong grasp of what Indian telecommunications customers required and derived satisfaction from Tejas's decision to split with Sycamore and focus on building products to satisfy those Customer Purchase Criteria (CPC). As he saw it, potential customers wanted "the lowest prices ('10% to 20% lower than China'), the highest quality ('higher than China'), and the most up-to-date technology with the broadest functionality ('same as in the West')." And once Tejas had decided to focus on meeting these CPC, Deshpande "then choose which path to take, although I privately hoped they would choose to take the high-risk/high-reward path of becoming a product company."[56]

To achieve its strategic goals, Tejas needed capital. Specifically, it raised $29 million in three rounds of equity investments reflecting increasing valuations—Nayak claimed that the Series C share price was "several times" that of its Series A round. And Tejas negotiated lines of credit to finance its inventories and receivables. The first round came from the previously described $5 million from Deshpande and Sycamore. The second one was in January 2002, in which Deshpande, Intel Capital, and IIML (an Indian venture capital fund for infrastructure development affiliated with the IFC) invested $9 million.[57]

The third round came in December 2004, when Battery Ventures led a $15 million round that included IIML, Deshpande, Intel Capital, and a communcations-focused fund, Gabriel Ventures, as a new investor. According to Carl Stjernfeldt, who led the round for Battery Ventures and joined the Tejas board, the decision to invest in Tejas was a challenging one because of the newness of investing in an Indian start-up and the legal paperwork required to meet the needs of Battery's limited partners who wanted to enjoy the same investment conditions from India as they would get from a U.S. investment. Nevertheless, Stjernfeldt viewed Tejas has having many investment positives including a big potential market and an experienced management team.[58]

Stjernfeldt described his thinking as follows: "We led the early 2005 round of $15 million with a $10 million investment. It was our first investment in India and was outside of our mandate as a fund, so I spent a lot of time addressing the concerns of our investors (that they would not be liable for tax reporting in India, for example). I had identified the Indian telecommunications equipment market as an interesting one, and appreciated the fact that culturally India was more understandable and transparent than many other emerging markets, such as China."[59]

Stjernfeldt formed a very favorable impression of Tejas's management team. As he said, "I had heard about Tejas from two carriers in the West, so I decided to meet them in the summer of 2004. I found a very strong and balanced team, was impressed by the general management skills of Sanjay Nayak, the operational skills of Arnob Roy, and the technical stature of Kumar. I had not known that Desh Deshpande was involved, and this was an extra bonus, along with a very professional board of directors."[60]

Stjernfeldt then went on to explain some of the legal complexities he faced in investing in an Indian company. As he said, "After signing the term sheet in August, it took several months to close due to the complexity of making the legal documents of an Indian company reflect the protections and rights that VC investors require in the United States."[61]

Stjernfeldt felt some trepidation about his investment in Tejas because he decided to invest before having conducted a thorough examination of all the possible start-ups in India at the time. According to Stjernfeldt, "My only disappointment is that I do not see more product companies in India that we might invest in. Was Tejas a one-off that I luckily found? Or is it just a matter of time before we will see more high-potential product-based ventures in India? India's technical-service oriented labor market is losing its pricing advantage, and would benefit from high-value added businesses."[62]

Tejas's ability to apply to the emerging Indian telecommunications market teams' U.S. optical networking capabilities reveal important lessons for entrepreneurs:

Sometimes it makes sense to start a company with a vague idea and a great team. Deshpande's exceptional track record of starting and leading two highly successful optical networking companies gave him unusual flexibility to start with a vague idea of building a company in India and using that idea to recruit a top-notch executive team.

A start-up that locates itself in an emerging market can have an advantage over more established firms that operate remotely. Tejas's ability to spend significant time with customers to listen to their needs gave it a big competitive advantage. Tejas discovered that big potential customers had an important unmet need and that its competitors would have very little economic incentive to satisfy it. Thanks to Tejas's Bangalore location next to its potential customers and its willingness to build a company around meeting their needs, it was able to build a significant business.

A great team with a credible idea for winning in a rapidly growing market can ease the path to raising capital. Deshpande's track record and his ability to describe Tejas's market opportunity in a credible manner helped persuade Battery Ventures to invest despite the additional work it needed to do in order to satisfy the demands of its limited partners.

Sawyer Research Products Loses Its Investment to Russian Expropriation

Sawyer Research Products—a U.S.-based quartz manufacturer—invested $8 million in a Russian quartz crystal manufacturing plant. Once the formerly dormant defense facility was up and running with Sawyer's money and know-how, the Russian government used its court system to take control of the facility from Sawyer—leaving it $8 million poorer and leaving its IP in the hands of its former partners. With such examples of "creeping expropriation" why should any entrepreneur invest in Russia?

Gary Johnson, Sawyer Research's former CEO described his company's business in greater detail. As he explained, "Sawyer Research Products, Inc. is a global leader in the business and technology of single crystal piezoelectric materials, especially cultured quartz. Quartz is second only to the production of silicon in the ranking of crystal materials used in electronics. Quartz is the leading material used both to generate and to select electronic signals at a precise frequency. Common applications include telecommunications and digital electronics—mobile telephones and computers, for example. The optical properties of quartz are used in digital imaging and optical data storage applications."[63]

Sawyer decided to expand production of quartz crystals into Russia through a 1994 investment in what had been a moribund plant in Russia's Vladimir region. According to Johnson, "In 1994, Sawyer became a shareholder of Quartz Glass Plant ('QGP') in Goose Khrustalny in the Vladimir region and [later] invested over $8 million in the creation of a high technology piezoelectric quartz growing operation at QGP."[64]

Sawyer viewed QGP as a way to gain access to a high quality manufacturing facility at a low price. Johnson explained QGP's condition as follows: "The QGP facility was idled at the time of privatization in 1994 and was being plundered by local interests. The plant is a 300,000 square meter facility created mostly in the 1980's to supply the high purity glass required to manufacture semiconductor crystals, high quality optics, and other technical uses. At its peak, the plant employed more than 10,000 workers in eight workshops. One of the smaller of these, Workshop Five, contained eighty quartz growth vessels purchased in Japan that produced relatively low grade material that subsequently was crushed into sand as a feedstock for certain grades of glass used by other parts of the facility."[65]

Sawyer perceived several benefits of the QGP facility. According to Johnson, "The principal attractions for Sawyer of Workshop Five were relatively low operating costs, especially energy, the availability of highly skilled production and technical workers, and the availability of capital equipment at much less cost than new investment. Also, the utilization of this idle capacity would not add further to the excess capacity that existed in the quartz industry in 1994."[66]

Sawyer decided that the potential benefits of investing in the QGP plant outweighed the risks. However, it is clear that Sawyer's assessment may have been unduly biased by its perception of the artificial quartz market opportunity and Sawyer's previously successful international ventures. As Johnson explained, "Sawyer's assessment of the economic opportunity of exporting artificial quartz from Russia and Sawyer's international experience, especially success with a joint venture in Korea, and subsequent success with operations in China and Japan, overcame concerns about the investment climate."[67]

By 2007, Sawyer had decided to proceed with its QGP investment. Johnson described the investment as follows: "In July 1997, Sawyer decided to proceed and entered a 25-year lease contract with QGP. It invested over $3 million in capital improvements, renovations and start-up operations. The lease required Sawyer to rapidly payoff $1.5 million in social debt to help QGP, one of the largest enterprises in Vladimir, avoid bankruptcy. Including working capital and other necessary expenditures, Sawyer's investment exceeded $8 million."[68]

Unfortunately for Sawyer, this investment did not pay off. In fact, once Sawyer had written its checks, complied with its contractual obligations, and built a successful business, Russia expropriated QGP without making fair and just compensation to Sawyer. Johnson described the events in a surprisingly dispassionate manner as follows: "After meeting all legal obligations under the external management plan and contract obligations and establishing a successful business in the QGP facility through the Sawyer subsidiary ZAO 'Russian Quartz,' the Governor and Deputy Governor of the Vladimir administration launched a campaign using state institutions to oust Sawyer for the benefit of private interests represented in a new company, OAO 'Very Pure Quartz Glass' (VPQG)."[69]

How did Sawyer lose control of QGP? Russia used its legal system against Sawyer in ways that put Sawyer at an insurmountable legal competitive disadvantage. As Johnson explained, "The short answer is that Russian institutions failed. Their failure to protect Sawyer's property rights was neither simple nor unintended; indeed, they were co-opted into a sophisticated and systematic campaign to take control of Sawyer's $8 million investment."[70]

Johnson provided a systematic analysis of how the Russian legal system failed. As he argued, "Russia's legal system is being exploited in five different ways:

- Rent-seekers used their government positions and ability to influence official decision-making to create facts that put Sawyer, as a small foreign investor with no government access and no willingness to make special arrangements with the local government, permanently at a disadvantage.
- Effective collusion occurred between the local Vladimir administration and the local courts in both Vladimir and Nizhny Novgorod. This goes beyond "telephone justice" to a sophisticated system under which the judges are converted into legal advocates for one side in a commercial dispute, to a point where they provide one side legal advice, help them prepare evidence,

and otherwise form strategy. This has become so brazen that *ex parte* meetings between the judges and the other side in this dispute, VPQG, take place on a routine basis in full public view.

- After Sawyer defeated early attempts to invalidate the 25-year lease, the local administration requested the state prosecutor to become the advocate of VPQG, a private party in the name of protecting Russia's "state interests." Effectively, since that point the state has been acting as the law firm of one party in a commercial dispute.

- The defense mobilization law was used in an effort to re-nationalize QGP. Though Sawyer defeated this effort on the merits, this campaign effectively created a public perception that an American company was trying to control a national strategic asset. Eventually, the prosecutor withdrew defense mobilization claims.

- The use of bankruptcy law to (a) create a false bankruptcy (b) strip valuable assets from QGP and its shareholders, including, by the way, the 17.5% interest of the Russian Federation; and (c) finally, after withdrawing the defense mobilization claims the prosecutor turned to bankruptcy law to annul Sawyer's 25-year lease. This despite the fact that Sawyer had fulfilled all obligations under the external bankruptcy plan of QGP and the lease. Material compliance notwithstanding, the prosecutor eventually succeeded in invalidating the lease based on a technical point of bankruptcy law that according to experts is subject to broad interpretation. In the course of these long proceedings to the best of our knowledge no official questioned what state interests are invoked by the outcome of an interpretation of minutia in a bankruptcy regulation—a body of law widely believed to be dangerously vague and susceptible to abuse. Logically, the state interest is to insure that it is impossible to distort state interests for the benefit of a private party."[71]

These five means of exploiting the Russian legal system led Sawyer to lose its investment in QGP. As Johnson explained, "in May 2001, a federal appeals court declared Sawyer's 25-year lease invalid. In June 2001, Sawyer was removed from the factory, but was unable to take its assets, property and inventory. Since June 2001, though the local courts have ruled that Sawyer's property should be returned, these decisions have not been enforced. Most recently, the federal appeals court in Nizhny Novgorod was able to create a whole new fact and turn investor's rights inside out by ruling that Sawyer owes damages to VPQG because Sawyer unlawfully occupied Workshop Five for three years, the very time during which Sawyer renovated the plant and returned it to operation. Again, what is most telling is that this 'creeping expropriation' of Sawyer's investment has taken place in full public view."[72]

Once the local government had taken over QGP, the business failed. According to Johnson, "This takeover strategy was completed in June 2001 by the posting of a private security force to exclude Russian Quartz employees from the plant. Since that time, the export capability that Sawyer had created at Workshop Five— [generating revenues of] about $300,000 per month and rapidly increasing—has been reduced to almost nothing and the shop has lost its ability to produce world standard quartz on a reliable basis. Reports indicate that VPQG has failed in the market. We further understand that in recent months workers have not been paid fully and that layoffs are underway. In short, under VPQG management, the Workshop Five asset has been all but destroyed."[73]

Johnson examined what went wrong with the Sawyer investment in Russia and identified several beliefs—in legal strategy, outlook on life, and shared values—he had at the time of the investment that he now views as incorrect. More specifically, these include the following:

Legal strategy. As Johnson explained, one of these was "believing [we] could lose in local courts and win in higher courts." In retrospect, Johnson realized that Sawyer "needed to fight vigorously locally to avoid the situation in which the adversaries created a sufficient body of decisions to give cover to the higher courts."

Outlook on life. Moreover, Johnson's natural optimism caused him to assume that the situation would improve. As he wrote, "[We acted on the] belief that over time the situation—judicial independence, protection of investor rights, etc.—would improve. As we've seen that was not the case[.] The deterioration continues."

Shared values. Finally, Johnson initially believed that Russian business executives shared his goals. As Johnson wrote, "[We acted on the] belief that basically business was business and that Russian businessmen would pursue the same objectives as we. This basic philosophy had worked well in other Sawyer ventures in Korea, Japan, and China and in the business of the company to sell globally. For various reasons, Russians were different."[74]

Johnson expanded on how Russians differ and concluded that there might be some aspects of the national character and outlook on life that lead to different ways of conducting business. As Johnson explained, "There are a couple issues I picked up in the Russian 'character' (whatever that might be) that seemed to underlie a lot of business behavior. [I have noticed that many of the Russians with whom I have interacted have] different perceptions of time. [They seem to have] much less faith in the future than Americans tend to have. [They use a much] shorter investment horizon. [They want to] get [a return on their investment] now by any means possible. [They believe that] the future is short and present opportunities must be exploited now. Officials and business people share this view (as does the populace). [They are] fatalistic. [They act as though] only today matters. [And I think that this outlook on life] justifies corruption [in their minds]."[75]

Johnson concluded that Russia's legal system is manipulated by government officials to achieve their political aims. Moreover, he found that there are very few people there he trusts. According to Johnson, "[Outsiders seeking entry into Russian business should] trust only those with whom [they] have a direct relationship built from an introduction by a trusted intermediary. [In Russia] the rule of law does not work. [Power centers around] cults of personality [and] networks of support that band together [around those personalities]. [I found that you] can't trust your neighbor. [To operate in Russia, an outsider] must become part of [this] network. [I think that such networks are] common in authoritarian states where government uses citizen spies and corrupt systems to control [the] population and stay in power. [This method of popular control] leads to distrust of 'others,' 'clanishness' and ultimately nationalism. [And it] gives leaders [a] route to create common enemies of the 'others.' "[76]

Johnson believes that these Russian habits of behavior spring from a rich history of powerless individuals trying to survive in the face of powerful leaders. As Johnson explained, "[These ways of operating are a result of] lessons learned [by the] powerless [regarding how they ought] to deal with power (think peasants and czars, populace and party officials). [The powerless] created a 'jujitsu' in which power is used against the powerful—using the strengths of adversaries against them. Look at [Russia's] use of a Western veneer against Westerners. It isn't a coincidence that Potemkin villages[77] were born in Russia. Many Russian institutions are set up as Potemkin villages without [a] real commitment to [creating] civil society. [This is] a way for powerful to remain so. Russians have a very keen sense of where power lies and how to use that position. If they are in a power position—[they] dominate. If they are in a weaker position—[they] use the power of the powerful against them."[78]

In the case of Sawyer, Russia perceived itself as the weaker party and used its legal system to entice investment only to expropriate it. In Johnson's experience, Russia is unique in creating such a system. As Johnson explained, "As a group, I've never seen more people more adept at this. [Russia] set up a system that looks like the rule of law [so] Westerners will respect it. In [the] Sawyer dispute the U.S. government repeatedly said [it] couldn't intervene because it was in the courts—as though the courts deserved the same respect as those in the United States, Western Europe, Japan, etc. They never dealt with how it got there (corrupt prosecutorial system, which is a long tradition in Russia)."[79]

In Johnson's experience, the Russian approach to justice is unique. As he explained, "[I had] never [before] dealt with fundamental differences in the concept of courts. [I found that] Russian [courts] protect state interests (which typically were defined by prosecutor), rather than adjudicate according to laws. [Until Sawyer's involvement with the Russian legal system I] didn't recognize that laws were set up inconsistently and with such complexity that everyone was always in violation. Thus, the decision to prosecute (an executive decision) meant guilt. Many think Russia is lawless. [This is] not so. [In fact, Russia has] too many laws that are inconsistent. [Russia] often place[s] accumulation of power over business deals. [By contrast,] Americans [are] much more likely to value [closing a] deal rather than personal victory."[80]

Sawyer's experience with QGP in Vladimir suggests that it may be very difficult for a foreign entrepreneur to get a return on investment in Russia. As a result, it appears that the most important lesson of this case is that entrepreneurs must be willing to let hard-nosed analysis overcome their initial

instincts about an investment decision. It appears that Johnson came to a conclusion about investing in the QGP plant before an exhaustive analysis of the
potential risks. To be fair, his contacts in Russia probably realized that he was
strongly inclined to make the investment in QGP and gave him the answers he
wanted to hear. So how is an entrepreneur to know whether his or her instinct
and resistance to naysayers will ultimately lead to a money-winning or losing
investment?

Here are some steps Sawyer might have taken that might have led the company to pass on the QGP investment:

Find 10 other U.S. companies that had made investments in Russian operations. An
entrepreneur seeking to invest outside the home country should do what Sawyer
may not have done—find 10 companies that had done what Sawyer hoped to do.
At the time, it may have been difficult to find that many companies in Russia.
But the reasoning for suggesting 10 people is to make sure that a decision is not
biased by seeking out only the examples that confirm what an entrepreneur may
already have decided to do.

Talk with the CEOs of those companies to learn from their experience. Sawyer
should have spoken with the CEOs of these companies—asking them questions such as the following: Why did your company want to invest in Russia?
Which projects did you consider investing in there? What criteria did you use
to choose among the investments? Why did you pick the specific project in
which you invested? How did you analyze the risks and benefits of the investment? What were the terms of the investment? Has your company made or lost
money on the investment? How do you explain the outcome? What lessons
have you learned from the experience? What advice would you give a company considering an investment in Russia? Any entrepreneur should consider
exploring the answers to such questions before an investment outside their
home country.

Objectively weigh the results of this due diligence before deciding. It is likely that
if Sawyer had conducted such research before making its investment in QGP
that it would have been more aware of its inherent risk. Johnson's assumption
that his Russian partners would share his goal of creating a successful venture
and his belief that Sawyer could prevail in the Russian court system appear naive
in retrospect. Had he conducted interviews with other U.S. companies that had
invested in Russia, he may have been more aware of the risks. However, it may
have been better for Johnson to have hired a consultant to assess the decision so
he could receive a recommendation regarding the decision that was unbiased by
his natural optimism.

Campus Media Helps Intel Capital Sell Chips to Chinese Students

Not all corporate investment in new ventures meet the same fate as Sawyer
did in Russia. Intel Corp.'s venture capital arm, Intel Capital's, investment in
Chinese start-up Campus Media—which operates an advertising network in

university cafeterias across China—appears to be on track for a more favorable outcome. Intel Capital viewed Campus Media, which by 2006 had installed 7,000 TVs in 300 universities with a total enrollment of 4 million students that it used to show programming and advertising, as a creator of demand for Intel's chips.[81]

Moreover, Intel Capital chose China because it believes that China has the high-end consumers, large pool of engineering talent, and (unlike India) a very business-friendly government. Campus Media's then-CEO Pike Tse, a 38-year-old former Coca-Cola salesman, planned to turn his terminals into Internet access points as well. Tse chose Intel as an investor for its technical support and semiconductor know-how—and with these added capabilities Campus Media intends to flow with China's entrepreneurial ecosystem.[82]

An important reason that Intel Capital invested in China is that it perceived greater opportunities for growth as well as significant innovation that could grab a meaningful share of China's booming revenues. By mid-2006, Intel Capital saw greater innovation among Chinese start-ups and added four new investments from its $200 million Technology Fund.[83] In the course of a year, its China Technology Fund had made a dozen investments. The four new companies included Campus Media, Montage Technology Co. Ltd., Star Softcomm Pte Ltd. and Winking Entertainment Limited. As such Intel Capital's China Technology Fund had invested in 12 Chinese companies in the year following its June 2005 inception. Intel was making these latest investments, together with earlier announced funding in 50 Chinese start-ups and companies, to foster Chinese innovation in cellular communications, broadband deployment, software applications, and semiconductor design.[84]

Cadol Cheung, managing director, Intel Capital Asia Pacific, elaborated on Intel's objectives for such investments. He pointed out that in 2006 Intel typically invested between $1 million and $5 million in each company—focusing on its efforts to foster Chinese innovation in technology hardware, software, and services. Cheung was growing concerned about rising private company valuations in China. However, he believed that thanks to Intel Capital's reputation with Chinese entrepreneurs—which began investing there in 1998—it could continue to make sound investments that met its strategic and financial criteria. Specifically, Cheung believed that Chinese entrepreneurs valued Intel Capital's capabilities at company-building, technology validation and global "matchmaking" with potential customers or business partners. And in the case of Campus Media, Cheung suggested that the company would also provide an interesting opportunity for Intel marketing campaigns to target hard-to-reach university students across China.[85]

The big lesson of this case is that entrepreneurs seeking investment from corporate venture capital funds must understand those funds' objectives. While a traditional VC's primary objective is to generate high returns for their partners, a corporate VC may exist to create companies that will buy more of the company's products or services. Campus Media's capital raise from Intel Capital was mutually beneficial because Campus Media provided Intel Corp. access to an attractive market—Chinese students—that it otherwise would have had difficulty reaching.

And Campus Media received many benefits from the Intel Capital investment—credibility, access to its network, and marketing support. Entrepreneurs seeking capital from outside their home countries should seek out investors who can create these mutually beneficial outcomes.

Changyou's Blockbuster IPO Is an Oasis in the Desert

While Campus Media has yet to pay off for Intel Capital, some China-based start-ups have generated attractive returns for investors. By the spring of 2009, the market for U.S. technology-based initial public offerings had been moribund for at least 18 months. Into this IPO desert stepped a Chinese company with a successful nine-year Nasdaq listing, Sohu.com. In early April 2009 Sohu.com sold shares of its online video gaming subsidiary, Changyou.com Ltd., and those shares spiked 25% when they first started trading.[86]

The rationale for taking this subsidiary public was to motivate the people who ran the subsidiary by tapping into investor hunger for growth and satisfying that demand with shares of Changyou and its online video gaming business. Specifically, Sohu took Changyou public because Changyou's manager wanted a share of its profits and an IPO would make stock options available to him and his staff. So a Chinese company tapped a moribund U.S. IPO market and achieved a significant stock market victory in the bargain.[87]

While Changyou was highly valued in the stock market, it trailed its peers. In April 2009, its stock traded at 7 times earnings—but this value was roughly at the mid-range of competitors but below the 11 or 12 earnings multiple of top Chinese gaming companies like Giant, Netease, and A Perfect World.[88]

Changyou's IPO was not done primarily for the money though. Instead, Sohu's decision to take its gaming division public may have been less about timing or the division's success than about Sohu's internal politics. According to Sohu Chief Executive Charles Zhang, in 2004 Sohu hired an executive, Wang Tao, from competing Internet portal Sina to boost its wobbly gaming division. Tao's hiring agreement included the provision that he would share in his division's profit and revenue.[89]

As Changyou's revenue has grown to account for half of Sohu's earnings, Zhang says the company decided to take its gaming division public and create stock option incentives—as a way to retain skilled game designers like Wang and attract new talent. As Zhang said, "With Wang, we just found the right person, and so we gave him all the right incentives. That's why we're making him a millionaire with this IPO."[90]

Wang, and the development team he brought to Sohu between 2004 and 2009, helped make Changyou the fourth most popular gaming site in China's online game market, behind firms like Netease, Giant, and A Perfect World. Changyou's revenues came from the sale of virtual items related to its most popular game, "Tian Long Ba Bu," which had 800,000 simultaneous users at peak times. And Changyou's ties with Sohu gave it an advantage over competitors—directing Sohu's 30 million unique daily visitors to Changyou's new games boosted the odds that Changyou would be able to add to its list of highly popular game titles.[91]

As of April 2008, Changyou was overly dependent on its one hit—Tian Long Ba Bu. According to RBC Capital Markets analyst Stephen Ju, Changyou's future success depends on the combination of two corporate capabilities—Wang Tao's game design skills with Sohu's immense Web traffic. According to Ju, "Sohu's game division began as a kind of skunkworks project and blossomed into this great business. But having one of the biggest Web portals in China pointing traffic in your direction doesn't hurt either."[92]

Thus Zhang's decision to spin off Changyou represents a calculated gamble that its publicly traded shares will provide a highly compelling financial incentive for Changyou's game designers to come up with another hit. In so doing, Sohu merged two key elements of the entrepreneurial ecosystem—financial markets and human capital. More specifically, Zhang decided to use his access to the IPO market to give his top Changyou game developers a chance to get rich.

What can entrepreneurs learn from Changyou's experience? Very few entrepreneurs can find themselves in Sohu's position of being able to use its access to the IPO market during a long down-period to motivate its most valuable employees. But the Changyou case does highlight two important lessons:

Give top performing people a chance to profit from their success. Entrepreneurs must know which of their people are contributing most heavily to their success and take pains to give them a chance to profit from their contribution to the company. In Sohu's case, its access to Nasdaq and the ability to list Changyou there made it possible to provide top game developers with stock options linked to that division's results. But entrepreneurs who lack such access can use other ways to reward key employees—such as profit sharing or bonus plans linked to achieving performance milestones.

Think globally about how to deliver those incentives. Zhang set an example for other entrepreneurs—to look globally for opportunities to reward top talent. Zhang rewarded Changyou employees with a Nasdaq listing of his China-based company. But an Indian entrepreneur might try to list shares of a key division in London to reward its Bangalore-based engineers. And a U.S.-based start-up staffed by Indian ex-pats might seek private capital from an Indian corporation. While such combinations would not work for every entrepreneur, Zhang's success with Changyou suggests that there is a benefit in thinking globally about rewarding top talent.

Focus Media Rewards Private Equity through Quick Thinking

Changyou is hardly the only successful Chinese start-up. In fact, there are many others that succeeded in making the journey from a glimmer in the eye of an ambitious entrepreneur to a successful initial public offering followed by revenue and profit growth. Focus Media exemplifies this pattern. In 2003, Jason Jiang was an unknown Chinese entrepreneur with a then-strange idea to sell ads in elevator lobbies. Then he persuaded the venture investors to back him. By 2006, Jiang's company, Focus Media Holding Ltd., had a market capitalization of almost $2.9 billion. Its share price had quadrupled since its IPO in July 2006 on the Nasdaq Stock Market. Jiang's personal fortune of more than $700 million included a 25% stake in his company.[93]

Jiang has risen quickly in China where not long ago getting rich quickly was not celebrated. However, by 2006, the 33-year-old Jiang was a Chinese celebrity—one of a small group of young entrepreneurs pursuing China's rising consumer class, rather than relying on its traditional economic role as a center of low-cost manufacturing. Jiang's name is on a list of top-10 "IT Young Spirits" posted on a Web site run by the Shanghai Municipal Committee. And China's state-owned newspapers featured profiles recounting his rise to wealth.[94]

Jiang's success with Focus Media established a template that other investors—particularly private equity investors and venture capitalists coming to China—hoped to emulate. Focus Media's quick success contrasted with many previous Chinese ventures that grew quickly but failed to deliver high investment returns. By paving the way for other start-up companies, Jiang proclaimed that he was making it possible for China's new entrepreneurs to "inject new dynamics into the Chinese economy."[95]

Jiang emerged into the entrepreneurial stratosphere on the wings of his own talent. He is the only child of a middle-class couple. His father was an accountant, and his mother managed a state-run grocery store. He attended a teachers' college in Shanghai and was preparing to become an elementary school instructor. While a student, he wrote poems and recited them at public readings. Jiang enjoyed debate as a first-year student and he engaged upper class men in discussions on philosophy and literature, according to Alan Ji, a college friend who is Focus Media's head of public relations. Jiang later won election as president of the student union.[96]

Focus Media's business of advertising initially grabbed Jiang's attention in college. To earn some money, he began selling print ads for an advertising company, and he quickly became its top salesman. After graduation, he founded an Internet advertising firm. In 2003, he left that business to found Focus Media. Jiang believed that the emergence of newly affluent Chinese required advertisers to find better ways to target customers, many of whom spent more time at the office than at home. To reach these people he wanted to sell advertisements on a network of electronic billboards installed at elevator lobbies in office buildings in Shanghai and Beijing.[97]

In 2003, Jiang struggled to keep the money-losing Focus Media in business. It was quickly using up the seed capital that Softbank China Venture Capital had invested, was operating at a net loss for the year, and was in desperate need of more money.[98]

By December 2003, Jiang decided he would try to satisfy this need for capital by trying to persuade a private equity fund to write Focus Media a multimillion dollar check. He flew to Beijing to visit the senior partner at CDH Fund, a private equity firm. He arrived there on a cold afternoon without an overcoat, according to Wu Shangzhi, the CDH partner. Dismissing Wu's concerns that he would catch a cold, Jiang began explaining Focus Media's business strategy.[99]

With Focus Media's back against the wall, Jiang was able to persuade CDH that he understood both the strengths and weaknesses of Focus Media's business strategy. According to Wu, Jiang spoke passionately. He also displayed an understanding that Focus Media would face challenges with its then-current business strategy. For example, since Focus Media already controlled 70% of the Shanghai market and a big share of Beijing's major office complexes, it would have trouble growing unless it could expand into new markets.[100]

But Wu was impressed by Jiang's ideas about how to overcome Focus Media's weaknesses. Jiang wanted to sustain the company's growth by establishing franchises in secondary cities in China, such as Changsha and Tianjin, with the hope of buying and integrating them into the parent company once they became financially viable. Jiang also claimed that although Focus Media had lost money for 2003, it had become profitable in November and December. But what finally convinced Wu was Jiang's willingness to share the risks he was asking investors to take.[101]

To that end, Jiang agreed that Focus Media would earn $10 million in net profit in 2004 and that CDH could reduce its capital commitment if Focus Media did not achieve the target. Wu recalled that Jiang told him: "If I don't achieve what I set out, I will suffer." By the end of the meeting Wu agreed to invest $12 million—twice what Jiang had been seeking to raise.[102]

Focus Media ended up exceeding its 2004 financial targets. Revenue grew quickly in 2004, and the company earned several million more than the $10 million earnings target he had set with Wu. By November 2004, Goldman Sachs, venture capital fund 3i Group and United China Investment Ltd. provided $30 million. Focus Media's summer 2005 IPO raised $171 million—reaping significant returns for its investors. In January 2006, Focus Media raised $295 million in a secondary offering on Nasdaq that yielded $40 million for Jiang and more than $100 million combined for Goldman Sachs and CDH.[103]

Like Changyou, Focus Media was able to enrich its investors through a Nasdaq-listed IPO. In both cases, it appears likely that the higher level of corporate governance and the greater liquidity of Nasdaq made it possible to attract significant capital investment from credible sources. But Focus Media was unique in the sense that the entrepreneur who came up with the initial idea for the company was able to overcome initial start-up hurdles, raise fresh capital, manage a successful IPO, and continue to run the company for years after taking it public.

The most important lesson an entrepreneur can draw from the Focus Media case is that a flexible mind is critical for overcoming the obstacles to achieving start-up success. Jiang took a new idea and made it work in some of China's largest cities. Yet he realized that unless he changed the idea, Focus Media would not be able to continue to grow. To that end, he decided that franchising his idea to smaller cities would be the key to sustaining his company's growth and persuading a private equity investor to buy a piece of his company. Jiang's intellectual flexibility—which enabled him not to be locked into the idea that future success depended on replicating a previously successful strategy—is an attribute that every entrepreneur should seek to develop.

Dangdang Books Profit for Western VCs

Not all of China's successful start-ups spring from original ideas such as Focus Media's strategy of displaying advertising to office workers. Many successful Chinese start-ups take ideas that have proven successful in the United States and adapt those ideas to the Chinese market. Rebecca Fannin, author of *Silicon Dragon: How China is Winning the Tech Race*, highlights the role of Silicon Valley VC in financing the growth of China's technology companies. Fannin also points out the role of Chinese entrepreneurs who return to China after spending time in the United States, which are dubbed "sea turtles"—a play on words that sounds like "coming home" in Chinese.[104]

Fannin suggests that it is becoming increasingly popular for sea turtles to start companies in China, get financing from Silicon Valley, and take the venture public on Nasdaq. According to Fannin, "The 'in' thing among bright, young Chinese techies is to draw up a business plan, get financing, scale the start-up to sizeable revenues and profits, and then go public in the United States. There are a few who have listed in China, especially Hong Kong, but the gold standard is really seen as the Nasdaq or the New York Stock Exchange. There are already more than 65 companies trading on the Nasdaq and the New York Stock Exchange, and doing very well out of it."[105]

Not surprisingly, many of the sea turtles have been heavily influenced by their experience in the United States and see an opportunity to make quick money by copying a successful U.S. business model and applying it to the Chinese market. Since U.S. investors understand those successful models, they perceive a relatively limited risk as long as they are betting on an entrepreneur with whom they feel comfortable. One such "copycat" is Peggy Yu, cofounder of a Chinese version of Amazon, online bookseller Dangdang.com.[106]

Dangdang.com faced significant competition in 1999 from dozens of other Amazon clones in China. But Yu succeeded by offering the widest possible selection of books—by 2008 its titles numbered 200,000—and it used marketing innovations such as steep discounts—important in China where low-priced pirated copies are popular—and making the site user-friendly.[107]

Dangdang.com also benefited from its harvest of venture capital. Specifically, it raised $40 million in VC from the United States and China, which enabled Dangdang.com to grow while many of those Chinese competitors collapsed following 2000's dot-com crash.[108] Its initial venture money came from IDG, Softbank, and Luxembourg Cambridge Holding Group—followed in late 2003 by an $11-million injection from the U.S.-based Tiger Technology Fund. And in July 2006 it secured $27 million in third round funding from San Francisco Bay Area VCs Doll Capital Management (DCM), Walden International, and Alto Global Investment, each taking a 12% stake.[109]

Another advantage for Dangdang was the surprising failure of Amazon to compete effectively in China. Initially Amazon fumbled its China venture after acquiring the Joyo site and then failing to support it properly—by June 2008, the Joyo site had recovered but remained unprofitable. In June 2008, Dangdang (which means "worthy" in Chinese) had nearly 13 million registered customers, compared with Joyo's 11 million. Again, following Amazon's trail, Dangdang began to add general merchandise to its sales site in 2004, and by 2008 nonbook items accounted for about 40% of sales, compared with 25% for Joyo.[110]

Although there are similarities between Amazon and Dangdang, Yu adapted its business strategy to many of the limitations of the Chinese consumer industry—including a far less developed payments and delivery infrastructure. According to Fannin, "Dangdang has faced some very Chinese problems. First, credit cards have not really caught on in China, so Dangdang used money orders, which are very popular. More recently, they have added a cash-on-delivery service. Then there is the obstacle that the postal service in China is less than reliable, so Dangdang used couriers—bicycles—early on, and now cars. In many ways, Peggy Yu and Dangdang have benefited from being a few years behind the West in this area. They could cherry-pick from a lot of things that others had tested in very elaborate and expensive ways, and decide what to do and not do."[111]

Yu offers two important insights for entrepreneurs:

- *In seeking U.S. venture capital, the odds of success rise if an entrepreneur can compare her start-up to a U.S. success story.* Particularly in China, which has a reputation for weak IP protection, a U.S.-based VC is likely to lack confidence in the chance to earn a profit from investing in a technology-based start-up. So Yu was clever to develop a start-up that based its strategy on Amazon.com, which had amply rewarded its early investors. And Yu's firm depended for its success on many factors that were not related to technology—such as solving China's specific infrastructure challenges including its weak distribution and payment networks.
- *To copy a U.S. model successfully, an entrepreneur must provide unique value to the consumer.* Yu was not the only entrepreneur seeking to create a Chinese version of Amazon. But she did a better job than her peers of understanding the needs of the Chinese consumer for wide selection and low prices. As a result, Dandang prevailed over the competition and rewarded its investors. Her lesson is that one of the universal rules of competition is giving customers more of what they want than competitors. And to do that, an entrepreneur must start with a detailed understanding of how a customer will choose among those competitors.

Bain Capital Blue-Printing Spurs Portfolio Company Growth

Chinese entrepreneurs such as Li and Zhang who have already enjoyed successful relationships with private capital providers are well-versed in the lessons for building effective VC firm ties. However, start-up CEOs who aspire to work with leading Western private capital providers must realize that some private equity firms that invest in China expect their portfolio companies to follow their specific management disciplines along with their investment. Chinese entrepreneurs may benefit from gaining insight into these expectations before they accept Western capital.

One leading Western private equity firm, Bain Capital, has a clear idea of how it likes to work with portfolio companies in China—and that process generally starts with deploying people who speak Mandarin. According to Bain Capital's Jing Huang, "My preference is for local talent because they can override psychological barriers more easily than foreigners in China. Local entrepreneurs still regard even people from Taiwan, Hong Kong or Singapore as outsiders because they speak Mandarin with an accent. All people in our Shanghai office are 100 per cent mainland Chinese nationals or people who grew up in China. It may be of interest that for one of our portfolio companies, before closing the deal, all transactions were conducted in Mandarin: most materials provided by the company were in Chinese though Bain Capital internal communications leading to our approval process were in English. As we entered the post-deal, 'blue printing process' [a plan for improving the portfolio company's value], the team realized that one of the founders spoke very good English. If we knew that, we would have asked him to present to our partners in English! This came as a positive surprise."[112]

Bain Capital differentiates itself from many of its private equity competitors by getting involved with portfolio companies at an earlier stage. Jing characterized other VC firms in China as being more interested in later stage investments because of a lower appetite for risk. According to Jing, "I feel that VC firms in China tend to conduct later stage deals (by Silicon Valley standards) in which they do not create companies that create technologies, but rather back up a team that applies certain technologies. In effect, they invest in applications in the service industry that uses technology rather than the technology companies per se."[113]

However, Jing believes that these competitors are taking on a different risk by delaying investment until later in a company's development process. As Jing explained, "In a way, one risk that VC firms take when paying a high valuation for companies that are making a small profit is scalability of that profit. In China, many start-up companies keep their operational costs low, so they can be profitable with revenue of only $15 million. However, by U.S. standards, if a VC firm can be evaluated on profits only, then they are in their later stage of evolution."[114]

Bain Capital does not necessarily agree with this strategy because it raises numerous important questions for investors. According to Jing, these questions include the following: "Can the [portfolio company's] profit grow from $1 million to $10 million or to $100 million? Can the company become significant enough for an IPO? This kind of evolution draws both market risks and operational risks—not trivial considerations. Also, many smaller companies are especially vulnerable to sudden, unexpected regulatory changes that might prohibit certain business expansion. In such cases, although they make $2 million to $3 million per year, the scale of their business is unattractive to big-time investors or even the public market. In effect, they can linger in business though they do not die.

The major gamble for VC firms with the appetite to invest at a 20x or 30x Price/ Earnings ratio is whether their investment will quadruple over the next two years. Do they want to take this risk?"[115]

Bain Capital places tremendous emphasis on the blue-printing process mentioned above. And this process can add value to a portfolio company if the CEO is willing to accept Bain Capital's management discipline. As Jing explained, "Bain Capital's style adopts active involvement in portfolio management, which may or may not be welcome by entrepreneurs. The 100-day blue-printing process and budgets for management improvement highlighted how often these requirements shock entrepreneurs. They are accustomed to having fixed asset capital expenditures—buying machines, building facilities, buying land, and maybe paying for software—but consulting services such as those by McKinsey, Bain and BCG frighten them."[116]

Jing tends to shun investing in entrepreneurs who simply expect a capital provider to write a check and let the founders run the business. Jing explained: "From the start of negotiations, it is clear that such entrepreneurs just want your capital. You will be welcome to attend the Board meetings, but other than that, do not bother anyone! Such entrepreneurs would probably not become our partners."[117]

By 2007, Bain Capital had three portfolio companies in China, each of which bought into the blue-printing process. As Jing pointed out in June 2007, "In each case, we conducted or are conducting a 100-day blue-printing process. One company has completed the process. The entrepreneurs were skeptical first and asked, 'In what way does this foreign consulting firm know more about our industry than us?' We had to explain our development strategy for a complete business survey to identify the company's current shortcomings and to find out how to improve business practice and how to track performance. After completion, the entrepreneurs were very happy. In the final session, the founders reflected that the results exceeded their expectations and they want to repeat the process again next year. They have referred another company to us. At one of the first meetings, the firm inquired about our blue-printing process, because they understood that Bain Capital has a reputation for improving operations post-investment."[118]

The Bain Capital case illustrates an extreme example of an investor getting involved in managing its portfolio company. Such aggressive intervention makes sense given Bain Capital's genesis as the investment arm of management consultant, Bain & Co. which had a reputation for taking over the day-to-day management of its client companies.

Although extreme, the Bain Capital case offers an important lesson for entrepreneurs: *Be sure you're comfortable with the way your capital provider works with its portfolio companies.* As we've seen in this chapter, some venture capital firms prefer to install their own CEO and let that person take the lead in running the company. Others, like Bain Capital, appear to want a partnership that involves providing a very structured approach to managing. Different entrepreneurs are comfortable with different approaches. And they should pick a capital provider whose style of working with portfolio companies best fits with their preferences.

Worksoft's Sea Turtles Bring Home Venture Gold

Worksoft is an example of a company that raised VC from a Silicon Valley firm and is staffed by sea turtles. Despite the differences between the Chinese and U.S. entrepreneurial ecosystems, the Silicon Valley VC felt comfortable investing because Worksoft was doing outsourcing work for U.S. companies and those sea turtles were steeped in U.S. business culture.

Worksoft operates out of Beijing doing work for U.S. companies. For example, its employees work with PCs and cell phones testing the phones' games under a contract with San Diego, CA-based Qualcomm. In another Worksoft office, engineers modify Peoplesoft software for China's market. And its Beijing office is so steeped in Western business culture that its conference rooms are named for towns in the Silicon Valley. One of its investors is a Silicon Valley venture capital firm, DCM, which invested in Worksoft with the idea of taking it public on Nasdaq.[119]

DCM made its investment in Worksoft in April 2005 despite all the significant differences between China and the United States. After all, Chinese accounting practices, language, legal structure, and culture are different from those in Western markets. But DCM found in Worksoft some factors that reduced its perceived risk. First, Worksoft performs work for U.S. companies, which can provide credible references. And Worksoft's managers are Chinese nationals who went to college or worked in the United States for years. For example, Jeff Wu, a Worksoft vice president, earned a master's in computer science at the University of Southern California and worked at EDS and Ariba before returning to China.[120]

A few months after receiving DCM's capital, Worksoft was planning for very rapid growth after operating as a family business for a decade. In May 2005, it had 800 employees but its offices were half empty as it planned to grow to 1,200 employees by the end of 2005 and an ultimate goal of 4,000 people. As Stanley Zhou, then–Worksoft's chief financial officer, said, "We want to become the largest outsourcing company in China." Such rapid growth represented a major shift for Chinese technology companies.[121]

Worksoft had operated without significant growth ambitions for its first decade. Chris Chen, Worksoft founder and CEO, explained: "In China, a typical software company has maybe 100 people. Worksoft was one of these for six or seven years." Chen earned a master's in engineering from Huazhong University of Science and Technology and briefly worked in the United States writing software for Wescom, then returned to China. In 1995, he started Worksoft with friends and family money—as is typical of Chinese start-ups.[122]

Worksoft remained a small family company until 2002 when the demand for outsourcing accelerated. Chen saw this demand as an opportunity. According to him, "We had to decide whether to grow fast or keep it as is. We decided to grow fast. But to do that, we needed capital and international expertise."

By early 2004, Worksoft started seeking venture funding and asking for meetings with the VCs. With some VCs and Chinese start-ups making financial killings through IPOs, excitement on both sides was building.[123]

And for Chinese entrepreneurs, U.S. venture money was the only option to finance rapid growth. That's because few other funding options exist for Chinese start-ups. Chinese banks rarely lend money to them. And an organized VC community did not exist in China. The best entrepreneurs could hope for was corporate VC—for example, Legend Holdings, parent of PC maker Lenovo, invested in start-ups—but only rarely in Chinese companies.[124]

But in order to attract U.S. VC, Chinese companies needed to change the way they operated. According to Andrew Hu, Beijing-based Asia/Pacific president of U.S. tech company Wyse, "Creditworthiness of Chinese start-ups is not there yet." Many companies keep two or three sets of books using different accounting methods. One set of books might be for government officials to see and minimize tax liabilities. Other practices, such as intellectual property protection, can be a sticky issue between Chinese and U.S. firms.[125]

But Chen wanted to raise U.S. VC money so in 2004 he asked his U.S.-educated team to change Worksoft to meet the requirements of U.S. VCs. DCM, which had made eight investments in China between 1999 and 2005, took Worksoft's bait. According to DCM cofounder David Chao, who moved to the United States from Japan at 13 and earned a degree in economics and East Asian studies, explained, "We are probably the most exposed (U.S. VC firm) to China and one of the few that has made money."[126]

Why did DCM invest in Worksoft? There are several reasons: its software outsourcing is a proven business strategy in China; it has been in business for 10 years; and its management team—including its VP, CFO, and COO and others—was educated and worked in the United States before becoming "sea turtles."[127]

DCM was able to overcome the challenges of conducting due diligence in light of China's eclectic accounting practices. Since contract law isn't well developed in China, Chinese often rely on handshakes and personal influence in business deals, making it harder to conduct such due diligence based on reviewing paperwork. To overcome these due diligence challenges, DCM coinvested with Legend Holdings—wagering that it would have better contacts and more insight into due diligence. Ultimately, DCM and Legend invested an undisclosed amount in Worksoft with the intention of conducting a 2007 IPO.[128]

And Worksoft actually achieved its goal—although under a different name. In December 2007, the newly named VanceInfo Technologies Inc. raised $65 million in an IPO of its American Depositary Shares on the New York Stock Exchange. On their first day of trading Vanceinfo shares rose 15.2% from their initial offering price of $8.50. VanceInfo's venture capital backers—DCM, Sequoia Capital China, and Legend Capital—all benefited from this rise. Although Microsoft and IBM were its two biggest customers in June 2007—accounting for 40% of its net sales—VanceInfo had increased its customer count from 66 in 2004 to 187 as of September 30, 2007.[129]

And by January 2010, its share price had risen 101% from its IPO price to over $20 a share and its financial results were solid—having generated $105 million in sales and $16 million in net profit for the first nine months of 2009.[130]

Like Focus Media, Worksoft is a Chinese start-up that made it from concept to successful IPO and beyond. But Worksoft's differences from Focus Media yield some important lessons. Worksoft was pursuing a strategy of outsourcing to U.S. companies, which had proven successful in India; whereas Focus Media was pioneering a completely new business strategy. Since Worksoft's strategy had been validated by Indian outsourcers, it was able to appeal to U.S. VCs who were looking for a proven business strategy to capture China's growth.

For entrepreneurs, it's worth emphasizing that Worksoft was able to benefit from the specific methods that DCM used to limit its perceived risk of investing in the company. In addition to what DCM perceived as its proven business strategy, Worksoft also benefited from what must have been a positive reference that it received from DCM's coinvestor Legend Capital. For entrepreneurs seeking capital from foreign providers, Worksoft's most valuable lesson is that different capital providers evaluate whether to invest differently. An entrepreneur should pick capital providers whose decision criteria fit with what their start-up can offer.

Implications for Entrepreneurs

What should entrepreneurs in new companies and industries do to profit from the globalization of entrepreneurship? While start-ups change too rapidly to follow any kind of rigorous methodology, the cases detailed earlier in the chapter suggest a series of general management imperatives that an entrepreneur might follow to improve the odds of success. And entrepreneurs ought to pursue these imperatives in a logical sequence. However, given the need to adapt to rapidly changing circumstances in order to build their companies, this sequence should not be pursued too rigorously.

What follows are six management imperatives we believe will help CEOs to take advantage of the globalization of entrepreneurship.

1. *Build a top-notch management team with cultural bridging experience.*

    The Tejas and Sonoa cases illustrate the power of pulling together an excellent team of managers as a starting point for forming a new venture. In some respects, such thinking may seem illogical since a management team that might excel in one industry might fail in another. In other words, some might think that picking the industry should precede the selection of the management team.

    However, for an entrepreneur it is far more important to find a team of people who are likely to be able to take an idea and turn it into a successful company. The entrepreneur is likely to have a track record of previous industry experience and as a result, should have a network of people who can help build a new company.

    As such, an entrepreneur is better off building an excellent team first and only then trying to pick an industry that is likely to value that team's capabilities. Since most entrepreneurs try to create new companies, and in some cases, new industries, to focus initially on the market might be difficult since there would be very little solid data on which to base an analysis.

For CEOs seeking to capitalize on the globalization of entrepreneurship, it helps to build a team that has experience working and/or studying in the country in which the start-up hopes to raise capital and go public, the country where the start-up hopes to develop its product, and the country where it expects to sell that product. In other words, the team should be familiar with the entrepreneurial ecosystem in all the countries where its key stakeholders are located. And that familiarity should be based on the team's deep experience in those countries.

2. *Identify a rapidly growing market that can benefit from the management team's competitive strengths.*

Once the management team is assembled, the entrepreneur should start to think about new market opportunities where the team's capabilities will give the start-up a competitive advantage. In the case of Tejas Networks, it was clear that optical networking would be a good focus given the team's strengths. However, Deshpande decided to focus that skill on optical networking for Indian telecommunications carriers. And given that its competitors did not operate in India, Tejas's optical networking skills had the distinct potential to win against those remote competitors.

By contrast, Tutor Vista clearly had no prior experience offering remote tutoring services to American students. However, Ganesh developed a general notion that there would be an opportunity to focus on solving the problem of weak secondary education in America. And due to his prior success with start-ups, he had the confidence and ability to attract the people and the capital needed to develop a solution to that general problem.

3. *Talk to potential customers to gain deep insights into their unmet needs.*

Given the challenge of quantifying the size and growth of an emerging market opportunity, the best way for an entrepreneur to decide whether to develop a product targeting that market is to talk with customers. In the Dangdang.com, Tejas Networks, and Tutor Vista cases it is clear that the entrepreneurs invested a significant amount of time talking with potential customers. These conversations yielded important insights into unmet customer needs, what competitors were or were not offering to satisfy those needs, and how best to position a new product or service.

4. *Raise Angel capital to finance a prototype of a product/service that will satisfy those unmet needs.*

Once an entrepreneur has analyzed the results of the customer research, the next step is to raise the money needed to develop a prototype of the solution to the customer's problem. As we saw in the cases of Tutor Vista and Tejas Networks, raising such Angel capital can come from a handful of wealthy individuals—many of whom are part of the start-up management team—who have significant capital from prior start-up successes.

In most cases, it is useful to seek Angel investors who have good contacts among venture capital firms. Often such Angel investors have helped enrich venture capitalists due to their prior success. And if the Angels are enthusiastic about their latest start-up, they can attract the interest of the deeper-pocketed venture capital firms.

Despite these contacts, venture capitalists will generally not invest without some proof that the concept will work. That is, many of the successful entrepreneurs featured in this chapter used the Angel capital to build a prototype. Of course, in addition to helping generate VC enthusiasm, such prototypes help a start-up to get customer feedback, which can lead to product refinements.

5. *Pick venture capital firms who can provide the additional skills needed for the company to succeed.*

As we saw in many of the case studies reviewed in this chapter, successful entrepreneurs see VCs as closing the gap between the skills of the management team and the requirements for winning in the selected market. With many of the start-ups we examined, such as Tutor Vista, Focus Media, and Worksoft, the choice of VCs helped boost the start-ups' credibility with potential customers and provided these ventures with the money they needed to grow.

6. *Use the capital to build the company and take it public.*

The final imperative for entrepreneurs is to use that capital to build the company to the point where it can be taken public. As we saw with many of the cases profiled above—such as the Bain Capital Blue-Printing and Sonoa cases—there are different ways that entrepreneurs work with capital providers.

In many cases, the capital providers install a CEO with whom they have worked in the past. These CEOs are in a position to figure out a growth plan—including developing specific milestones for helping the company boost revenues. Such CEOs should review their plans with the board, which will include the VCs, and take their advice to help them achieve the goals and adjust if they encounter challenges.

Other capital providers, such as Bain Capital, clearly have a far more structured methodology that they use in working with a portfolio company. While some entrepreneurs will welcome this more structured approach, most capital providers prefer to let a trusted CEO do the heavy lifting of developing and executing the growth strategies for their companies.

Conclusion

Entrepreneurs seeking to tap into the benefits of globalization have many options. They can perform each of their critical business activities—such as raising capital, building their management team, hiring workers, designing and building their products, seeking customers, and providing postsales service—in different countries. But our research suggests that certain combinations of locating activities seem to boost the odds of success. For example, in many cases, it makes sense to raise capital and go public in the United States—and yet for designing, building, and servicing new products or providing customer service it makes more sense to locate the activity in an emerging market near sources of inexpensive labor and customers. While there is no single best way for a CEO to succeed in a start-up, the six management imperatives we outlined can help entrepreneurs forge a profitable path through the complex thicket of globlization.

10

Seeking Congruencies and Resolving Conflicts among Ecosystem Participants

Capital flows change the entrepreneurial ecosystem by altering the way economic actors think about two fundamental business decisions:

- How best to allocate resources—or Where to invest; and
- How to pay for those investments.

The cases we've examined reveal that global capital flows open up a far broader range of investment opportunities and threats than had existed before capital flowed so freely around the world. That's because global capital flows enable entrepreneurs and managers in mature businesses to find new growth all around the world by serving new consumers and/or tapping cheap, skilled human capital. And we've explored cases in which such capital flows have opened up pockets of growth that have rewarded investors and executives.

But there is a flip side to capital flows. We've seen cases that reveal that capital flows can go awry—making it profitable for capital providers to supply capital to investments that would otherwise be difficult to justify. These cases suggest that capital is subject to Say's Law—the idea that supply creates its own demand. Many cases were a failure, as we found, because there was more capital that wanted to find a home than there were profitable investments that needed that capital. As a result, that surplus capital found its way into risky investments, the collapse of which led to a rapid drop in asset prices and economy.

Our general finding is that when the right entrepreneurial ecosystem (EE) elements work in harmony, the odds that good investments will get funded will be increased. To explain these elements we introduce the concept of EE triads—which are combinations of EE participants who are directing an investment with the help of two EE elements that, in this case, help the EE participant achieve success. How does this apply to our work? In 22 out of 47 cases we explored, investors and managers achieved a successful outcome—such as an initial public offering or an acquisition that boosted the acquirer's sales and profits.

It turns out that a small number of common EE triads helped explain the success. One of the most common triads associated with successful investments was Mature Company Manager/Government Policymaker/Financial Markets (MGF) that prevailed in three of the success cases. Simply put, in these three cases, a manager of a mature company completed an acquisition to strengthen its competitive position with assistance from government policymakers in the target company's country—who permitted the deal to go through—and the global financial markets, which provided the debt financing to help complete the acquisition.

Another common success triad features an entrepreneur as its driving force. In 3 of the 22 success cases, the triad of Entrepreneur/Venture Capitalist/Financial Markets (EVF) helped explain the success of a start-up. In the EVF cases, we saw that cooperation among two EE participants—entrepreneurs and venture capitalists—contributed to a venture's success. In many of these cases, the entrepreneur sought out venture capitalists that he believed would help make the start-up more competitive. However, achieving the ultimate success of an initial public offering depended on the help of an EE element—financial markets' appetite for the common equity of these ventures.

We also explored cases in which the wrong combination of EE participants and elements resulted in failure. Of the eight failure cases, two were due to one triad. This most common failure triad was Government Policymaker/Private Equity/Financial Markets (GPF). In the GPF cases, it appears that private equity investors were lured into investing in that country's companies with no objection from the government; however, thanks to a collapse in the financial markets in one case or a sudden reversal in government policy in the other, those investments ended up losing a significant amount of value. The other six failure cases resulted from unique combinations of EE participants and elements.

Exploring these success and failure cases from the perspective of these triads—as well as the other 17 cases whose outcome is somewhere between those two poles—can yield valuable insights for EE participants. To help focus this discussion, the remainder of this chapter develops lessons through the following methodology:

- Recap the successful and unsuccessful case studies;
- Highlight the key lessons learned from each;
- Develop specific recommendations for all participants on how best to find common ground and overcome conflicts;
- Outline scenarios for how the partnerships are likely to evolve;
- Suggest ways to structure the partnership to create greater value for all participants; and
- Present a methodology that all participants can use to forge more profitable partnerships within the evolving EE.

Success Cases

Recap of Successful Case Studies

What factors contributed to the 22 successful cases we examined? The two most common success triads were MGF and EVF. To examine why these two triads are most commonly associated with successful outcomes, we recap one notable success from each of the two triads.

We encountered a particularly successful MGF case study in chapter 8—Mittal Acquires Sicartsa—that illustrated the profits that flow to a skilled acquirer of undermanaged assets in a country with untapped profit potential. Mittal's CEO, the manager of a leading company in a mature but rejuvenating industry, was able to work with the Mexican government to address labor issues with a Mexican steel company to create a powerful presence in the rapidly growing Mexican market. The MGF triad worked here because of the alignment of three forces: a rejuvenating industry that needed new capacity, the availability of cheap, idle steel producing capacity, and Mittal's ability to access the capital needed to buy that capacity and revive it.

And in chapter 9, we saw how the capital can flow from West to East when a company is formed that meets Western demands with Western-trained managers who can harness lower cost Eastern resources. Worksoft is an example of a company that used the EVF triad to succeed. It raised VC from a Silicon Valley firm and is staffed by the Western-trained managers who were able to persuade Western VCs to take a chance on their Chinese start-up. And the Western VCs took that chance for two reasons—they perceived a big opportunity to meet the needs of Western companies using lower cost Chinese resources and they were persuaded that Worksoft's managers could span both business cultures. That bet paid off because Worksoft's business performance proved those assumptions to be correct.

Key Lessons Learned

These two cases from the success triads suggest different lessons for EE participants. Nevertheless, both cases reveal one of the most important lessons for achieving success—the presence of an entrepreneurial CEO who sets and executes a strategy for growth. To satisfy the entrepreneurial designation, such a CEO must exhibit a variety of traits including having a compelling vision for the company—whether it's mature or a start-up—and the ability to attract, retain, and motivate a top executive team to achieve that vision.

Another common lesson of both success triads is that in order to forge a successful growth strategy, an entrepreneurial CEO must make the right choices. Specifically, that CEO must decide which elements of the EE to emphasize in the pursuit of the growth strategy and which EE participants the CEO should partner with in order to execute that strategy. This is where the lessons learned from each of triads must be explored distinctly.

The case of Mittal's acquisition of Sicartsa reveals some important insights about how a CEO can make choices about which EE elements to emphasize and which EE participants the CEO should partner with. This case illustrates the benefits of an MGF triad—although it might make sense to think of it as an Mature Company Manager/Government Policymaker/Financial Markets/Corporate Governance (MGFC) quadrad to include the role of Mittal's superior corporate governance. Here are the key lessons:

Mittal's successful growth strategy depended on its entrepreneurial CEO. Lakshmi Mittal had the idea that Mittal Steel could achieve profitable growth by acquiring an underperforming steel plant that would give it a foothold in the rapidly growing Mexican market. This lesson is not that useful for most CEOs because if a CEO does not exhibit the entrepreneurial traits we outlined above, the incumbent cannot learn them. Nevertheless, this is useful for a board because it suggests if a company needs growth, the CEO should be replaced with an entrepreneurial one.

Mittal was able to assure Mexican policymakers that its presence there would be beneficial. Although the Mexican government had originally invested billions in the Sicartsa plant, its management let down the government. In fact, Mexican government officials publicly blamed the management and employees of the factory for the losses, and decided to privatize both Sicartsa factories in 1991. Based on its reputation for turning around Iscoot, a steel mill in Trinidad, the Mexican government invited Mittal to participate in the Sicartsa bid.

Mittal has superior corporate governance. Mittal was bringing not just money but valuable management skill that would help boost Sicartsa's value. Mittal and the Mexican government recognized that Mittal's management techniques were superior to those in Mexico. Such corporate governance would help Mittal to boost sales, profits, and employment at the plant.

Mittal uses its superior corporate governance to enlist capital providers to help finance the acquisition. Moreover, Mittal could persuade global capital providers that its superior corporate governance would enable it to pay back lenders and/or investors. This—coupled with Mittal's NYSE listing—gave it access to capital and the credibility of Wall Street advisors who could analyze its expansion plans and support its stock as a currency for consolidation. Moreover, Mittal believed that it could earn back the price premium it paid to get control of the Mexican production capacity by tapping the Mexican steel market's relatively rapid growth and by cutting inefficiency.

The Worksoft case presents the advantages of an EVF triad. This is a particularly powerful one because Western venture capital firms are eager for growth and markets such as China and India can supply that growth more readily than the United States. Therefore, if entrepreneurs in those rapidly growing markets can build ventures that appeal to those Western VCs, they are likely to be able to raise capital and sell initial public offering (IPO) shares in the West. This is helpful for all participants because Nasdaq is still considered the best place in the world for a technology IPO.

In the case of Worksoft, the success of its EVF triad reveals three key lessons:

Pursue a business strategy that will appeal to Western VCs. Worksoft was fotunate—from the perspective of raising Western VC—that it offered outsourcing services to U.S. companies. This strategy appealed to Silicon Valley VCs for three reasons. First, such VCs are comfortable with the idea of outsourcing work to lower-labor-cost locations—such as India. Second, VCs perceive the opportunity to tap rapid growth in China. Finally, VCs considered it far easier to obtain objective customer references from Worksoft's well-known American corporate clients. The lesson for global entrepreneurs is that it helps to get well-known Western VCs to provide capital if the goal is a Nasdaq IPO.

Help Western VC bridge the gap between the U.S. market and the country where the start-up operates. In the Worksoft case, the Western VC that decided to invest in the company, DCM, was not comfortable checking references on Worksoft's people. In order to overcome the risk of weak due diligence prior to investing, DCM decided to partner on its Worksoft investment with Legend Capital, a Chinese company. Presumably, Legend Capital offered excellent references on Worksoft's team. The lesson for entrepreneurs is to structure the business and encourage partnerships that raise a potential VC investor's confidence in the start-up.

Build a venture that meets Nasdaq listing requirements. Although Worksoft was focusing its efforts on satisfying the requirements of its corporate customers, management maintained a long-term focus on doing what would be needed to list its shares on Nasdaq. After a name change to VanceInfo and a solid earnings track record, the former Worksoft listed its shares and watched them rise 101% between its December 2007 IPO and mid-January 2010. If an entrepreneur follows the first two lessons, the odds increase that the start-up will be able to tap the Nasdaq for its IPO.

How Participants Can Find Common Ground and Overcome Conflicts

The success cases are particularly helpful because they illustrate how participants can work together effectively to achieve results that make them all better off. It is easy in retrospect to recognize the benefits that success yielded for all participants—in the Worksoft case, the company founders and employees, VC investors, and IPO stock investors all ended up wealthier. And the Mittal/Sicartsa case reveals that Mittal executives and employees benefited from the deal as did the Mexican government and the people who worked in the Sicartsa plant thanks to its improved economic performance.

But at the beginning of a partnership, the players do not know how things will work out. So what can these participants do to increase the chances for success? The most important thing they can do is to agree on one or two common objectives—the achievement of which drives the partnership. In some cases, such as Worksoft, all parties—for example, Worksoft executives, the VC firms, and presumably the IPO investors—shared a single common objective that was to build Worksoft into a company with the scale and service quality needed to go public and continue serving its customers.

With Mittal/Sicartsa, the objectives differed for each participant. Mittal wanted a profitable way to tap the rapidly growing Mexican market. The Mexican government wanted to put life back into the Sicartsa plant so it could employ more people and generate tax revenues for the region. As it happened, Mittal and the Mexican government were able to find a way to achieve both objectives—by letting Mittal acquire Sicartsa and applying its proven turn-around expertise.

Both cases reveal that the party initiating a partnership is doing so because it cannot achieve its objective without the help of a partner. The Worksoft founders realize that they cannot grow and achieve liquidity for their sweat equity without a Silicon Valley VC. And Mittal understood that it would not be able to gain access to the rapidly growing Mexican market without the willing cooperation of the Mexican government. But in both cases, we saw that the partnership initiators—the CEOs of each company—needed to overcome the risks that those potential partners perceived in order to gain their participation.

The two CEOs had different risk mitigation strategies for the different partners. For example, to encourage DCM to invest in Worksoft, its CEO needed to address at least two major areas of uncertainty: DCM's potential discomfort with the viability of Worksoft's business strategy and DCM's perceived inability to get an objective assessment of Worksoft's strengths and weaknesses. As mentioned above, DCM perceived that Worksoft's business strategy of outsourcing to U.S. companies had already been validated in India so Worksoft had already managed that potential area of conflict before DCM considered investing. DCM felt confident that it could get an objective assessment of Worksoft from the customer perspective by talking with its U.S. clients.

However, DCM took the initiative to manage the second area of risk—the difficulty of getting an objective read on Worksoft's strengths and weaknesses—by coinvesting with Legend Capital. DCM assumed that Legend Capital, with its base in China and a broad network of government and business contacts, would be in a strong position to gain the kind of objective assessment of Worksoft—including its executives and staff—that DCM could not have obtained.

These two cases reveal an important lesson for entrepreneurs seeking to find common ground and resolve conflicts with partners. It is better to identify and discuss potential sources of risk at the beginning of the partnership. Such frank, up-front exchanges set a tone at the beginning of a partnership that will help partners address and resolve the inevitable challenges they will encounter as they travel further along the path to achieving their shared objectives.

Although we do not know all the challenges that Worksoft and Mittal faced in their partnerships, we believe that this open approach to potential conflicts is superior to the alternatives. Such alternatives, which we will see in the next section on the failure cases, include ignoring potential risks and sources of conflict in the eagerness to close a deal or simply assuming that such conflicts can be ironed out later. In general, we believe that a systematic and data-driven approach to partnerships is better than one driven by gut instinct alone.

Inconclusive Cases

As noted above, 17 of the 47 cases we discussed in previous chapters did not have a clear conclusion. In some cases, we decided it was too early to tell whether the company would succeed or fail. In other cases, we observed a mixture of success and failure. We noticed that some common triads emerged from our analysis of the inconclusive cases. The most common of these was Entrepreneur/Venture Capital/Human Capital (EVH) that occurred four times. And of the remaining inconclusive cases, two of them were associated with the Government/Venture Capital/Human Capital (GVH) triad and two others emerged from the MGF triad.

While there were other triads and quadrads associated with other inconclusive cases, these three triads reveal some interesting trends. The four EVF cases were start-ups led by Indian entrepreneurs who had successfully obtained Silicon Valley VC and used largely Indian professionals to build their product or deliver their service. Yet in each case, the company had yet to achieve a successful outcome for investors—possibly due to the global economic contraction or a flaw in the company's business strategy.

The other two inconclusive triads—GVH and MGF—reveal different reasons for not reaching a conclusion. In the GVH cases, which involved the governments of China and India attempting to create biotechnology and nanotechnology industries, respectively, in their countries, we saw the difficulty of attracting significant venture capital to tap a country's human capital when there is insufficient entrepreneurial talent in the industries. In the MGF cases, we noted that although global acquisitions had been completed, the assumptions of industry growth that underpinned the decision to acquire had backfired—leaving the acquirer in a more precarious financial condition than before.

Recap of Inconclusive Case Studies

We next briefly recap one case study from each of the three triads mentioned above to examine lessons learned and provide some thoughts on how participants can find common ground. For the EVH triad, we recap the Tutor Vista case; from the GVH case we reexamine the India nanotechnology case; and for the MGF triad we take a fresh look at the Vale de Rio/Inco case.

Tutor Vista, which we discussed in chapter 9, seemed to do everything right. Its CEO was a successful serial entrepreneur from India who analyzed the biggest social and political issues in the United States and concluded that education was an area of opportunity. But the CEO went further—conducting in-depth market research with potential parent and student clients—and developed a popular service. He realized that in order to persuade American families to pay $300 a month for this service, he would need credibility and he got this by persuading top tier U.S. VC firms to invest. Then he hired and trained skilled Indian tutors and expanded the service. As of January 2010; however, Tutor Vista remained a private company.

India's effort to create a nanotechnology industry, analyzed in chapter 4, illustrates the challenges of a government—rather than entrepreneurs—trying to drive the creation of a new industry. Nanotechnology has yet to emerge from the science project phase into an industry with significant revenues. As a result, despite India's efforts to attract foreign capital, it has not been able to build a strong cadre of strong nanotechnology start-ups. Instead, India has attracted partnerships with Western companies seeking to tap India's talent to experiment in an effort to create saleable products. If nanotechnology indeed becomes an industry with a solid record of product sales, it may have an edge in attracting venture capital to fund future start-ups. However, for the time being an Indian nanotechnology cluster remains out of reach.

Finally, the Vale de Rio/Inco merger—discussed in detail in chapter 5—is an example of a deal that was successfully completed but boosted the acquirer's share of what turned out to be a declining industry. This case illustrates how a rare credit rating upgrade for Brazilian mining company Vale de Rio (Vale) gave it the capital to acquire a Canadian nickel mining company, Inco. After acquiring Inco, Vale applied its more harmonious labor-management techniques to the formerly rancorous Inco work environment. Ultimately, however, this deal had a less than sanguine ending as declining nickel prices soured the deal.

Key Lessons Learned

These three cases offer different lessons for EE participants. The Tutor Vista case suggests a variety of steps they can take to increase their odds of a successful investment. The Indian nanotechnology example illustrates the challenges a country can encounter if it depends too heavily on government to create a new industry. And the Vale/Inco case provides a mixed set of lessons—some about positive steps participants can take and others about the risks of betting too heavily on a potentially volatile industry.

As we mentioned, it's too early to know at this point whether Tutor Vista will reward its venture capital investors. However, Ganesh's progress so far suggests important lessons for entrepreneurs:

Test potential market opportunities with in-depth market research. Often entrepreneurs perceive an opportunity in a new country but fail to conduct the customer research needed to test whether that opportunity will really support a start-up. Ganesh clearly gained valuable insights into the willingness of American parents and their children to pay for tutoring offered by Indian teachers. Although such services had never before been offered, Ganesh's primary research revealed that his idea could work.

Partner to gain access to the complete bundle of capabilities required to succeed in the business. Ganesh realized that he could not succeed alone. Instead, it was clear that he would need to partner with others in order to make Tutor Vista a success. Interestingly, he viewed his Silicon Valley venture investors as a way to gain the credibility needed to persuade American consumers to pay a significant monthly fee for its service.

Pick the key VC contact carefully and keep that VC up to speed with the venture's activities. Ganesh learned that he had to pick a VC carefully—investing time to make sure he was comfortable with the person from the firm who would be managing the investment. Ganesh also recognized that he needed to keep the person informed about the company's activities and seek advice on how to achieve their mutually agreed-upon goals.

The Indian nanotechnology case—with its inconclusive outcome—raises an important question for policymakers: If they wish to create a new industry, who are the right partners to engage and how should policymakers sequence those partnerships? India did some things right—it had built up a strong base of human capital in the form of researchers who could apply nanotechnology to different industrial challenges. And ultimately India's efforts to attract investment may pay off.

However, India may have to wait a long time for the desired payoff. The reality remains that nanotechnology seems not to have reached the scale and growth that some proponents had anticipated. As a result, it has not yielded venture-backed start-ups that have profited from nanotechnology through IPOs. In defense of India's efforts, it is often difficult to know when or if a new technology will gain market acceptance. For example, it took around 25 years from the time the Internet was invented by the U.S. Department of Defense and the time it became a commercialized service.

Nevertheless, a better route for the Indian government may have been to try to identify and partner with corporate investors, venture funds, and entrepreneurs who were enthusiastic about nanotechnology in India. If India had worked with such partners, it may have been able to identify what conditions it could change in its EE to attract nanotechnology-oriented capital and entrepreneurs to India instead of to other countries. Simply put, it may have increased India's odds of success if it had tried to make itself into the world's ripest Petri dish in which to grow a new nanotechnology industry.

The Vale/Inco case offers many useful lessons to acquirers. Brazil's drive to privatize enabled Vale to shift its corporate governance model to one focused on rapid shareholder value creation from one that emphasized employment of Brazilian citizens. That shift to a shareholder focus also pushed Vale's management to expand globally and diversify its sources of income. Thanks to its willingness to upgrade its EE, Vale management recognized that it would need to reduce its cost of capital and it set out on a winning campaign to achieve that objective. As a result, Vale was able to offer a competitive bid that captured Inco. And Vale used its skills at harmonizing with communities and workers to integrate the Inco deal effectively.

One negative point of the Vale/Inco deal is that it boosted Vale's dependence on nickel prices. When such prices rise, Vale benefits more than it did prior to the merger. However, during periods of economic contraction when nickel prices fall, Vale suffers disproportionately. As of January 2010, Vale was benefiting from rising metals prices as an expected economic recovery boosted demand for its products, and hence its financial outlook.

How Participants Can Find Common Ground and Overcome Conflicts

These three inconclusive cases suggest different ways that participants can find common ground and overcome conflicts by trying to seek shared objectives that will make all participants better off. In some of the cases, it is easier to imagine that common ground than in others. For example, Tutor Vista's customers, executives, and venture investors will all be better off if Tutor Vista is able to expand its customer base globally. India achieved some success by resolving the potential conflict between venture capitalists and corporate investors by favoring the corporations that were willing to contract with Indian workers to provide nanotechnology services. By contrast, a decline in nickel prices put Vale and its workers in the former Inco facilities at odds with one another. Vale may seek to cut Inco staff to offset the declining revenues resulting from declining prices and demand for nickel.

Let's examine each case in more detail to explore the lessons that might be gained for EE participants seeking to find common ground and head off conflicts.

The Tutor Vista case certainly has the potential for conflict. One example was its CEO's decision to expand into the Indian tutoring market by acquiring bricks-and-mortar tutoring schools there. While this idea was clearly in conflict with its U.S. strategy, Tutor Vista's CEO was able to persuade the board—which represented the interests of its venture capital investors—that this deal made sense because it would provide access to the much larger and more rapidly growing market in India.

Tutor Vista's CEO offers two important lessons about how to avoid conflict with the board. One is to cultivate a good relationship with board members—particularly those representing investors—and spend time consulting with them in order to sustain their confidence. The other is to agree on a concrete way to measure whether an investment opportunity makes sense. It appears that Ganesh had agreed with his board that if a good business case could be made—which may have included an assessment of the attractiveness of the market, the target's competitive position, and the potential to earn a positive net present value—then the board would make the capital available. This case suggests that agreeing on such decision criteria can help avoid conflicts among participants.

The Indian nanotechnology case reflects an inherent—and potentially irresolvable—conflict between government policymakers and private investors and entrepreneurs. The policymakers need to win elections in order to stay in power. In order to do so, they must advocate policies that benefit their particular voters. If, for example, an Indian policymaker supports the construction of a nanotechnology design plant on a farmer's field in his district, then the policymaker runs the risk of losing the electoral support of the farmers whose land will be used for the plant.

From the venture capitalist's perspective, that location might be ideal because it is close to a large group of skilled workers and it has relatively low taxes and other operating costs. But a new nanotechnology facility that might be ideal for the private investor or entrepreneur might well cause the government official to get voted out of office. These differences in what motivates government officials and capital providers make it difficult for these partners to find common ground.

In contrast to the model of venture-backed technology-based entrepreneurship, renting Indian human capital to U.S. companies—through IT or pharmaceutical research and testing—appears to be a more well-tolerated way for India to engage with Western companies. Thus it appears more natural that a partnership emerged between those Western companies, India's nanotechnology-trained engineers, and Indian policymakers acting as the broker between the two.

Finally, the Vale/Inco deal reveals that government policymakers can find common ground with outside-the-country acquirers seeking a stake in their domestic firms. Such outside capital providers have the potential to induce xenophobic responses from some government officials who hope to defeat incumbent officials by scaring the local populace with stories about how the foreign capital will cut jobs and how the challengers can protect the populace from that external threat.

In order to stem such capital-impeding forces, acquirers must be able to counteract such fear mongering with rational arguments. In the case of Vale, it had a compelling track record of managing labor relations more effectively than Inco. Therefore, the Canadian government came to the conclusion that the local nickel mines would operate more profitably and with less labor-management conflict if Vale acquired them.

The lesson here—as we saw in the Mittal/Sicartsa case—is that when an acquirer seeks to find common ground with policymakers in a new country, the acquirer must bring capabilities that those policymakers value. In the Vale case, the valued capability was its demonstrated ability to manage labor relations— which solved a difficult problem facing Canadian policymakers. Thus those policymakers were able to convince the local populace that it would be better off accepting the Vale bid.

Failure Cases

As we discussed above, the previous chapters highlighted eight failure cases—two of which were due to one triad—GPF. Of the GPF failure cases, a clear pattern emerges—governments can lure foreign capital by tapping into decision makers' irrationality. As we'll explore, that irrationality can take different forms—for example, Sovereign Wealth Funds (SWFs) from countries such as China wanted to invest in U.S. financial institutions because they believed it would enhance their prestige. And a U.S. fund manager who traded in Russian stocks thought he was held in high esteem by Russia's leaders as he built up his wealth. Both cases resulted in failure due to the gap between reality and expectations.

Recap of Failure Case Studies

While Russia and the United States are at different stages of their economic development, they both succeeded in luring outside capital only to disappoint it—either wilfully in the case of Russia or in the wake of an unintended but costly financial collapse in the case of the United States.

Russia has repeatedly been able to lure in foreign capital from Western investors. Based on the cases we explored here—Hermitage, Sawyer and TNK-BP—the Western investors believed that their Russian partners would share their investment and reap their share of the long-term returns. However, sooner or later, once the Western investors had invested their capital, they discovered that their interests diverged and that the Russian partners enjoyed an insurmountable home field advantage. The result was that the Russian investors took as much of that capital as they could—through a combination of manipulating the legal system and personal threats against the investors. While the investors escaped with their lives, they ended up poorer and wiser.

The United States followed a different path to failure when it came to attracting foreign capital and then losing it. It allowed SWFs to invest in U.S. companies despite the emergence of protectionist voices from some parts of the U.S. political spectrum in early 2008. It turns out that SWFs' investments in U.S. financial institutions were not a threat as much as they were a sign of a market top. After losing significant sums on these investments, SWFs are no longer interested in being played for fools. The result is that the United States decided to sell bonds to finance a $23.7 trillion bailout of its collapsing financial system since SWFs would not step in after they were burned the first time.

Key Lessons Learned

Both these cases offer useful lessons. The Browder case suggests that it is possible for foreign capital providers to make profitable investments in Russia but they should do so only if they can get their money out of Russia immediately after making it. The SWF case suggests that in the short term, the United States was wise to keep its more xenophobic tendencies from blocking foreign capital flows. However, SWF investors watched their newly acquired equity, for example, in Blackstone Group stock, decline quite rapidly. The resulting embarrassment put the kibosh on future SWF investing in the United States. Perhaps the ultimate lesson is that foreign capital providers should not be blinded by their emotions when it comes to investing; instead they should exercise rigorous due diligence before investing.

Browder's Russian odyssey reveals important weaknesses in Russia's EE. In general, cases like Browder's are likely to repel others who might consider investing in Russia. Investors who might hope to earn attractive profits from investing in Russia's energy companies to profit from a rise in demand for oil and gas are likely to view these EE weaknesses as deal killers. Vivid examples of Russia's willingness to encourage foreign capital investment then to expropriate it through corporate raids suggest profound weaknesses in EE components such as corporate governance and financial markets. These weaknesses are likely to repel foreign capital investment.

When it comes to SWFs, the United States and the SWFs ought to learn a basic lesson from their investments in the late 2000s: SWF investments only work when both the capital provider and recipient end up better off. And while there is a strong element of luck in any investment, much detailed investment analysis was left undone. It appears that the United States may have panicked in allowing SWFs to provide capital to its weakened financial institutions. This might have unwittingly put partial sovereignty of those banks in the hands of countries that did not share United States' interests. At the same time, the capital providers may have allowed their pride at being asked to invest in such prestigious institutions to get in the way of conducting due diligence before making these investments. For both parties, cooler heads should have prevailed.

How Participants Can Find Common Ground and Overcome Conflicts

When failures on the scale of these cases occur, they suggest that nothing could have been done to find common ground and overcome conflicts. In the Hermitage Capital case, it is clear that Browder may have brought on the hostility of the Russian power structure by being so openly critical of some of Russia's corporate governance practices.

Perhaps if Browder had been able to earn high investment returns while at the same time behaving in a way that did not antagonize Russia's political elite, he might have been able to profit without losing his firm and risking his life. However, based on the other failure cases we discussed that involve Russia, it appears unlikely that Russia will change its EE to satisfy foreign capital providers.

Nor does the United States appear eager to change its practices to find common ground with foreign capital providers. On the one hand, it does not raise very high barriers to foreign investment and has largely avoided using such investment as a reason to stoke public fear of foreigners. On the other hand, the United States leaves those foreign capital providers on their own when it comes to assessing the potential returns from those investments.

In many cases, this results in a situation in which the United States courts foreign investment most aggressively at the point in the economic cycle when such investment may be far from the best opportunity for foreign capital providers. Simply put, the United States hopes to attract capital from overseas at times when U.S. investors are far more wary—and knowledgeable—about the potential risks in the U.S. investment climate than are their foreign counterparts.

In the SWF case, this leads to a situation in which the interests of the capital source countries were at odds with those of the capital destination country—the United States. And over the long run, it is better when the interests of the capital source and destination countries are aligned than when they are at odds with each other. The SWF case suggests that the United States knew that getting SWF capital was a zero sum game that would benefit the United States at the time of the investment while costing the capital providers significant losses soon thereafter. As a result, SWFs are likely to be shy when it comes to such future investments in the United States.

Scenarios for Partnership Evolution

Nevertheless, partnerships almost never work out as planned. And, therefore, they ought to consider multiple scenarios. For example, while partners tend to feel most comfortable discussing the optimistic scenario in which their objectives are achieved quickly, they may feel significant pain in discussing what they will do if reality falls far short of the results they expect.

In most cases, it is better for partners to consider—as they are negotiating the terms of their partnership—what they would do under different scenarios rather than trying to restructure their partnership after an unexpected surprise. Nevertheless, participants cannot anticipate all the possible opportunities and/ or threats that might arise during the life of a partnership. And this means that partners must develop good enough relationships to react quickly and effectively to such unanticipated changes.

Despite the challenges, partners should anticipate how their partnerships will evolve while they are negotiating the terms of their partnership. And a methodology for such anticipation can help identify some of the most important ways that circumstances might change in a partnership so that the partners can prepare related contingency plans.

To that end, here is a six step methodology that partners might consider following to develop scenarios for partnership evolution:

- Form scenario-planning team;
- Identify key areas of uncertainty;
- Construct many different scenarios that combine these areas;
- Estimate the probability of the different scenarios;
- Develop contingency plans for the most likely scenarios; and
- Monitor weak signals and adjust scenarios and contingency plans accordingly.

Form Scenario-Planning Team

The first step in considering different scenarios for a partnership is forming a team of people who can represent the viewpoints of all partners. And as a partnership evolves, it might add new members whose views ought to be incorporated into the process of scenario planning. The scenario-planning team should agree on the goals of their work and a methodology for achieving it. And they may wish to consider hiring an outsider to lead the process in order to assure that the scenarios stress objective analysis and deemphasize the biases of the team members.

Identify Key Areas of Uncertainty

Once the scenario-planning team is formed, it should begin its work by considering which areas of uncertainty might have the biggest impact on the partnership. Such areas might include changes in economic growth rate assumptions, a shift in government policies resulting from newly elected leaders, changes in demand and/or pricing for a key product or input to the partnership's production process, the emergence of a particularly threatening competitor or new technology, or a sudden drop in the availability of capital.

Construct Many Different Scenarios That Combine These Areas

The scenario-planning team should use these areas of uncertainty as building blocks for constructing scenarios. For the six variables mentioned above, the team could construct a variety of scenarios assuming different levels of change for each variable. One scenario, we could call it the *Global Crisis Scenario*, might look as follows:

- *Economic growth rate assumptions.* From +4% GDP growth to –6% GDP contraction;
- *Government policies.* From low taxes and light regulation to very high taxes and tight government regulation;
- *Product demand and product and input pricing.* From high product demand, rising prices and low input costs to slumping product demand, declining prices, and rising input costs;
- *Competitors and technologies.* From no threatening competitors and little technological change to two rapidly growing competitors taking market share through disruptive technologies; and
- *Availability of capital.* From ample, cheap capital to scarce, expensive capital.

The scenario-planning team would develop many such scenarios in a fairly exhaustive manner in order to avoid overlooking any possibilities.

Estimate the Probability of the Different Scenarios

The scenario-planning team will not be able to manage so many different scenarios. This is why it must try to decide which scenarios are most likely to occur so it can focus on the most probable ones. Alternatively, it can focus on the ones with the highest expected value (EV)—the product of the probability of each scenario and its likely benefit or cost. And the scenario team might wish to focus on those scenarios with both the most positive and most negative EVs.

This step is among the most difficult for the scenario-planning team. The reason is that nobody can predict the future and the members of the team may have a significant vested interest in putting a greater probability on scenarios that will lead to success than on those that might lead to failure. To overcome such potential biases, the team can hire an outside facilitator who would interview experts on the scenario variables who have no stake in the outcome of the partnership. While such experts might ultimately fail to predict the future, their objectivity would help the team make more accurate probability estimates.

Develop Contingency Plans for the Most Likely Scenarios

The scenario-planning team might use the foregoing analysis to select between three and five scenarios on which to focus. The team would develop plans for how it might change the partnership's strategy in response to each scenario. For example, it would develop a contingency plan for the Global Crisis Scenario mentioned above, which would involve steps to raise reserve capital before a financial crisis and plan for rapid cost cutting.

Such contingency plans would also help the scenario-planning team to structure their partnership agreements to anticipate putting the contingency plans into action. To that end, the scenario-planning team might recommend modifying the partnership agreement to include the possibility of cost cuts or rapid boosts to liquidity through borrowing or selling common shares.

Monitor Weak Signals and Adjust Scenarios and
Contingency Plans Accordingly

Once the partnership has launched, the scenario-planning team should monitor the variables on which it based its scenarios. To that end, the team should identify weak signals—those that might help the team anticipate changes that would affect the success of the partnership before conditions changed radically. If these weak signals suggested that the scenarios for the partnership were not consistent with what the team had anticipated, the scenario-planning team should adjust the partnership's contingency plans accordingly.

Structuring Partnerships for Greater Value

While the foregoing methodology can help partners to anticipate what might go wrong and prepare for those contingencies, the question remains how best to structure partnerships to enhance their value. In the next section of the chapter we'll discuss a methodology to that effect. But value is an amorphous concept and in order for partners to use it, they must first define it in a useful manner.

To that end, we introduce here the concept of *Drivers of Partnership Value* (DPVs). DPVs are the specific variables that partners use to track whether their partnership is getting better or worse. DPVs are closely linked to the objectives that each partner brings to the partnership. And they vary for each project and partner. Therefore, each case requires a distinct analysis to identify its particular DPVs for each partner.

As we alluded to earlier in this chapter, the key to a successful partnership is for the partnership driver—whether it's an entrepreneur, a mature company manager, or a private equity firm—to have a clear and effective vision for what capabilities the partnership will require in order to succeed. In the Tutor Vista case, Ganesh realized that the company needed U.S. credibility in order to persuade American families to spend $300 per month on an India-based academic tutoring service. Since Ganesh was able to structure his partnerships to make all partners better off, he gained their enthusiastic contributions to Tutor Vista.

The Tutor Vista case illustrates the importance of pinpointing the DPVs for each partner. Here we use a broad concept of what constitutes a partner—specifically, we focus not only on those company stakeholders who seek to profit from investing in the company but also on those who will benefit from it in other ways. We use this broader definition of partners because understanding the DPVs of all these "partners" helps the CEO to craft a value-enhancing strategy for all of them. Conversely, leaving off noninvestment partners from consideration puts the company at risk.

What follows is a list of Tutor Vista's partners and what we imagine would be their DPVs:

- *Venture capital investors.* Obtaining high returns through an IPO or acquisition; adding value by providing customer leads, hiring executives, and guiding management team.
- *Company founders.* Realizing their vision for the company, creating a great place to work that motivates top people, earning high returns through IPO or sale.
- *Tutors.* Working in a pleasant environment with opportunities for advancement; earning competitive wages; feeling of helping people and working with good colleagues.
- *American parents.* Ensuring that their children do well on standardized tests to increase their chances of college admission; paying a reasonable amount for effective tutoring services.
- *American students.* Keeping parents off their back while getting the help they need to improve their test scores.

The value of articulating such DPVs becomes clear as participants attempt to structure their partnership to enhance value. If participants understand each other's definitions of value, then they can take actions designed to make the partnership more valuable for each of them. In some cases, their interests could conflict. However, with an initial understanding of their DPVs, the partners will be more likely to avoid such conflicts and instead craft strategies intended to make all participants better off.

Methodology for Enhancing Partnership Profitability

The way to enhance the profitability of a partnership depends on who is driving it. We devoted chapters to how various EE participants—policymakers, capital providers, managers in existing industries, and entrepreneurs—can take advantage of the lessons from the case studies we presented featuring these participants.

We will now explore ways to enhance the partnerships formed among these different participants. As we have alluded earlier, each partnership is different and even among partnerships made up of the same triads, there are likely to be unique differences not only in the DPVs of each participant but also in the strategies that could be crafted to increase them. Rather than catalogue lists of ways to enhance partnerships for each triad, we introduce a general methodology that we believe will help participants to take a fresh look at each new partnership and maximize its value.

Our methodology for enhancing partnership profitability includes the following six steps:

- Form partnership profitability team;
- Identify DPVs for each participant;
- List capabilities required for partnership to gain market share;
- Assess the partnership's capability gap(s);
- Develop strategies to close the capability gaps; and
- Implement strategies.

Form Partnership Profitability Team

The partnership profitability team (PPT) would consist of the most senior people from all the partners. The team's charge would be to agree on the partnership's goals, set the strategy for achieving those goals, monitor the implementation of that strategy, and make adjustments as appropriate. The team would agree on a charter and use a commonly understood methodology, such as the one we articulate below.

Identify DPVs for Each Participant

The PPT's first task would be to define what value means for each partner. To that end, we would advise the PPT to use a broader definition of partner. This should include not only those who have the biggest financial interest in the outcome of the partnership but also those who are critical to the long-term operation of the business who will not make outsized gains if it succeeds—by that we refer to customers, employees, and suppliers.

To identify each partner's DPV, the PPT should conduct in-depth interviews with each partner. Such interviews would vary in focus, depending on the partner. For example, an interview with a VC would focus on their investment criteria, their return objectives, their industry focus, and their business objectives. By contrast, an interview with a customer would focus on the ranked purchase criteria they use to select among competing suppliers and their unmet needs.

List Capabilities Required for Partnership to Gain Market Share

The PPT should next explore the capabilities that the company will need to gain market share. To accomplish this, the PPT should identify which competitors are doing the best job of satisfying the customers' DPVs—as identified in the previous step—growing the fastest and gaining the most market share. The PPT should further analyze these top performing competitors to analyze the specific activities they rely on to help them achieve top performance. The result of this analysis should be a list of capabilities and the specific tactics that these winning competitors use within each capability.

Assess the Partnership's Capability Gap(s)

The PPT would then take steps to close the capability gaps identified in the previous step. The ways to close the capability gap vary depending on the industry, the country, and the company. One example from the cases we explored is the Mittal/Sicartsa deal in which Mittal's CEO recognized that there was an opportunity to take advantage of Mexican steel industry growth but that it lacked the low-cost manufacturing resources in Mexico that would be required to exploit that opportunity. Mittal viewed the Sicartsa acquisition as a way to close its capability gap.

Develop Strategies to Close the Capability Gaps

As Mittal's CEO did—working in conjunction with its board, capital providers, Sicartsa management, and Mexican government officials—the PPT must develop strategies to close the capability gaps identified above. Such capability gaps would vary depending on many factors such as the industry, country, company, customers DPVs. And so would the means of closing those gaps. However, the case studies we explored in this book suggest that in addition to acquisitions, there might be many ways to close the capability gaps.

There are many ways that the PPT can use to close the company's capability gaps. They include the following:

- Hiring a CEO with the experience to craft strategies to take market share from the most prominent competitor;

- Seeking venture capital from a U.S. VC with strong capabilities in the industry, an outstanding reputation in financial markets, and good connections with leading investment banks;
- Partnering with an outside firm that specializes in specific critical functions where the company is weak—such as engineering, advertising, low-cost manufacturing, or logistics; or
- Forming an agreement with local government officials to endorse a merger and offer tax breaks in exchange for a willingness to maintain a specific level of employment within the territory in which the company operates.

Implement Strategies

The PPT would then proceed to implement the strategies to close the company's capability gaps. In general, the PPT ought to work with those partners who might be added to the team to close the capability gaps to strike mutually profitable agreements. Such agreements should make it clear how both parties will measure and award the success or failure of the relationship. More specifically, the agreement should make it clear under what conditions the partners can deal with contingencies along the lines identified earlier in the chapter—such as replacing key executives, changing strategy, and exiting the partnership.

Once such strategies are implemented, the new partners should join the PPT and monitor the implementation of the strategy on a regular basis. If it appears that a fundamental change is about to occur in the industry, the PPT should reexamine the strategy and adjust it accordingly.

Conclusion

The EE is a new framework for helping policymakers, capital providers, and business leaders to rethink their business. The emergence of global capital flows as a force for change carries with it both opportunities for growth and risks of loss. By defining the EE, showing how it plays out in 47 different cases and charting how the changing EE affects these participants, we have offered a guide on how to capture the opportunities and skirt the pitfalls. It is up to you to decide how best to apply these ideas. Please let us know what works and what does not.

Acknowledgments

Peter

This book would not have been possible without the help of many people. Srini Rangan was willing to take a chance on collaborating with me in my first effort to coauthor a book. He contributed generously his ideas and time from the day we first decided to try to develop a book proposal right up until its publication. I am looking forward to working with him to help make the world aware of the ideas in this book.

My family has also helped to make this book possible. My wife, Robin, cheerfully offered to read and comment on our book proposal and key chapters of the book. My brothers Bill and Jamie introduced me to their colleagues in the private equity and venture capital communities. My children helped provide valuable research support. And my parents continue to offer cherished encouragement—this book is codedicated to them.

Srini

Many things in life are not possible without the help of others. Writing a book is often seen as a lonely effort but that view obscures the fact that authors too benefit from the help of others. It has been the case with this work as well. The time has come to acknowledge those who helped us in this endeavor.

My first debt of gratitude goes to my coauthor, Peter Cohan. From the time we started discussing the topic of global capital flows and their impact on entrepreneurial ecosystems, Peter has been the one to keep us on track. His has been the voice of practicality that has leavened the tone and tenor of the book. More often than not, he ensured that my academic theorizing was grounded in empirical findings.

The second person to whom I owe a debt of gratitude is my wife, Sudha. She ensured that I pursue my book planning and writing in peace. Amidst all my work, I rarely had time to focus on anything relating to the home front. As always, she cheerfully carried the burdens of hearth and home with nary a complaint. I dedicate this book to her.

I also wish to acknowledge the financial support of Babson College that ensured that this long planned book project actually came to fruition.

Peter and Srini

We are both grateful to the many people who shared their insights into capital flows and entrepreneurship throughout the development of this book. These include Jonathan Roosevelt, Gautam Prakash, Robert Scannell, Ray Smilor, Martin Kenney, Rafiq Dossani, Frank Lavin, Raj Judge, Krishnan Ganesh, Gary Johnson, Michael Greeley, and Chet Kapoor.

Finally, we are grateful for the efforts of everyone at Palgrave Macmillan including our editor Laurie Harting and her able assistant Laura Lancaster for their enthusiasm for this project and their capable efforts to bring it to fruition.

Notes

Chapter 1   Introduction

All URLs are current as of March 5, 2010. Some articles, such as those from Knowledge@ Wharton, are accessible online after registration at the site.

1. See *Wall Street Journal*, *Emerging Markets Flows Forecast to Rebound*, October 3, 2009, http://online.wsj.com/article/SB125456954928261737.html?mod=googlenews_wsj
2. Gray, Tim. "How to Gauge the Rush to Emerging Markets." *The New York Times*, January 10, 2010, http://www.nytimes.com/2010/01/10/business/mutfund/10global.html?hp=&pagewanted=print.
3. It is quite likely that there are other factors as well that shape capital flows but we believe that these are the most critical ones.
4. Heliotropism—derived from the Greek words for sun and growth—is a process by which certain plants change the position of their flowers or leaves so they will receive the maximum amount of sunlight as the sun moves from east to west during the day. By capital heliotropism we imply that firms, industries, and even countries are all shaped by capital flows.
5. Chandler, Clay. "Wireless Wonder: India's Sunil Mittal." *Fortune*, January 12, 2007, http://money.cnn.com/magazines/fortune/fortune_archive/2007/01/22/8397979/index.htm
6. In 1997, Wal-Mart entered the German market by acquiring the 21-unit Wertkauf hypermarket and the 74-unit Interspar hypermarket chain. In July 2006, Wal-Mart's German experiment ended when it sold its remaining 85 stores after losing $1 billion.
7. VentureWire, April 12, 2007.
8. "Harvard Business School Association (HBSA) Investing in Emerging Markets—Highlights." e-mail to Srinivasa Rangan from Peter Cohan, March 14, 2007.
9. Prayag, Anjal, "Accenture on Course to Hit 35,000-Headcount," *Hindu Business Line*, August 28, 2007, http://www.blonnet.com/2007/08/28/stories/2007082851660400.htm
10. Coy, Peter and Mandel, Michael. "Private Equity vs. China." *BusinessWeek*, April 5, 2007, http://www.businessweek.com/bwdaily/dnflash/content/apr2007/db20070405_214446.htm?chan=top+news_top+news+index_top+story
11. Although we have not explored it in detail, we believe that the global auto industry may at such a strategic inflection point at the time of writing. Witness how companies in India and China, both domestic and foreign-owned, have been innovating in the automotive sector and their likely long-term impact on the global auto industry.
12. Alaric Nightingale and Matthew Craze, "Arcelor Mittal Buys Villacero Units for $1.4 Billion," *Bloomberg News*. December 20, 2006, http://www.bloomberg.com/apps/news?pid=20601086&sid=aj5LKRHVFeUQ&refer=latin_america
13. Ross Kerber, "International Public Offering," *Boston Globe*, January 28, 2007, http://www.boston.com/business/articles/2007/01/28/international_public_offering/

14. "Wipro Acquires Majority Stake in Spectramind for Rs 4.07 Billion," *Rediff*, July 19, 2002, http://www.rediff.com/money/2002/jul/19wipro.htm

Chapter 2   Capital Rising: Globalization, Capital Flows, and the Emerging New Entrepreneurial Ecosystems

1. *Wall Street Journal*, Review & Outlook, September 15, 2009.
2. Two good examples of such a benign view of globalization are the works by J.N. Bhagwati (2004), *In Defense of Globalization*, Oxford: Oxford University Press and M. Wolf (2004), *Why Globalization Works*, Yale: Yale University Press.
3. See, for example, B. Setser (2005), "The Economic Outlook," *Testimony before Joint Economic Committee of the U.S. Congress*, October 20, 2005.
4. See, for example, G. Mastel (2006), "Why We Should Expand Trade Adjustment Assistance," *Challenge*, 49 (4), 42–57.
5. See UNCTAD (1999), *World Investment Report: FDI and the Challenge of Development*, Geneva: UNCTAD.
6. See A. Rugman (1999), "Multinational Enterprises and the End of Global Strategy," *Proceedings of the 25th European International Business Association (CEIBA) Conference*, UMIST, Manchester, United Kingdom and A.M. Rugman and J.R. D'Cruz (1997), "The Theory of the Flagship Firm," *European Management Review*, 15(4) (August), 403–411.
7. See M.E. Porter (1990), *The Competitive Advantage of Nations*, New York: Free Press and E.W. Hill and J.F. Brennan (2000), "A Methodology for Identifying Drivers of Economic Development," *Economic Development Quarterly*, 14 (1).
8. See Andy Grove (1999), *Only the Paranoid Survive*, Broadway Books, New York: Random House
9. M. Yoshino and U.S. Rangan (1996), *Strategic Alliances: An Entrepreneurial Approach to Globalization*, Boston: HBS Press, p. 54.
10. Jeffrey T. Macher and David C. Mowery, eds. (2008), *Innovation in Global Industries: U.S. Firms Competing in a New World*, Washington, DC: National Academic Press.
11. Jeffrey T. Macher and David C. Mowery, "Introduction," in Jeffrey T. Macher and David C. Mowery, op. cit.
12. GEM Report (2009), Babson College, p. 4.
13. Ibid., p. 7.
14. GEM Report (2009) uses classifications such as "factor driven," "efficiency driven," and "innovation driven" to distinguish between developing and developed economies drawing from M.E. Porter et al., eds. (2002), *The Global Competitiveness Report 2001–2002*, New York: Oxford University Press.
15. J.A. Schumpeter (1934), *Theory of Economic Development: An Inquiry into Profits, Capital, Credit, Interest, and the Business Cycle*, Cambridge, MA: Harvard University Press.
16. J.A. Timmons and S. Spinelli (2003), *New Venture Creation: Entrepreneurship for the 21st Century*, 6th ed. New York: McGraw-Hill Irwin.
17. See, for instance, World Competitiveness Reports of recent years.
18. See, M.E. Porter (1990), *Competitive Advantage of Nations*, New York: Free Press.
19. See R. Whitley (2003), "How National Are Business Systems? The Role of Different State Types and Complementary Institutions in Constructing Homogenous Systems of

Economic Coordination and Control," Paper presented to the Workshop on National Business Systems in the New Global Context, Oslo, May 8–11, 2003 (*mimeo*).

20. See D.C. North (1987), "Institutions, Transaction Costs, and Economic Growth," *Economic Inquiry*, July and U.S. Rangan (2005), *Russia and the WTO: A National Business System Perspective*, in M.L. Bruner and V. Morozov, eds. (2005), *Market Economy in Post-Communist Russia*, Leeds, England: Wisdom House.

21. See R. Whitley (1992), *European Business Systems*. London: Sage and C. Lane (1995), *Industry and Society in Europe*, Edward Elgar: Aldershot.

22. See E.T. Hall (1984), "Patterns of Economic Policy: An Organizational Approach," S. Bornstein, D. Held, and J. Krieger, eds., *The State in Capitalist Europe*, London: Unwin Hyman, 124–138; E.T. Hall (1986), *Governing the Economy*, London: Oxford University Press; K.A. Thelen (1991), *Union of Parts: Labor Politics in Postwar Germany*, Ithaca, NY: Cornell University Press; and O.E. Williamson (1986), *The Economic Institutions of Capitalism*, New York: Free Press.

23. See G.S. Becker (1993), *Human Capital*, 3rd ed. Chicago, IL: University of Chicago Press and T.A. Kochan and P. Osterman (1994), *The Mutual Gains Enterprise: Forging a Winning Partnership Among Labor, Management & Government*, Boston, MA: Harvard Business School Press.

24. The current debates in the United States over healthcare reform do have the issue of United States' ability to be a world-class economic power with its current system of healthcare as a key driver of arguments.

25. See M. Maurice, F. Sellier, and J-J. Silvestre (1986), *The Social Foundations of Industrial Power: A Comparison of France and Germany*. Cambridge, MA: MIT Press.

26. See W.C. Kester (1993), "Banks in the Board Room: Germany, Japan, and the United States," Samuel L. Hayes, III, ed., *Financial Services: Perspectives and Challenges*, Boston: Harvard Business School Press, pp. 65–92. Also reprinted in *Global Finance Journal*, 5 (2), 181–204.

27. Many observers have noted how the junk bond market creation led to a veritable entreprencurial explosion in the United States in the 1980s and early 1990s, although, in later years, junk bond markets may have encouraged extreme risk taking.

28. *Keiretsus* and *Zaibatsus* are Japanese corporate arrangements with several closely related firms linked through cross-shareholdings and through a common bank. *Chaebols* are Korean conglomerates, often family owned. *Grupos* are Latin American analogues of *chaebols*. See M.L. Gerlach (1992), *Alliance Capitalism: The Organization of Japanese Businesses*, Berkeley, CA: University of California Press for the role of keiretsus in Japanese industrial organization.

29. See R. Coase (1937), "The Nature of the Firm," *Economica*, 4 (16), 386–405 and Hernando De Soto, (2000), *The Mystery of Capital: Why Capitalism Triumphs in the West and Fails Everywhere Else*. New York: Basic Books.

30. T. Ochoa and M. Rose (2002), "The Anti-Monopoly Origins of the Patent and Copyright Clause," *Journal of the Patent and Trademark Office Society*, 84: 909.

31. The story of Google draws heavily from T.R. Eisenmann and K. Herman (2006), *Google Inc.*, Harvard Business School, Case Study # 9-806-105.

32. The story of Infosys draws heavily from A. Nanda and T. DeLong (2002), *Infosys Technologies*, Harvard Business School, Case Study # 9-801-445.

33. See U.S. Rangan and J.D. Parrino (2008), "Going Abroad through Acquisitions: An Exploratory Analysis of Indian Companies' Recent International Expansion," *International Journal of Indian Culture and Business Management*, 1 (3), 335–353.

Chapter 3   The Impact of the Entrepreneurial Ecosystem on Countries

1. Andrew Kramer, "Empires Built on Debt Start to Crumble," *New York Times*, October 18, 2008, http://www.nytimes.com/2008/10/18/business/worldbusiness/18oligarch.html
2. "World Investment Report (2008)," UNCTAD, September 24, 2008, http://www.unctad.org/Templates/webflyer.asp?docid=10503&intItemID=1528&lang=1#endnote1#endnote1
3. "Foreign Direct Investment May Have Peaked in 2007, Annual Report Reveals," UNCTAD, September 24, 2008, http://www.unctad.org/Templates/webflyer.asp?docid=10500&intItemID=1528&lang=1.
4. "Sovereign Wealth Funds Beginning to Play Major Role in Foreign Direct Investment through Mergers and Acquisitions," UNCTAD, September 24, 2008, http://www.unctad.org/Templates/webflyer.asp?docid=10478&intItemID=1528&lang=1
5. *"Global Development Finance 2008,"* worldbank.org, June 10, 2008, http://econ.worldbank.org/WBSITE/EXTERNAL/EXTDEC/EXTDECPROSPECTS/EXTGDF/EXTGDF2008/0,,menuPK:4989774~pagePK:64167702~piPK:64167676~theSitePK:4989766,00.html
6. "APER 2008 Mid-Year Review," *Centre for Asia Private Equity Research*, June 2008, http://www.asiape.com/?Publications:Asia_Private_Equity_Review:APER0806MY
7. Scott Austin, "A Chinese Venture-Capitalist Gold Rush Beyond the Olympics," *VentureWire*, August 19, 2008, http://blogs.wsj.com/deals/2008/08/19/a-chinese-venture-capitalist-gold-rush-beyond-the-olympics/
8. "Venture Capital Flows to India Slightly Down at $158 Million in April-June," *domain-b.com*, July 15, 2008, http://www.domain-b.com/finance/financial_services/20080715_venture_capital.html
9. "Foreign Direct Investment May Have Peaked in 2007, Annual Report Reveals."
10. "Financial Crisis, Economic Downturn Affecting Firms' Plans for Future Foreign Investment," September 24, 2008, http://www.unctad.org/TEMPLATES/webflyer.asp?docid=10510&intItemID=1528&lang=1
11. Scott Kirsner, "Investing Further Afield," *Boston Globe*, May 4, 2008, http://www.boston.com/business/articles/2008/05/04/investing_further_afield/
12. Ibid.
13. Ibid.
14. Ibid.
15. Ibid.
16. Ibid.
17. Antonio Regaldo, "Brazilian Mining Titan Takes On Global Giants," *Wall Street Journal*, April 25, 2008, p. A1.
18. Ibid.
19. Ibid.
20. Ibid.
21. Ibid.
22. Ibid.
23. Ibid.
24. Ibid.
25. "Fitch Upgrades Vale's Ratings to 'BBB' & 'AAA (bra)'; Outlook Stable," *Reuters*, May 26, 2009, http://www.reuters.com/article/pressRelease/idUS215019+26-May-2009+BW20090526.

26. Vale (VALE) NewsBite—VALE Hits 52-Week High," Market Intelligence Center, January 4, 2010, http://www.marketintelligencecenter.com/articles/1019434

27. Peter S. Goodman, "When Foreigners Buy Factories: 2 Towns, 2 Outcomes," *New York Times*, April 7, 2008, http://www.nytimes.com/2008/04/07/business/07sale.html

28. Ibid.

29. Ibid.

30. Ibid.

31. Ibid.

32. Clifford J. Levy, "An Investment Gets Trapped in Kremlin's Vise," *New York Times*, July 24, 2008, http://www.nytimes.com/2008/07/24/world/europe/24kremlin.html

33. Ibid.

34. Ibid.

35. Ibid.

36. Ibid.

37. Ibid.

38. Ibid.

39. Ibid.

40. Ibid.

41. Ibid.

42. Ibid.

43. Ibid.

Chapter 4   The Impact of the Entrepreneurial
Ecosystem on Growing Industries

1. Vinish Kathuria and Vandita Tewari, "Venture Capitalists and Biotech Sector—Discovering the Potential." *Hindu Business Line*, December 29, 2004, http://www.blonnet.com/2004/12/29/stories/2004122900200900.htm

2. Ibid.

3. Rumman Ahmed, "Biocon Second Quarter Net Profit Almost Triples," *Wall Street Journal*, October 22, 2009, http://online.wsj.com/article/SB125619831922100859.html?mod=googlenews_wsj

4. "Profiles in Innovation: Building Biotech in Bangalore—Kiran Mazumdar-Shaw," *Wipo Magazine*, September 2005, http://www.wipo.int/wipo_magazine/en/2005/05/article_0001.html?

5. Ibid.

6. "Podcast: Biocon's Kiran Mazumdar-Shaw: 'More Indian Biotech Firms Will Be Able to Fund Discovery-Led Programs,'" *India Knowledge@Wharton*, January 11, 2007 http://knowledge.wharton.upenn.edu/india/article.cfm?articleid=4144

7. Ibid.

8. "Biocon eyes more buys to boost growth," *Economic Times*, February 27, 2008, http://economictimes.indiatimes.com/News/Biocon_eyes_more_buys_to_boost_growth/articleshow/2820122.cms

9. "NPIL Reshuffles Top Deck," *Economic Times*, June 17, 2006, http://economictimes.indiatimes.com/News/News_By_Company/Companies_A-Z/N_Companies_/Nicholas_Piramal/NPIL_reshuffles_top_deck/articleshow/1655803.cms

10. Ibid.

11. Gregory Roumeliotis, "India's Nicholas Piramal Buys Pfizer's UK Manufacturing Plant," *Outsourcing-pharma.com*, June 15, 2006, http://www.outsourcing-pharma.com/Contract-Manufacturing/India-s-Nicholas-Piramal-buys-Pfizer-s-UK-manufacturing-plant

12. Emilie Reymond, "Nicholas Piramal Eyeing US Acquisition," *Outsourcing-Pharma*.com, February 1, 2007, http://www.outsourcing-pharma.com/Contract-Manufacturing/Nicholas-Piramal-eyeing-US-acquisition

13. "Venture Investments Boost China Biotech Industry," *China Venture News*, August 22, 2005, http://www.chinaventurenews.com/50226711/venture_investments boost _china_biotech_industry.php

14. Ibid.

15. JEN LIN LIU, "Venture Capitalists Shun Chinese Biotech," *Nature*, November 6, 2003 http://www.nature.com/bioent/bioenews/112003/full/bioent778.html

16. Ibid.

17. Ibid.

18. Ibid.

19. Terry Collins, "China's Biotech Industry: An Asian Dragon Is Growing," *Eurekalert,org*, January 2008, http://www.eurekalert.org/pub_releases/2008–01/pols-cbi010108.php

20. Ibid.

21. Vivek Srivastava, "Reaching the Critical Mass in Indian Nanotechnology Industry," *Nanotechechnology Now*, June 18, 2007, http://www.nanotech-now.com/columns/?article=069

22. Ibid.

23. Ibid.

24. Ibid.

25. Ibid.

26. "Indian Biotech Industry on High-Growth Curve," *BioPharm Bulletin*, July 24, 2007 http://biopharminternational.findpharma.com/biopharm/News/Indian-Biotech-Industry-on-High-Growth-Curve/ArticleStandard/Article/detail/443625

27. "India-Preferred Partner for Biotech Industry?," *Dance with Shadows*, October 17, 2006, http://www.dancewithshadows.com/pharma2/india-biotech-growth.asp

28. Ibid.

Chapter 5   The Impact of the Entrepreneurial Ecosystem on Maturing and Rejuvenating Industries

1. "Over to Chinese MNCs." *AsiaTimesOnline*, April 1, 2005, http://www.atimes.com/atimes/China/GD01Ad07.html

2. Kalpana Shah, "Accenture Shifts Growth to India," *Red Herring*, January 29, 2007. http://www.redherring.com/Home/20989

3. Jane Spencer and Loretta Chao, "Lenovo Goes Global, but Not without Strife," *Wall Street Journal*, November 4, 2008, Technology Main; B1

4. Ibid.

5. Ibid.

6. Ibid.

7. Ibid.

8. Ibid.

9. Ibid.

10. Ibid.

11. Ibid.

12. Ibid.

13. Stephen Pritchard, "Bill Amelio: The Boss Who's Breaking Free of a Big Blue Shadow," *Independent UK*, April 1, 2007, http://www.independent.co.uk/news/people/profiles/bill-amelio-the-boss-whos-breaking-free-of-a-big-blue-shadow-442674.html

14. Ibid.

15. Sumner Lemon, "Lenovo's Amelio Resigns, Yang Returns as CEO," *IDG News Service*, February 5, 2009, http://www.pcworld.com/article/158966/lenovos_amelio_resigns_yang_returns_as_ceo.html

16. Jena McGregor, "The Issue: For Cognizant, Two's Company," *BusinessWeek*, January 17, 2008, http://www.businessweek.com/managing/content/jan2008/ca20080117_999307.htm

17. Ibid.

18. Ibid.

19. Ibid.

20. Sriram Srinivasan and KS Vasanth, "Giving Back to Society Is What You Are About," *Business OutlookIndia*, http://business.outlookindia.com/newolb/article.aspx?100214

21. Ibid.

22. Ibid.

23. "Wipro's Azim Premji on Leadership, Global Expansion, and the U.S. IT Shortage," June 12, 2008, *Knowledge@Emory*, http://knowledge.emory.edu/article.cfm?articleid=1152.

24. Ruth David, "Wipro's CEO Sees India's Global Future," *Forbes*, August 13, 2007, http://www.forbes.com/2007/08/05/wipro-azim-premji-oped-cx_rd_0813premji_print.htmlQ&A.

25. "Wipro Chairman Azim Premji: 'The Next Challenge Is to Globalize Our Leadership Much More,'" *India Knowledge@Wharton*, June 12, 2008, http://knowledge.wharton.upenn.edu/india/article.cfm?articleid=4297

26. "Dell, Inc. Key Financial Ratios," *Moneycentral.com*, December 3, 2008, http://moneycentral.msn.com/investor/invsub/results/compare.asp?Page=InvestmentReturns&Symbol=DELL

27. "Accenture Limited, Key Financial Ratios," *Moneycentral.com*, December 3, 2008, http://moneycentral.msn.com/investor/invsub/results/compare.asp?Page=InvestmentReturns&symbol=acn

28. Jeremy Kahn, "As Clients Cut Back, So Do Indian Outsourcers," *New York Times*, December 4, 2008, http://www.nytimes.com/2008/12/04/business/worldbusiness/04rupee.html

29. Ibid.

30. *Gross, Daniel, "The Bottom-Feeder King," New York Magazine,* May 21, 2005, http://nymag.com/nymetro/news/bizfinance/columns/moneyandmind/10279/

31. Ibid.

32. Ibid.

33. "The physical internet: A survey of logistics," *The Economist*, June 17, 2006, http://www.manovich.net/physical_internet.pdf

34. "Q&A: India's Tata Motors Chief Ratan Tata," *Auto Observer*, January 11, 2008, http://www.autoobserver.com/2008/01/qa-indias-tata-motors-chief-ratan-tata.html

35. Ibid.

36. Anand Giridharadas, "Four Wheels for the Masses: The $2,500 Car," *New York Times*, January 8, 2008, http://www.nytimes.com/2008/01/08/business/worldbusiness/08indiacar.html?pagewanted=print

37. Ibid.

38. Ibid.

39. Ibid.
40. "Q&A: India's Tata Motors Chief Ratan Tata."
41. Ibid.
42. Bellman, Eric, "Tata Halts Work on Indian Auto Plant, Citing Protests," *Wall Street Journal,* August 30, 2008, http://online.wsj.com/article/SB122001852872983281. html?mod=googlenews_wsj.
43. "Tata Motors moves Indian Nano plant," *Cleantech,* October 7, 2008, http://www. cleantech.com/news/3648/tata-nano-be-built-gujarat-not-west-bengal
44. "On the Record with Mauricio Botelho, President & CEO, Embraer," Aviation Week, June 17, 2001, http://www.aviationweek.com/shownews/01paris1/newsmk09.htm
45. Lynch, David J. "Comeback Kid Embraer Has Hot Jet, Fiery CEO to Match," *USA Today,* March 7, 2006, http://www.usatoday.com/money/industries/manufacturing/ 2006–03–07-embraer-usat_x.htm
46. Ibid.
47. "Embraer CEO Sees Airlines Facing Scarce Financing," *Reuters.com,* September 29, 2008, http://www.reuters.com/article/idUSSIN34712020080929
48. Ibid.
49. "This CEO Wants to Hold Chinese Products to a Haier Standard," *Knowledge@Wharton,* April 11, 2001 http://knowledge.wharton.upenn.edu/article.cfm?articleid=342
50. Ibid.
51. Ibid.
52. Ibid.
53. Ibid.
54. Ibid.
55. Ibid.
56. Ibid.
57. Ibid.
58. Kathleen Kingsbury, "China's Aircraft Industry Gets Off the Ground, *Time,* October 11, 2007, http://www.time.com/time/magazine/article/0,9171,1670256,00.html
59. "Embraer," *Googlefinance.com,* December 8, 2008, http://finance.google.com/ finance?q=NYSE:ERJ and "The Boeing Company," *Googlefinance.com,* December 8, 2008, http://finance.google.com/finance?q=ba

Chapter 6   Implications for Policymakers

1. The concept of Israel as a start-up nation is based on Dan Senor and Saul Singer, "Start-up Nation: The Story of Israel's Economic Miracle" (Twelve, 2009).
2. Clay Chandler, "Wireless Wonder: India's Sunil Mittal." *Fortune,* January 12, 2007, http://money.cnn.com/magazines/fortune/fortune_archive/2007/01/22/8397979/ index.htm.
3. Dan Pine, "'Start-Up Nation': Author Spreads the Word on Israel's Advances," Jweekly.com. January 14, 2010, http://www.jweekly.com/article/full/41065/start-up-nation-author-spreads-the-word-on-israels-advances/.
4. "Nonfiction Reviews: 9/7/2009," *Publisher's Weekly,* September 7, 2009, http://www. publishersweekly.com/article/CA6687582.html.
5. Ibid.
6. Ibid.
7. Charles Forelle, "The Isle That Rattled the World," *Wall Street Journal,* December 27, 2008, http://online.wsj.com/article/SB123032660060735767.html

8. Ibid.
9. Ibid.
10. Ibid.
11. Ibid.
12. Ibid.
13. Ibid.
14. Ibid.
15. Ibid.
16. Ibid.
17. Peter Cohan, "Asian Sovereign Wealth Funds and the Implications for the World Economy," *Forum for American/Chinese Exchange at Stanford (FACES)*, April 14, 2008.
18. Landon Thomas, "To Court or Shun the Wealth of Nations," *New York Times*, April 2, 2008, *www.nytimes.com/2008/04/02/business/02foreign.html*
19. Peter Cohan, "Profit-Wealthy Asia and Middle East Collect Their Pound of Flesh from Debt-'Wealthy' UBS," *BloggingStocks*, December 10, 2007, http://www.bloggingstocks.com/2007/12/10/profit-wealthy-asia-and-middle-east-collect-their-pound-of-fle/
20. Peter Cohan, "Does the Fed view Sovereign Wealth Funds as Greater Fools?," *BloggingStocks*, April 15, 2008, http://www.bloggingstocks.com/2008/04/15/does-the-fed-view-sovereign-wealth-funds-as-greater-fools/
21. Joe Nocera, "How India Avoided a Crisis," *New York Times*, December 20, 2008, http://www.nytimes.com/2008/12/20/business/20nocera.html?ref=business&pagewanted=print
22. Ibid.
23. Ibid.
24. Ibid.
25. Ibid.
26. Ibid.
27. Ibid.
28. Ibid.
29. Ibid.
30. Ibid.
31. Peter Cohan, "Satyam: 'India's Enron,'" *BloggingStocks*, January 7, 2009, http://www.bloggingstocks.com/2009/01/07/satyam-indias-enron?icid=sphere_wsj_teaser
32. Cohan, "Satyam: 'India's Enron.'"
33. Cohan, "Satyam: 'India's Enron.'"
34. Peter Cohan, "Will Accenture and IBM Pick Up Satyam's Slack?," *BloggingStocks*, January 9, 2009, http://www.bloggingstocks.com/2009/01/09/will-accenture-and-ibm-pick-up-satyams-slack/
35. Ibid.
36. Niraj Sheth, Jackie Range, and Romit Guha, "Satyam Abandons Deals, as Investors See Conflict," December 17, 2008, *Wall Street Journal*, http://online.wsj.com/article/SB122953447984014593.html?mod=googlenews_ws
37. Peter Cohan, "Why Do We Do Business with Russia?." *BloggingStocks*, August 6, 2008, http://www.bloggingstocks.com/2008/08/06/why-do-we-do-business-with-russia/
38. Peter Cohan, "Tell Me Again, Why Do We Do Business with Russia?," *BloggingStocks*, August 15, 2008, http://www.bloggingstocks.com/2008/08/15/tell-me-again-why-do-we-do-business-with-russia/

39. Cohan, "Why Do We Do Business with Russia?."
40. Gregory White and Guy Chazan, "Misreading the Kremlin Costs BP Control in Russia Venture," *Wall Street Journal*, December 16, 2008, http://online.wsj.com/article/SB122939129977609281.html
41. Ibid.
42. Ibid.
43. "TNK-BP," *APS Review Downstream Trends*, August 18, 2008, http://www.entrepreneur.com/tradejournals/article/print/183314472.html
44. Ibid.
45. Ibid.
46. Ibid.
47. "Bharti Wal-Mart Joins Hands with Government of Punjab to Launch Training Institute in Punjab," *Walmartstores.com*, November 12, 2008, http://walmartstores.com/FactsNews/NewsRoom/8772.aspx
48. Ibid.
49. "Wal-Mart, Indian Firm in Deal," *Los Angeles Times*, August 7, 2007, http://articles.latimes.com/2007/aug/07/business/fi-walmart7
50. Ibid.
51. Ibid.
52. Ibid.
53. Ibid.
54. "CIA World Fact Book," *CIA.gov*, December 18, 2008, https://www.cia.gov/library/publications/the-world-factbook/.
55. Josh Lerner, "Boulevard of Broken Dreams: Why Public Efforts to Boost Entrepreneurship and Venture Capital Have Failed—and What to Do About It," Princeton University Press, 2009, http://press.princeton.edu/titles/8984.html.
56. Ibid.

Chapter 7   Implications for Capital Providers

1. Marc Gunther, "Buffett Takes Charge," *Fortune*, April 13, 2009, http://money.cnn.com/2009/04/13/technology/gunther_electric.fortune/index.htm?postversion=2009041305
2. Ibid.
3. Ibid.
4. Ibid.
5. Ibid.
6. Ibid.
7. Ibid.
8. Ibid.
9. Ibid.
10. David Barboza, "Banks Face Big Losses From Bets on Chinese Realty," *New York Times*, April 3, 2009, http://www.nytimes.com/2009/04/03/business/global/03realestate.html?ref=business&pagewanted=print
11. Ibid.
12. Ibid.
13. Ibid.
14. Ibid.
15. Ibid.

16. Russell Flannery, "China's New Investor Class," *Forbes*, November 3, 2006, http://www.forbes.com/2006/11/03/neil-shen-ctrip-biz_06china_cz_rf_1103shen.html

17. Ibid.

18. Ibid.

19. Ibid.

20. Ibid.

21. Ibid.

22. "China or India: Which Is the Better Long-Term Investment for Private Equity Firms?," *Knowledge@Wharton*, April 26, 2006, http://knowledge.wharton.upenn.edu/article.cfm?articleid=1456

23. Ibid.

24. Ibid.

25. Ibid.

26. Ibid.

27. Matt Richtel, "Looking for Best Place to Take a Company Public, Some Look Overseas," *New York Times*, December 22, 2006. http://www.nytimes.com/2006/12/22/business/worldbusiness/22venture.html?dlbk=&pagewanted=print

28. Ibid.

29. Ibid.

30. Ibid.

31. Ibid.

32. Ibid.

33. Ibid.

34. Sri Rajan and Ashish Singh, "Making Private Equity Work in India," *Business Standard*, March 19, 2007, http://www.bain.com/bainweb/publications/publications_detail.asp?id=25711&menu_url=publications_results.asp

35. Ibid.

36. "PE Investment in India to Fall by a Third in 2009," *Reuters*, February 20, 2009, http://www.reuters.com/article/idUSBOM13611820090219

37. Ibid.

38. John Satish Kumar, "Private-Equity Firms Form Syndicates for India Acquisitions," *Wall Street Journal*, February 17, 2009, http://online.wsj.com/article/SB123485625532898181.html?mod=googlenews_wsj

39. Ibid.

40. Ibid.

41. "Why Are Private Equity Firms Looking Hard at India? Ask Warburg Pincus," *Knowledge@Wharton*, November 2, 2005, http://knowledge.wharton.upenn.edu/article.cfm?articleid=1305

42. Ibid.

43. Ibid.

44. Ibid.

45. Ibid.

46. Ibid.

47. Ibid.

48. Ibid.

49. Alexander Haislip, "Ajit Nazre: The Man Behind Kleiner Perkins' First Big Hit in India," *Venture Capital Journal*, March 1, 2007, http://74.125.47.132/search?q=cache:wXLeuTOuE_MJ:www.vcjnews.com/story.asp%3Fstorycode%3D41525+Ajit+Nazre:+the+man+behind+Kleiner+Perkins%27+first+big+hit+in+India&cd=1&hl=en&ct=clnk&gl=us

50. Ibid.
51. Ibid.
52. Ibid.
53. Ibid.
54. Ibid.
55. Ibid.
56. Ibid.
57. Peter Cohan, "Interview with Michael Greeley," May 12, 2009.
58. Ibid.
59. Ibid.
60. Ibid.
61. Ibid.
62. Ibid.
63. Ibid.
64. Ibid.
65. Ibid.
66. Ibid.
67. Ibid.
68. Ibid.
69. Ibid.
70. Ibid.
71. Ibid.
72. Ibid.
73. Anu Partanen, "'Entrepreneur' Means Little in France," *Fortune*, April 9, 2009, http://money.cnn.com/2009/04/08/technology/french_entrepreneurs.fortune/index.htm?postversion=2009040907
74. Ibid.
75. Ibid.
76. Ibid.
77. "Private Equity Abroad: Despite the Credit Crunch, Opportunities in Developed Markets Are Waiting," *Knowledge@Wharton*, May 6, 2008, http://knowledge.wharton.upenn.edu/article.cfm?articleid=1954
78. Ibid.
79. Ibid.
80. Ibid.
81. Ibid.
82. Ibid.
83. The capital receptivity index (CRI) lets capital providers quantify the openness to global capital flows of a country's corporate governance, financial markets, human capital, and IP regime. Capital providers can construct the CRI by conducting primary research into the specific drivers of each of these four EE elements. They can score each country on each of the drivers on a scale of 1 = hostile to 5 = highly welcoming. For instance, capital providers might score Indian minority shareholder rights as a 3 based on a review of how Western PE and VC firms have fared in their minority investments there. Capital providers would repeat this analysis for each of the drivers of the 4 EE elements and divide the total score by 95 (the total number of EE drivers: 19, x the maximum score on each: 5). As they compare the CRI across countries, capital providers can develop a fact-based assessment of the opportunities and risks of investing in the different countries.

84. "Chasing Deals among India's Fast-Growing Small and Midsize Businesses," May 17, 2007, *India Knowledge@Wharton* http://knowledge.wharton.upenn.edu/india/article.cfm;jsessionid=a830ec3a7444e53770bf7e576a3564324b72?articleid=4193

85. Ibid.

86. Ibid.

87. Ibid.

88. Peter Cohan interview with investment banker familiar with S&Y's thinking, April 27, 2009.

89. Ibid.

90. Ibid.

91. Ibid.

92. Ibid.

93. Ibid.

94. Ibid.

95. Ibid.

96. Ibid. As we'll see below, one of MOVCAPL's investments was a leading company in the Indian market for plastic household goods that the investment banker referred to as "India's Rubbermaid."

97. "Chasing Deals among India's Fast-Growing Small and Midsize Businesses."

98. Ibid.

99. Ibid.

100. Ibid.

101. Ibid.

102. Ibid.

103. Ibid.

104. Ibid.

105. Ibid.

106. Ibid.

107. Ibid.

108. Ibid.

109. Peter Cohan interview, Ibid.

110. Ibid.

111. Ibid.

112. Ibid.

113. Ibid.

114. "Chasing Deals among India's Fast-Growing Small and Midsize Businesses."

115. Ibid.

116. Ibid.

117. Ibid.

118. Ibid.

Chapter 8   Implications for Managers in Existing Industries

1. Alaric Nightingale and Matthew Craze, "Arcelor Mittal Buys Steel Plants from Grupo Villacero," *Bloomberg News.* December 21, 2006, http://www.iht.com/articles/2006/12/20/bloomberg/bxsteel.php

2. "Arcelor, Mittal Buy Mexico's Sicartsa," *AP*, December 20, 2006, http://www.thefreelibrary.com/Arcelor%2c+Mittal+buy+Mexico's+Sicartsa-a01611343034

3. Ibid.
4. Ibid.
5. Ibid.
6. Paul Maidment, "Japan Tobacco Deal Is All About Russia," *Forbes*, December 15, 2006, http://www.forbes.com/2006/12/15/russia-japan-tobacco-biz-comm_cx_pm_1215tobacco.html
7. Ibid.
8. Ibid.
9. Don Hedley, "Consolidation Endgame in Sight—But Is There One More Big Throw of the Dice?," *Euromonitor*, July 27, 2007, http://www.euromonitor.com/Consolidation_endgame_in_sight_but_is_there_one_more_big_throw_of_the_dice
10. Maidment.
11. Ibid.
12. City Staff, "Japan Tobacco Buys Gallaher for £7.5bn," *Independent UK*, December 16, 2006, http://www.independent.co.uk/news/business/news/japan-tobacco-buys-gallaher-for-16375bn-428722.html
13. "Japan Tobacco Inc Says Gallaher Group Takeover Completed," *Bloomberg*, April 19, 2007, http://www.taipeitimes.com/News/worldbiz/archives/2007/04/19/2003357338
14. Saritha Rai, "Tata Steel Buying Corus for $12 Billion," *New York Times*, January 31, 2007, http://www.nytimes.com/2007/01/31/business/worldbusiness/31steel.html
15. Nevin John, "Tata Steel Plans to Restructure Corus' Europe Operations," *Business Standard*, May 2, 2009, http://www.business-standard.com/india/news/tata-steel-plans-to-restructure-corus-europe-operations/356862/
16. V. Phani Kumar, "India's Tata Group Goes Global, One Buy at a Time," *Market Watch*, March 4, 2008, http://www.marketwatch.com/news/story/indias-tata-group-looks-go/story.aspx?guid=%7BB3435835-8935-4090-86DE-76870C062E17%7D&print=true&dist=printMidSection
17. Ibid.
18. Ibid.
19. Ruth David, "Tata Acquires Euro Steelmaker Corus," *Forbes*, October 22, 2006, http://www.forbes.com/2006/10/22/tata-corus-mna-biz-cx_rd_1022corus.html
20. Kumar.
21. Ibid.
22. Ibid.
23. Hasan Suroor, "Tatas Acquire Corus Group," *Hindu*, October 21, 2006, http://www.hindu.com/2006/10/21/stories/2006102112710100.htm
24. Suroor.
25. David.
26. Suroor.
27. Suroor.
28. David.
29. " Tata Steel Restructures in Tune with Corus," *Indian Express*, November 29, 2007, http://www.indianexpress.com/news/Tata-Steel-restructures-in-tune-with-Corus/244622/
30. Ibid.
31. Manas Chakravarty and Mobis Philipose, "Can Tata Steel Cut Corus Costs," *Livemint*, December 15, 2008, http://www.livemint.com/2008/12/15223910/Can-Tata-Steel-cut-Corus-costs.html
32. Ibid.

33. John.
34. Ibid.
35. Ibid.
36. Michelle R. Smith, "Lottery Companies Lottomatica and Gtech Strike $4.65 Billion Deal," *Associated Press*, January 10, 2006
37. William M. Bulkeley, "Italy's Lottomatica To Buy Gtech For $4.8B," *Dow Jones News Service*, January 10, 2006
38. Bulkeley.
39. Smith.
40. Ibid.
41. Ibid.
42. Andrew Frye, "FOCUS: Lottomatica Seen Digesting EUR4B Gtech Takeover," Dow Jones International News, January 11, 2006.
43. Ibid.
44. Nigel Tutt, "FOCUS Lottomatica's GTECH Deal Wins Strategy, Price Plaudits, Some Div Worries," *AFX Asia*, January 11, 2006
45. "Lottomatica Announces Positive 2009 First-Quarter Results," Lottomatica Group, April 28, 2009, http://www.lottomaticagroup.com/eng/investor/documents/cs/lot-tomatica_positive_2009_%20first-quarter_results.html
46. "Turner to Retire as CEO of Lottomatica and GTECH," *Providence Business News*, November 9, 2007, http://www.pbn.com/stories/28253.html
47. "HM Rivergroup PLC Announces the Acquisitions of Houghton Mifflin Company and Riverdeep Holdings Limited in $5.0 Billion Combination," *Houghton Mifflin Co.*, November 29, 2006, http://www.hmco.com/company/investors/invest/ir_release_112906.html
48. "Riverdeep Buys Houghton Mifflin for $1.8B," *eSchool News*, December 4, 2006 http://www.eschoolnews.com/2006/12/04/riverdeep-buys-houghton-mifflin-for-1-8b/
49. "HM Rivergroup PLC Announces the Acquisitions of Houghton Mifflin Company and Riverdeep Holdings Limited in $5.0 Billion Combination."
50. Ibid.
51. Ibid.
52. "Riverdeep Buys Houghton Mifflin for $1.8B,"
53. Ibid.
54. "HM Rivergroup PLC Announces the Acquisitions of Houghton Mifflin Company and Riverdeep Holdings Limited in $5.0 Billion Combination."
55. Kathleen Barrington, "Hard Questions for Riverdeep Investors," *Businesspost*, March 4, 2007, http://archives.tcm.ie/businesspost/2007/03/04/story21459.asp
56. Ibid.
57. Ibid.
58. Barry O'Halloran, "Moody's Withdraws Credit Rating for Houghton Mifflin," *Irish Times*, May 12, 2009, http://www.irishtimes.com/newspaper/finance/2009/0512/1224246324510.html
59. John Waggoner, "Sabic Taking the Right Path," *Gulfnews.com*, September 22, 2007, http://www.gulfbase.com/site/interface/NewsArchiveDetails.aspx?n=44329
60. Claudia H. Deutsch, "General Electric to Sell Plastics Division," *New York Times*, May 22, 2007, http://www.nytimes.com/2007/05/22/business/22plastics-web.html
61. Ibid.

62. Ibid.
63. Scott Stafford "a plastics wrap The buyer, Sabic, Plans to Retain Berkshires Employees and Taps a GE Official as CEO," *Berkshire Eagle*, May 22, 2007, http://www.berkshireedc.com/index.php?nav_id=31&story_id=37
64. Ibid.
65. Diane Grassi, "Saudi Takeover of GE Plastics Flies under Radar, *OpEd News*, July 3, 2007, http://www.opednews.com/articles/opedne_ diane_ m__ 070703 _saudi _ takeover_of_ge.htm
66. GE Plastics had contracts with the Department of Transportation (DOT), the Department of Defense (DOD), the Department of Homeland Security (DHS), the Federal Emergency Management Agency (FEMA), the Federal Aviation Agency (FAA), and the National Aeronautics and Space Administration (NASA) according to Grassi.
67. Grassi.
68. Ibid.
69. Anousha Sakoui, "Sabic Innovative Plastics Plans Bond for GE Plastics Purchase," *MarketWatch*, July 24, 2007, http://www.marketwatch.com/news/story/Sabic-innovative-plastics-plans-bond/story.aspx?guid=%7B956CECB0-ACCA-4C8E-A29C-125912D76114%7D
70. "Sabic Reports Preliminary Consolidated Financial Results for Q1," *AME Info*, April 22, 2009, http://www.ameinfo.com/193580.html
71. Ibid.
72. "FACTBOX-Key features of Vodafone deal for Hutch Essar," *Reuters*, February 12, 2007, http://www.reuters.com/article/idUSL1286291920070212
73. Ibid.
74. Ibid.
75. Ibid.
76. P.R. Venkat and Shaleen Agrawal, "India Panel OKs Vodafone Stake Buy In Hutchison Essar," *Dow Jones Newswire*, April 28, 2007, http://www.cellular-news.com/story/23429.php
77. HS Rao, "Vodafone Pays $10.9 bn to Complete Hutch-Essar Deal," May 9, 2007, *Livemint*, http://www.livemint.com/2007/05/09174440/Vodafone-pays-109-bn-to-comp.html
78. Lilly Peel, "Sarin Leaves Vodafone on Profit High," *Times*, May 27, 2008, http://business.timesonline.co.uk/tol/business/industry_sectors/telecoms/article4010641.ece
79. Douglas Hamilton, "Expansion Strategy Pays for Vodafone," *Herald*, May 20, 2009, http://www.theherald.co.uk/business/comment/display.var.2509167.0.Expansion_strategy_pays_for_Vodafone.php

Chapter 9   Implications for Entrepreneurial Managers in New Firms and Industries

1. Peter Cohan interview with Krishnan Ganesh, June 10, 2009
2. "The Outsourcerer," *Economist*, June 21, 2007, http://www.economist.com/people/displaystory.cfm?story_id=9358954
3. Ibid.
4. Ibid.
5. Ganesh interview, Ibid.
6. Ibid.
7. Ibid.

8. Ibid.
9. Ibid.
10. Ibid.
11. Ibid.
12. Ibid.
13. Ibid.
14. Ibid.
15. Ibid.
16. Ibid.
17. Ibid.
18. Ibid.
19. Ibid.
20. Ibid.
21. Ibid.
22. Ibid.
23. Ibid.
24. Ibid.
25. "Sonoa Systems Raises $10 Million Series C Financing," *Sonoa Systems Website*, October 5, 2008, http://www.sonoasystems.com/about-us/news-and-events/news-articles/20081006
26. Peter Cohan interview with Chet Kapoor, June 25, 2009.
27. Ibid.
28. Ibid.
29. Ibid.
30. Ibid.
31. Ibid.
32. Ibid.
33. Ibid.
34. Ibid.
35. Ibid.
36. Ibid.
37. Ibid.
38. Ibid.
39. Ibid.
40. Daniel J. Isenberg, "Tejas Networks India Pte.—A Venture in India," *Harvard Business*, December 11, 2006, Publisher case number 9-807-058
41. Ibid.
42. Ibid.
43. Ibid.
44. Ibid.
45. Ibid.
46. Ibid.
47. Ibid.
48. Ibid.
49. Ibid.
50. Ibid.
51. Ibid.
52. Ibid.
53. Ibid.
54. Ibid.

55. Ibid.
56. Ibid.
57. Ibid.
58. Ibid.
59. Ibid.
60. Ibid.
61. Ibid.
62. Ibid.
63. Gary R. Johnson, "The Vladimir Investment Dispute: Good Governance and Investor's Rights," *25th Annual Conference on American-Russian Relations*, April 12–14, 2002.
64. Ibid.
65. Ibid.
66. Ibid.
67. Ibid.
68. Ibid.
69. Ibid.
70. Ibid.
71. Ibid.
72. Ibid.
73. Ibid.
74. Gary R. Johnson, "Follow up," *E-mail from Gary Johnson to Peter Cohan*, May 11, 2009.
75. Gary R. Johnson, "Russia Thoughts," *E-mail from Gary Johnson to Peter Cohan*, May 4, 2009.
76. "Russia Thoughts."
77. Potemkin villages were purportedly fake settlements erected at the direction of Russian minister Grigory Potyomkin to fool Empress Catherine II during her visit to Crimea in 1787. According to this story, Potyomkin, who led the Crimean military campaign, had hollow facades of villages constructed along the desolate banks of the Dnieper River in order to impress the monarch and her travel party with the value of her new conquests, thus enhancing his standing in the empress's eyes. "Did 'Potemkin Villages' Really Exist?," *Straight Dope*, November 14, 2003, http://www.straightdope.com/columns/read/2479/did-potemkin-villages-really-exist
78. "Russia Thoughts."
79. Ibid.
80. Ibid.
81. Bruce Einhorn, "To China, with Venture Capital." *Business Week*. July 24, 2006, http://biz.yahoo.com/special/multi080206_article4.html
82. Ibid.
83. "Intel Capital Invests in China's Innovation," *China Venture News*, June 30, 2006, http://www.chinaventurenews.com/50226711/intel_capital_invests_in_chinas_innovation.php
84. Ibid.
85. Ibid.
86. Andy Greenberg, "Sohu's Ambitious Stepchild," *Forbes*, April 2, 2009 http://www.forbes.com/2009/04/02/changyou-sohu-games-technology-internet-changyou.html
87. Ibid.
88. Ibid.
89. Ibid.

90. Ibid.
91. Ibid.
92. Ibid.
93. Laura Santini, "Young Entrepreneurs Go After China's Gold," *Wall Street Journal*, May 11, 2006 http://online.wsj.com/public/article/0,,SB114731156985249787-VT7W YMY69KOwTXHuOcpqynDZKgY_20060517,00.html?mod=regionallinks
94. Ibid.
95. Ibid.
96. Ibid.
97. Ibid.
98. Ibid.
99. Ibid.
100. Ibid.
101. Ibid.
102. Ibid.
103. Ibid.
104. Derek Parker, "Made in China," *CIO Magazine*, June 24, 2008, http://cio.co.nz/cio.nsf/depth/44E8E597ACCAD803CC257471000F6C57
105. Ibid.
106. Ibid.
107. Ibid.
108. Ibid.
109. "Red Herring Finance Report," *Red Herring*, July 16, 2006 http://www.redherring.com/Home/17603
110. Parker.
111. Ibid.
112. Shaun Rein, "Venture Capital and Private Equity Opportunities in China," *Seeking Alpha*, June 19, 2007, http://seekingalpha.com/article/38778-venture-capital-and-private-equity-opportunities-in-china
113. Ibid.
114. Ibid.
115. Ibid.
116. Ibid.
117. Ibid.
118. Ibid.
119. Kevin Maney, "Chinese Start-Ups Open Arms to Venture Capital," *USA Today*, May 29, 2005, http://www.usatoday.com/money/world/2005-05-09-china-cover_x.htm
120. Ibid.
121. Ibid.
122. Ibid.
123. Ibid.
124. Ibid.
125. Ibid.
126. Ibid.
127. Ibid.
128. Ibid.
129. "VanceInfo IPO Off To Strong Start," *Seeking Alpha*, December 13, 2007 http://seekingalpha.com/article/57157-vanceinfo-ipo-off-to-strong-start
130. VanceInfo, *GoogleFinance*, July 2, 2009, http://www.google.com/finance?q=vit

Index